BEGIN WITH

PRAISE

INSPIRATIONS FROM
DUA AL-IFTITAH

AYATOLLAH
MUNEER ALKHABBAZ

TRANSLATED BY MOHAMED ALI ALBODAIRI

THE
MAINSTAY
FOUNDATION

Author: Sayyid Muneer Al-Khabbaz

Translated by: Mohamed Ali Albodairi

© 2021 The Mainstay Foundation

Printed in the United States.

ISBN: 978-1943393282

To the Master of the Time.

May God hasten his emergence.

Contents

About the Author

Sayyid Muneer Al-Khabbaz was born in Qatif, Saudi Arabia in 1384 AH (1964 CE). At the age of 14, Sayyid Muneer traveled to the Holy City of Najaf to begin his training within the Islamic seminary. Not long after, he migrated to the city of Qum, Iran, when the Baathist Regime in Iraq began tightening its crackdown on the Islamic seminary.

In the year 1402 AH (1981 CE), Sayyid Muneer returned to Qatif for personal reasons and continued his studies there. One year later, he traveled to Damascus, Syria, to study in the Islamic seminary there under the tutelage of His Eminence Sayyid Jamal Al-Khoei. Finally, in 1405 AH (1984 CE), he returned to the Holy City of Najaf to continue his studies. There, he studied under some of the most respected scholars of the Islamic seminary, including Grand Ayatollah Sayyid Abulqasim Al-Khoei and Grand Ayatollah Sheikh Murtada Al-Boroujerdi. With the recommendation of another one of his tutors, Sayyid Habib Hussainyan, Sayyid Muneer also began to study under the tutelage of Grand Ayatollah Sayyid Ali Al-Sistani, benefitting much from his lessons in the principles of jurisprudence, as well as his extensive examination of modern sciences and their correlation with Islamic sciences.

Sayyid Muneer then moved back to Qum, where he studied under Grand Ayatollah Wahid Khorasani for several years. He also studied extensively under the tutelage of Grand Ayatollah Mirza Jawad Tabrizi, who became a guide and mentor for the remainder of his life. Before his passing, Grand Ayatollah Tabrizi gave Sayyid Muneer an endorsement as a jurist capable of deducing Islamic laws from their sources.

In 1418 AH (1997 CE), Sayyid Muneer began teaching Advanced Seminars (*Bahth Kharij*) in jurisprudence. He is known by his students for his eloquence, as well as his encouragement of discussion and debate. He is an avid lecturer and an author, with multiple works published for a varied readership.

Translator's Preface

The Holy Month of Ramadan is a season of worship and spirituality. God Almighty prescribed fasting during this Holy Month as a means for us to reach the highest of virtues through obedience and worship. It is a month whose "days are the best of days." We must seize the opportunity and utilize this month for our spiritual growth, seeking closeness to God Almighty.

But how do we do this? Where do we begin?

In the supplication of Du'a al-Iftitah, the Imam teaches us to recite "O' God, I begin exaltation with Your praise!" The Imam teaches us that when we begin any endeavor, it should start with remembering and praising God.

This supplication is attributed to the Imam of our time, Imam al-Mahdi (a). It is narrated by way of Uthman ibn Saeed, the first of Four Ambassadors – the four individuals that were explicitly appointed by Imam al-Mahdi (a) to represent him during the initial years of his occultation. The supplication is recited every night in the Holy Month of Ramadan, and is one of the most prominent of the daily deeds of the month.

The supplication contains ethical, spiritual, and theological principles from the wellspring of the Ahl al-Bayt. Like many other supplications attributed to our Immaculate Imams, its teachings are varied and its meanings are deep. The primary emphasis of Du'a al-Iftitah revolves around understanding God's divine attributes, and using exaltation and praise as a means of connecting with Him.

This book, *Begin with Praise: Inspirations from Du'a al-Iftitah*, is based on a set of lectures delivered by Sayyid Muneer al-Khabbaz in the Holy Month of Ramadan, 1422 AH. It contains a plethora of philosophical and spiritual theories, which are properly analyzed and explained. The Sayyid delves deep into each segment of the supplication to derive pearls of wisdom for the reader. The pure spiritual teachings of this supplication are clearly expounded, with our contemporary reality always in mind. The book tackles some of the prevalent spiritual diseases of the day, and uses the supplication to draw the spiritual antidote.

Sayyid Muneer al-Khabbaz is a prominent Shia scholar, thinker, and lecturer. He has dedicated his life to the study of Islam, studying under some of the most prominent scholars in the holy cities of Najaf and Qum. His teachers include Grand Ayatollah Sayyid Ali al-Sistani, the leading scholar of the Islamic seminaries today. Sayyid Muneer not only studied the science of usul under Grand Ayatollah al-Sistani, but benefited from his extensive examination of modern sciences and their correlation with Islamic sciences.

Alongside his exemplary scholastic credentials, Sayyid Muneer al-Khabbaz travels the world as a preacher and lecturer. The topics of his lectures range from the spiritual and theological, to the philosophical and scientific. He is also an accomplished author, with writings ranging from textbooks in the science of usul to critiques of New Atheism and addressing contemporary anti-religious trends.

I have personally benefitted from Sayyid Muneer's books and lectures. Most impactful were his books *The Mahdi: Understanding the Awaited One* and *Religion: Between Scientific Findings and Atheist Claims* (not to mention this book now between the reader's hands). I have also had the honor of attending his lectures and discussions, and sitting down with him one to one. In all of this, he never ceases to be broad-minded, thoughtful, and poignant.

This thoughtfulness and wisdom will be plain to the reader when going through this book. The reader will gain greater appreciation for Du'a al-Iftitah and the many deep meanings enfolded in its verses. The reader will find this wisdom especially poignant during the Holy Month of Ramadan. The daily recitation of the supplication, along with the deeper understanding provided by this book, will surely help the reader ascend to new spiritual heights.

Mohamed Ali Albodairi,

The Mainstay Foundation's Translation and Editorial Team

The Supplication

In the Name of God, the Most Beneficent, the Most Merciful

اللَّهُمَّ إِنِّي أَفْتَتِحُ الثَّنَاءَ بِحَمْدِكَ، وَأَنْتَ مُسَدِّدٌ لِلصَّوَابِ بِمَنِّكَ

O' God, I begin exaltation with Your praise! You support [the believers on the path] to truth with Your grace.

وَأَيْقَنْتُ أَنَّكَ أَنْتَ أَرْحَمُ الرَّاحِمِينَ فِي مَوْضِعِ العَفْوِ وَالرَّحْمَةِ، وَأَشَدُّ المُعَاقِبِينَ فِي مَوْضِعِ النَّكَالِ وَالنِّقِمَةِ، وَأَعْظَمُ المُتَجَبِّرِينَ فِي مَوْضِعِ الكِبْرِيَاءِ وَالعَظَمَةِ.

And I have come to know with certainty that You are the most merciful in disposition of forgiveness and clemency! [Still, You] are the sternest exactor at the time of exemplary punishment and chastisement, and the most dominant Lord in the domain of majesty and greatness.

اللَّهُمَّ أَذِنْتَ لِي فِي دُعَائِكَ وَمَسْأَلَتِكَ، فَاسْمَعْ يَا سَمِيعُ مِدْحَتِي، وَأَجِبْ يَا رَحِيمُ دَعْوَتِي، وَأَقِلْ يَا غَفُورُ عَثْرَتِي، فَكَمْ يَا إِلَهِي مِنْ كُرْبَةٍ قَدْ فَرَّجْتَهَا، وَهُمُومٍ قَدْ كَشَفْتَهَا، وَعَثْرَةٍ قَدْ أَقَلْتَهَا، وَرَحْمَةٍ قَدْ نَشَرْتَهَا، وَحَلْقَةِ بَلَاءٍ قَدْ فَكَكْتَهَا.

O' God, You have given me permission to invoke and beseech You. So, listen, O' all-Hearing, to my praise. Accept, O' all-Beneficent, my supplication. Discount, O' most-Clement, my shortcoming. O' God, how many a difficulty have You removed? How many a sorrow have You dispelled? How many a shortcoming have You discounted? How many a mercy have You spread? How many a woesome shackle have you unraveled?

الحَمْدُ لِلهِ الَّذِي لَمْ يَتَّخِذْ صَاحِبَةً وَلَا وَلَداً، وَلَمْ يَكُنْ لَهُ شَرِيكٌ فِي المُلْكِ وَلَمْ يَكُنْ لَهُ وَلِيٌّ مِنَ الذُّلِّ وَكَبِّرْهُ تَكْبِيراً.

All praise be to God, who has not taken unto Himself a wife, nor a son, and who has no partner in sovereignty, nor any protecting friend through dependence. Magnify Him with all magnificence.

الحَمْدُ للهِ بِجَمِيعِ مَحَامِدِهِ كُلِّها على جَمِيعِ نِعَمِهِ كُلِّها.

All praise be to God, with the entirety of all praise for the entirety of all His bounties.

الحَمْدُ للهِ الَّذِي لا مُضادَّ لَهُ في مُلْكِهِ وَلا مُنازِعَ لَهُ في أَمْرِهِ، الحَمْدُ للهِ الَّذِي لا شَرِيكَ لَهُ في خَلْقِهِ وَلا شَبِيهَ لَهُ في عَظَمَتِهِ

All praise be to God, who has no opposition to His rule, nor any challenge to His commands, nor a partner in His creation, nor is there anything similar to Him in His greatness.

الحَمْدُ للهِ الفاشِي في الخَلْقِ أَمْرُهُ وَحَمْدُهُ، الظاهِرِ بالكَرَمِ مَجْدُهُ، الباسِطِ بالجُودِ يَدَهُ، الَّذِي لا تَنْقُصُ خَزائِنُهُ، وَلا يَزِيدُهُ كَثْرَةُ العَطاءِ إلّا جُوداً وَكَرَما، إِنَّهُ هُوَ العَزِيزُ الوَهَّابُ.

All praise be to God, whose command and praise have proliferated throughout creation. His glory is evident through His magnanimity. His hands are open and overflowing with generosity. His vaults never diminish. His great bounties do not increase Him in anything but manifestations of His generosity and magnanimity. Surely, He is the mighty and the provider for all things.

اللّهُمَّ إِنِّي أَسْأَلُكَ قَلِيلاً مِنْ كَثِيرٍ، مَعَ حاجَةٍ بِي إِلَيْهِ عَظِيمَةٍ وَغِناكَ عَنْهُ قَدِيمٌ، وَهُوَ عِنْدِي كَثِيرٌ وَهُوَ عَلَيْكَ سَهْلٌ يَسِيرٌ.

O God, I ask for so little from so much [that You have] – while my need for it is so great, You have always been self-sufficient [without need for anything]. To me, it is so great, while to You, it is simple and effortless.

اللَّهُمَّ إِنَّ عَفْوَكَ عَنْ ذَنْبِي، وَتَجَاوُزَكَ عَنْ خَطِيئَتِي، وَصَفْحَكَ عَنْ ظُلْمِي، وَسَتْرَكَ عَلَى قَبِيحٍ عَمَلِي، وَحِلْمَكَ عَنْ كَثِيرِ جُرْمِي عِنْدَمَا كَانَ مِنْ خَطَأِي وَعَمْدِي، أَطْمَعَنِي فِي أَنْ أَسْأَلَكَ مَا لَا اسْتَوْجِبُهُ مِنْكَ

O' God, truly, when You forgive my sins, overlook my mistakes, pardon my transgressions, cover up my foul actions, and show forbearance in spite of my many crimes committed by me, both negligently and intently, I am tempted to ask for that which I do not deserve from You.

الَّذِي رَزَقْتَنِي مِنْ رَحْمَتِكَ، وَأَرَيْتَنِي مِنْ قُدْرَتِكَ، وَعَرَّفْتَنِي مِنْ إِجَابَتِكَ، فَصِرْتُ أَدْعُوكَ آمِناً، وَأَسْأَلُكَ مُسْتَأْنِساً، لَا خَائِفاً وَلَا وَجِلاً، مُدِلاً عَلَيْكَ فِيمَا قَصَدْتُ فِيهِ إِلَيْكَ،

You have blessed me through Your mercy, shown me Your omnipotence, and acquainted me with Your answers [for my prayers]. So, I persist in calling out, believing in You. I invoke You, talking familiarly, not afraid nor shy, but assured of Your love and kindness whenever I turn to You.

فَإِنْ أَبْطَأَ عَنِّي عَتِبْتُ بِجَهْلِي عَلَيْكَ، وَلَعَلَّ الَّذِي أَبْطَأَ عَنِّي هُوَ خَيْرٌ لِي لِعِلْمِكَ بِعَاقِبَةِ الْأُمُورِ

Yet, when [Your answer] is delayed for me, I blame You out of my ignorance – although perhaps the delay is a blessing for me. Surely, You alone know the consequence of all things.

فَلَمْ أَرَ مَوْلًى كَرِيماً أَصْبَرَ عَلَى عَبْدٍ لَئِيمٍ مِنْكَ عَلَيَّ يَا رَبِّ، إِنَّكَ تَدْعُونِي فَأُوَلِّي عَنْكَ، وَتَتَحَبَّبُ إِلَيَّ فَأَتَبَغَّضُ إِلَيْكَ، وَتَتَوَدَّدُ إِلَيَّ فَلَا أَقْبَلُ مِنْكَ، كَأَنَّ لِيَ التَّطَوُّلَ عَلَيْكَ، فَلَمْ يَمْنَعْكَ ذَلِكَ مِنَ الرَّحْمَةِ لِي وَالإِحْسَانِ إِلَيَّ، وَالتَّفَضُّلِ عَلَيَّ بِجُودِكَ وَكَرَمِكَ.

I know no generous master who is more forbearing to a miscreant servant that You are to me. O' Lord, You continue to invite me, but I continue to turn You down. You seek my love, while I seek Your displeasure. You show me affection, but I do not accept it from You. As if I have the right to be insolent towards You! Yet this did not stop You from having mercy on me, bestowing favors upon me, and blessing me from Your mercy and generosity.

فَارْحَمْ عَبْدَكَ الجَاهِلَ، وَجُدْ عَلَيْهِ بِفَضْلِ إِحْسَانِكَ إِنَّكَ جَوَادٌ كَرِيمٌ. الحَمْدُ للهِ مَالِكِ المُلْكِ، مُجْرِي الفُلْكِ، مُسَخِّرِ الرِّيَاحِ، فَالِقِ الإِصْبَاحِ، دَيَّانِ الدِّينِ، رَبِّ العَالَمِينَ.

So, have mercy on Your ignorant servant and be generous to him with Your favors and kindness; surely You are generous and kind. Praise be to God, the possessor of all sovereignty, the controller of ships, the disposer of winds, the creator of daybreak, the judge of faith, and the Lord of the worlds.

الحَمْدُ للهِ عَلَى حِلْمِهِ بَعْدَ عِلْمِهِ، وَالحَمْدُ للهِ عَلَى عَفْوِهِ بَعْدَ قُدْرَتِهِ، وَالحَمْدُ للهِ عَلَى طُولِ أَنَاتِهِ فِي غَضَبِهِ، وَهُوَ قَادِرٌ عَلَى مَا يُرِيدُ.

Praise be to God for His forbearance in light of His all-awareness. Praise be to God for His amnesty despite His omnipotence. Praise be to God for the long respite He allows in spite of provocation. Surely, He is able to do what He wills.

الْحَمْدُ للهِ خَالِقِ الْخَلْقِ بَاسِطِ الرِّزْقِ، فَالِقِ الإِصْبَاحِ، ذِي الْجَلَالِ وَالإِكْرَامِ، وَالْفَضْلِ وَالإِنْعَامِ، الَّذِي بَعُدَ فَلَا يُرَى، وَقَرُبَ فَشَهِدَ النَّجْوَى، تَبَارَكَ وَتَعَالَى.

Praise be to God, the creator of all creation, who makes sustenance freely available, who starts the day, the owner of glory, might, favors, and bounties. He is far from being visible [to the eye], yet so near that He hears every whisper. He is the most Blessed and High.

الْحَمْدُ للهِ الَّذِي لَيْسَ لَهُ مُنَازِعٌ يُعَادِلُهُ، وَلَا شَبِيهٌ يُشَاكِلُهُ، وَلَا ظَهِيرٌ يُعَاضِدُهُ، قَهَرَ بِعِزِّهِ الأَعِزَّاءَ، وَتَوَاضَعَ لِعَظَمَتِهِ الْعُظَمَاءُ، فَبَلَغَ بِقُدْرَتِهِ مَا يَشَاءُ.

Praise be to God, who has no equal to challenge Him, nor is there an image comparable to Him, nor a helper to assist Him. He dominates the powerful by His might, and disgraced are the great before His grandeur; so He, through His omnipotence, fulfills that which He wills.

الْحَمْدُ للهِ الَّذِي يُجِيبُنِي حِينَ أُنَادِيهِ، وَيَسْتُرُ عَلَيَّ كُلَّ عَوْرَةٍ وَأَنَا أَعْصِيهِ، وَيُعَظِّمُ النِّعْمَةَ عَلَيَّ فَلَا أُجَازِيهِ، فَكَمْ مِنْ مَوْهِبَةٍ هَنِيئَةٍ قَدْ أَعْطَانِي، وَعَظِيمَةٍ مَخُوفَةٍ قَدْ كَفَانِي، وَبَهْجَةٍ مُونِقَةٍ قَدْ أَرَانِي، فَأُثْنِي عَلَيْهِ حَامِداً وَأَذْكُرُهُ مُسَبِّحاً.

Praise be to God, who answers to me whenever I call Him, covers up my all my shortcomings while I disobey Him, and increases His blessings on me when I cannot repay Him. O' how many obvious favors has He granted me? From how many terrible dangers has He protected me? How many blossoming joys has He shown me? I sing His praises and recite His glorifications!

الحَمْدُ لِلهِ الَّذِي لا يُنْتَكُ حِجَابُهُ، وَلا يُغْلَقُ بَابُهُ، وَلا يَرُدُّ سَائِلَهُ، وَلا يُخَيِّبُ آمِلَهُ.

Praise be to God. None can pierce His veil. None can shut His [ever-open] doors. None who beseech Him are ever turned down. None who have hope in Him are ever disappointed.

الحَمْدُ لِلهِ الَّذِي يُؤْمِنُ الخَائِفِينَ، وَيُنَجِّي الصَّالِحِينَ، وَيَرْفَعُ المُسْتَضْعَفِينَ، وَيَضَعُ المُسْتَكْبِرِينَ، وَيُهْلِكُ مُلُوكًا وَيَسْتَخْلِفُ آخَرِينَ.

Praise be to God, who protects the frightened, helps the righteous, promotes the meek, demeans the arrogant, and destroys kings to replace them with others.

الحَمْدُ لِلهِ قَاصِمِ الجَبَّارِينَ، مُبِيرِ الظَّالِمِينَ، مُدْرِكِ الهَارِبِينَ، نَكَالِ الظَّالِمِينَ، صَرِيخِ المُسْتَصْرِخِينَ، مَوْضِعِ حَاجَاتِ الطَّالِبِينَ، مُعْتَمَدِ المُؤْمِنِينَ.

Praise be to God, breaker of tyrants, ender of oppressors, capturer of runaways, punisher of oppressors, aid to those who cry out for help, target of beseechers' requests, and patron of the faithful.

الحَمْدُ لِلهِ الَّذِي مِنْ خَشْيَتِهِ تَرْعَدُ السَّمَاءُ وَسُكَّانُهَا، وَتَرْجُفُ الأَرْضُ وَعُمَّارُهَا، وَتَمُوجُ البِحَارُ وَمَنْ يَسْبَحُ فِي غَمَرَاتِهَا. الحَمْدُ لِلهِ الَّذِي هَدَانَا لِهَذَا، وَمَا كُنَّا لِنَهْتَدِيَ لَوْلا أَنْ هَدَانَا اللهُ.

الحَمْدُ لِلهِ الَّذِي يَخْلُقُ وَلَمْ يُخْلَقْ، وَيَرْزُقُ وَلا يُرْزَقُ، وَيُطْعِمُ وَلا يُطْعَمُ، وَيُمِيتُ الأَحْيَاءَ وَيُحْيِي المَوْتَى وَهُوَ حَيٌّ لا يَمُوتُ، بِيَدِهِ الخَيْرُ وَهُوَ عَلَى كُلِّ شَيْءٍ قَدِيرٌ.

Praise be to God. Out of fear of Him, the heavens and their denizens quiver, the Earth and its inhabitants tremble, the oceans and all that swims in their depths shudder. Praise be to God, who has guided us to this. Certainly, we could not have been guided if God had not guided us. Praise be to God, who creates, but is not created, gives subsistence, but needs no provisions, gives food to eat, but takes no nourishment, and makes the living dead and brings the dead to life, while He is the ever-living – there is no death for Him. In His hands is all beneficence and He is able to do all things.

اللّٰهُمَّ صَلِّ عَلى مُحَمَّدٍ عَبْدِكَ وَرَسُولِكَ، وَأَمِينِكَ وَصَفِيِّكَ، وَحَبِيبِكَ وَخِيَرَتِكَ مِنْ خَلْقِكَ، وَحافِظِ سِرِّكَ وَمُبَلِّغِ رِسالاتِكَ، أَفْضَلَ وَأَحْسَنَ وَأَجْمَلَ وَأَكْمَلَ وَأَزْكى وَأَنْمى وَأَطْيَبَ وَأَطْهَرَ وَأَسْنى وَأَكْثَرَ ما صَلَّيْتَ وَبارَكْتَ وَتَرَحَّمْتَ وَتَحَنَّنْتَ وَسَلَّمْتَ عَلى أَحَدٍ مِنْ عِبادِكَ وَأَنْبِيائِكَ وَرُسُلِكَ وَصَفْوَتِكَ وَأَهْلِ الكَرامَةِ عَلَيْكَ مِنْ خَلْقِكَ.

O' God, send blessings on Muhammad – Your servant, messenger, trustee, friend, beloved, chosen among Your creatures, keeper of Your secrets, and deliverer of Your messages – the most superior, exquisite, beautiful, perfect, upright, prospering, pleasant, pure, sublime, and numerous amongst what You have blessed, sanctified, treated mercifully, dealt with affectionately, and saluted any of Your servants, prophets, messengers, friends, and those honored by You from among Your creatures.

اللّٰهُمَّ وَصَلِّ عَلى عَلِيٍّ أَمِيرَ المُؤْمِنِينَ، وَوَصِيِّ رَسُولِ رَبِّ العالَمِينَ، عَبْدِكَ وَوَلِيِّكَ وَأَخِي رَسُولِكَ وَحُجَّتِكَ عَلى خَلْقِكَ وَآيَتِكَ الكُبْرى وَالنَّبَأِ العَظِيمِ،

O' God, send blessings on Ali, the Commander of the Faithful, the successor to the Messenger of the Lord of the worlds, Your servant and representative, the brother of Your Messenger,

Your proof upon your creatures, Your greatest sign, and the
great news from You.

وَصَلِّ عَلَى الصِّدِّيقَةِ الطَّاهِرَةِ فاطِمَةَ سَيِّدَةِ نِساءِ العالَمِينَ، وَصَلِّ عَلَى
سِبطَيِ الرَّحْمَةِ وَإمامَيِ الهُدى الحَسَنِ وَالحُسَينِ سَيِّدَيْ شَبابِ أَهلِ الجَنَّةِ،
وَصَلِّ عَلَى أئِمَّةِ المُسلِمِينَ عَلِيِّ بنِ الحُسَينِ وَمُحَمَّدِ بنِ عَلِيٍّ وَجَعْفَرِ بنِ مُحَمَّدٍ
وَمُوسى بنِ جَعْفَرٍ وَعَلِيِّ بنِ مُوسى وَمُحَمَّدِ بنِ عَلِيٍّ وَعَلِيِّ بنِ مُحَمَّدٍ وَالحَسَنِ
بنِ عَلِيٍّ وَالخَلَفِ الهادِي المَهدِيِّ، حُجَجِكَ عَلَى عِبادِكَ وَأَمَنائِكَ فِي بِلادِكَ،
صَلاةً كَثِيرَةً دائِمَةً.

O' God, send blessings on the truthful and on pure Fatima, the
leader of the women of the worlds. O' God, send blessings on
the sons of 'the mercy unto the worlds,' the imams of
guidance, al-Hassan and al-Hussain, the leaders of the youth
of Paradise. O' God, send blessings on the imams of the
Muslims, Ali ibn al-Hussain, Muhammad ibn Ali, Jafar ibn
Muhammad, Musa ibn Jafar, Ali ibn Musa, Muhammad ibn
Ali, Ali ibn Muhammad, al-Hassan ibn Ali, and the rightly
guided successor, al-Mahdi – Your proofs over Your servants
and Your trustees on Your Earth – blessings which are
numerous and everlasting.

اللَّهُمَّ وَصَلِّ عَلَى وَلِيِّ أَمرِكِ القائِمِ المُؤَمَّلِ، وَالعَدلِ المُنتَظَرِ، وَحُفَّهُ بِمَلائِكَتِكَ
المُقَرَّبِينَ، وَأَيِّدهُ بِرُوحِ القُدُسِ يا رَبَّ العالَمِينَ. اللَّهُمَّ اجعَلهُ الدَّاعِيَ إلى
كِتابِكَ، وَالقائِمَ بِدِينِكَ، اسْتَخلِفهُ فِي الأرضِ كَما اسْتَخلَفتَ الَّذِينَ مِن قَبلِهِ،
مَكِّن لَهُ دِينَهُ الَّذِي ارتَضَيتَهُ لَهُ، أَبدِلهُ مِن بَعدِ خَوفِهِ أَمنا، يَعبُدُكَ لا يُشرِكُ
بِكَ شَيئاً. اللَّهُمَّ أَعِزَّهُ وَأَعزِز بِهِ، وَانصُرهُ وَانتَصِر بِهِ، وَانصُرهُ نَصراً عَزِيزاً،
وَافتَح لَهُ فَتحاً يَسِيراً، وَاجعَل لَهُ مِن لَدُنكَ سُلطاناً نَصِيراً.

O' God, send blessings on the custodian of Your matter, the longed-for guardian and the awaited justice. Surround him with Your closest angels and assist him by the Holy Spirit, O' Lord of the worlds. O' God, make him the caller unto Your Book and the patron of Your religion. Make him the successor of the Earth, as You made successors before him. Establish for him his faith, which You approved for him. Translate his fear into security, so that he may worship You and ascribe no partner to You. O' God, grant him might and grant might [to the believers] through him. Grant him victory and grant victory [to the believers] through him. Grant him a great victory and an effortless triumph. Grant him [these] through this manifest authority.

اللّٰهُمَّ أَظْهِرْ بِهِ دِينَكَ وَسُنَّةَ نَبِيِّكَ، حَتَّى لَا يَسْتَخْفِي بِشَيْءٍ مِنَ الْحَقِّ مَخَافَةَ أَحَدٍ مِنَ الْخَلْقِ.

O' God, empower Your religion and the tradition of Your prophet through him, such that he shall not hide any truth out of fear of any creature.

اللّٰهُمَّ إِنَّا نَرْغَبُ إِلَيْكَ فِي دَوْلَةٍ كَرِيمَةٍ، تُعِزُّ بِهَا الْإِسْلَامَ وَأَهْلَهُ، وَتُذِلُّ بِهَا النِّفَاقَ وَأَهْلَهُ، وَتَجْعَلُنَا فِيهَا مِنَ الدُّعَاةِ إِلَى طَاعَتِكَ، وَالْقَادَةِ إِلَى سَبِيلِكَ، وَتَرْزُقُنَا بِهَا كَرَامَةَ الدُّنْيَا وَالْآخِرَةِ.

O' God, we ask of you for an honorable era, wherein you distinguish Islam and its adherents and humiliate hypocrisy and its adherents. Allow us to be in it [i.e., that honorable era] amongst those who call toward Your obedience and the leaders in Your path. Bless us through it with the honor of this world and the next.

اللَّهُمَّ ما عَرَّفْتَنا مِنَ الحَقِّ فَحَمِّلْناهُ، وَما قَصُرْنا عَنْهُ فَبَلِّغْناهُ، اللَّهُمَّ ٱلْمُمْ بِهِ شَعْثَنا، وَأَشْعَبْ بِهِ صَدْعَنا، وَأَرْتِقْ بِهِ فَتْقَنا، وَكَثِّرْ بِهِ قِلَّتَنا، وَأَعْزِزْ بِهِ ذِلَّتَنا، وَأَغْنِ بِهِ عائِلَنا، وَأَقْضِ بِهِ عَنْ مُغْرَمِنا، وَاجْبُرْ بِهِ فَقْرَنا، وَسُدَّ بِهِ خَلَّتَنا، وَيَسِّرْ بِهِ عُسْرَنا، وَبَيِّضْ بِهِ وُجُوهَنا، وَفُكَّ بِهِ أَسْرَنا، وَأَنْجِحْ بِهِ طَلِبَتَنا، وَأَنْجِزْ بِهِ مَواعِيدَنا، وَاسْتَجِبْ بِهِ دَعْوَتَنا، وَأَعْطِنا بِهِ سُؤْلَنا، وَبَلِّغْنا بِهِ مِنَ الدُّنْيا وَالآخِرَةِ آمالَنا، وَأَعْطِنا بِهِ فَوْقَ رَغْبَتِنا،

O' God, allow us to bear what You have taught us of the truth, and teach us that which we have come short of. O' God, through him [i.e., al-Mahdi], unite our disunity, bond our rifts, remove our divisions, multiply our slightness, rectify our humility, support our destitute, shield our fugitives, mend our poverty, redress our shortcomings, ease our difficulties, brighten our faces, break our bondage, respond to our pleas, fulfill our promises, answer our calls, give us our requests, fulfill our hopes in this world and the hereafter, and give us more than what we seek.

يا خَيْرَ المَسْؤُولِينَ وَأَوْسَعَ المُعْطِينَ، اشْفِ بِهِ صُدُورَنا، وَأَذْهِبْ بِهِ غَيْظَ قُلُوبِنا، وَاهْدِنا بِهِ لِما اخْتُلِفَ فِيهِ مِنَ الحَقِّ بِإِذْنِكَ، إِنَّكَ تَهْدِي مَنْ تَشاءُ إِلى صِراطٍ مُسْتَقِيمٍ، وَانْصُرْنا بِهِ عَلى عَدُوِّكَ وَعَدُوِّنا، إِلهَ الحَقِّ آمِينَ.

O' best of those who are beseeched and the most abundantly giving. Through him, cure our chests [of psychological ills], remove the rancor in our hearts, guide us to what was disagreed upon of truth by Your leave – surely, You guide whomever You wish to the straight path. Support us with him over our enemies. God of truth, amen.

اللّٰهُمَّ إِنَّا نَشْكُو إِلَيْكَ فَقْدَ نَبِيِّنَا صَلَوَاتُكَ عَلَيْهِ وَآلِهِ، وَغَيْبَةَ وَلِيِّنَا، وَكَثْرَةَ
عَدُوِّنَا، وَقِلَّةَ عَدَدِنَا، وَشِدَّةَ الْفِتَنِ بِنَا، وَتَظَاهُرَ الزَّمَانِ عَلَيْنَا، فَصَلِّ عَلَى
مُحَمَّدٍ وَآلِهِ، وَأَعِنَّا عَلَى ذٰلِكَ بِفَتْحٍ مِنْكَ تُعَجِّلُهُ، وَضُرٍّ تَكْشِفُهُ، وَنَصْرٍ تُعِزُّهُ،
وَسُلْطَانِ حَقٍّ تُظْهِرُهُ، وَرَحْمَةٍ مِنْكَ تُجَلِّلُنَاهَا، وَعَافِيَةٍ مِنْكَ تُلْبِسُنَاهَا،
بِرَحْمَتِكَ يَا أَرْحَمَ الرَّاحِمِينَ

O' God, we complain to you of the departure of our Prophet –
may your blessings be upon him and his family – the absence
of our guardian [our Imam], the multitude of our enemies, the
slightness of our numbers, the hardship of sedition for us, and
the vicissitudes of time against us. So, send blessings on
Muhammad and on his family. Help us to overcome this state
of affairs through Your quickening of triumph, repelling of
misfortunes, inauguration of victories, and empowerment of
the authority of truth. Immerse us with the bestowal of Your
mercy. Dress us with the grant of Your health. By Your mercy,
O' most Merciful.

Connecting to the Divine

اللّٰهُمَّ إِنِّي أَفْتَتِحُ الثَّنَاءَ بِحَمْدِكَ

O' God, I begin exaltation with Your praise!

These words appear at the beginning of Du'a al-Iftitah, a supplication that our beloved Twelfth Holy Imam, may God hasten his emergence, taught us to recite throughout the Holy Month of Ramadan.

Praise, Gratitude, and Glorification

Our beloved Imams teach us to start our supplications by complimenting God Almighty. Our compliments can come in three forms: Praise[1], Gratitude[2], and Glorification[3].

Praise is a compliment given for a voluntary good. For example, if a child does well in school by dedicating to their studies, our compliments for such actions are called praise. We praise an individual who maintains their prayers on their prescribed times because such voluntary actions are praiseworthy.

God Almighty is truly deserving of our praise. He is absolute benevolence, and the benevolence of His attributes are an emanation of His omnibenevolence[4]. He is the source of all good, and thus worthy of all praise.

Gratitude is a compliment given in return for some boon or blessing. If your friend performs some favor for you, your compliment to them is gratitude.

Glorification is a compliment that signifies the subject's transcendence over all faults. When we describe God as being free of any ignorance

---

[1] *Praise: am expression of warm approval or admiration of. An expression of one's respect and gratitude towards (a deity) ...*

[2] *Gratitude: The quality of being thankful; readiness to show appreciation for and to return kindness.*

[3] *Glorification: The action of describing or representing something as admirable, especially unjustifiably. Praise and worship of God.*

[4] *Omnibenevolence: Perfect or unlimited goodness.*

and immune from any weakness, we are glorifying Him as our omniscient and omnipotent Lord.

Beginning and Ending with Praise

We notice that this supplication starts with praise to God Almighty – "O' God, I begin exaltation with Your praise!" Praise also comes at the conclusion of our supplications. The Holy Quran speaks of the residents of Paradise saying,

وَآخِرُ دَعْوَاهُمْ أَنِ الْحَمْدُ لِلَّهِ رَبِّ الْعَالَمِينَ

Their concluding call, 'All praise belongs to Allah, the Lord of all the worlds.'[5]

Why do we begin and end our supplications with praise?

We begin our supplications with praise because praise is the key to all other compliments and is the broadest amongst them. Both gratitude and glorification are reliant on praise. Without praise, there is no gratitude or glorification. If an individual does not realize the benevolence of their Lord, they will not be able to express gratitude to Him or glorify Him.

To understand His blessings, we must understand the benevolence of His actions – after all, His blessing to His creatures is a benevolent action. Our gratitude is praise for His blessings. Thus, we must realize the benevolence of His actions, so that we may understand that they are blessings. Once we understand how He has blessed us, we will be able to thank Him and show our gratitude. We can therefore see that gratitude is reliant on praise.

Glorification is also reliant on realizing God's benevolence. If an individual does not understand His omnibenevolence, they will not be able to realize His transcendence over all faults. His omnibenevolence requires that we understand His perfection. To compliment Him on His

---

[5] *The Holy Quran, 10:10.*

perfection is a form of praise. Thus, we can see that gratitude and glorification are reliant on praise.

Praise is also more encompassing than gratitude and glorification. It is not meant only for actions, but also as a compliment for God's divine attributes. As we said, praise is a compliment for a voluntary good. This does not stop at action, but extends to praise of His sublime attributes. He is all-good in His divinity. His all-goodness translates into what we understand as His divine attributes and benevolent actions. As such, God says in the Holy Quran:

قُلِ ادْعُوا اللَّهَ أَوِ ادْعُوا الرَّحْمَنَ ۖ أَيًّا مَّا تَدْعُوا فَلَهُ الْأَسْمَاءُ الْحُسْنَىٰ

Say, 'Invoke "Allah" or invoke "the All-beneficent." Whichever [of His Names] you may invoke, to Him belong the Best Names.'[6]

His absolute goodness translates into the goodness of His attributes and actions. Let us take as an example the following verse:

الَّذِي أَحْسَنَ كُلَّ شَيْءٍ خَلَقَهُ

[It is God] who perfected everything that He created[7]

Nothing emanates from Him but perfection. Our praise to Him, as well as our gratitude and glorification, comes from His sublime perfection.

Gratitude is specific praise for His blessings. Glorification is specific praise acknowledging His perfection. Praise is a broader form of complimenting His essence, attributes, and actions. As such, the Imam chose it as the opening of his exaltations to God.

All Praise is to God

When you praise an individual for a good quality or for a benevolent act, that praise ultimately returns to God Almighty. Any praiseworthy trait or action that we see in any of God's creatures are actually based in God's omnibenevolence. No one can do any good if God had not

---

[6] *The Holy Quran*, 17:110.

[7] *The Holy Quran*, 32:7.

blessed them with the ability to do good. The good and beauty that we see in creation is only a reflection and manifestation of God's ultimate good and beauty. Therefore, any praise made to any creature is, in essence, praise for God Almighty. That is why we read in the Holy Quran,

لَهُ الْمُلْكُ وَلَهُ الْحَمْدُ وَهُوَ عَلَىٰ كُلِّ شَيْءٍ قَدِيرٌ

To Him belongs all sovereignty and to Him belongs all praise, and He has power over all things.[8]

He holds the reins over all creation. Any beauty we see in anything is a result of His blessings and benevolence. This verse is an indication of the connection between God's supreme sovereignty[9], and the fact that all praise is due to Him. The linkage between the two comes from the fact that He has power over all things.

Praise without Glorification

In many instances, we find that praise and glorification are tightly linked. For example, we recite as part of our prayers during *rukoo'*, "I glorify my Great Lord and praise Him." Praise and glorification are deeply intertwined. As God Almighty says in the Holy Quran,

وَإِن مِّن شَيْءٍ إِلَّا يُسَبِّحُ بِحَمْدِهِ وَلَٰكِن لَّا تَفْقَهُونَ تَسْبِيحَهُمْ

There is not a thing but celebrates His praise, but you do not understand their glorification.[10]

God says that everything in the universe exalts Him with a mixture of praise and glorification. Yet in some instances, we find that praise is mentioned without glorification. As we read in the supplication, "O' God, I begin exaltation with Your praise!"

This is due to the different situations in which we are taught to recite these differing supplications. Our supplication in rukoo' comes from a testamentary position – we are attesting to God's benevolence and glory. Attestation requires the testimony to be complete. Making an

---

[8] *The Holy Quran, 64:1.*

[9] *Sovereignty: Supreme power or authority.*

[10] *The Holy Quran, 17:44.*

attestation about God requires that we describe Him as precisely as possible, while encompassing as many of His divine attributes as possible. Without glorification, praise becomes an imprecise form of exaltation.

When we praise God, we attest to His complete benevolence. When we glorify Him, we attest to His transcendence above any fault or deficiency. A precise and encompassing attestation must acknowledge both His complete benevolence as well as His perfection. As such, an attestation can only be as precise as required when it includes both praise and glorification.

When it comes to supplication, the situation becomes a little different. As God's creatures, it is He who blessed us with the opportunity to supplicate to Him. As Imam al-Sajjad teaches us to recite,

فَكَيْفَ لِي بِتَحْصِيلِ الشُّكْرِ، وَشُكْرِي إِيَّاكَ يَفْتَقِرُ إِلَى شُكْرٍ، فَكُلَّمَا قُلْتُ: لَكَ الْحَمْدُ، وَجَبَ عَلَيَّ لِذلِكَ أَنْ أَقُولَ: لَكَ الْحَمْدُ.

So how can I achieve thankfulness when my utterance of thanks to You is itself in need of thanks? Therefore, whenever I say, 'To you belongs all praise!', I am obliged to say, 'To you belongs all praise!'[11]

In every instance in which we are blessed with the ability to supplicate, we must be thankful and show our gratitude for that blessing.

When we recite the supplication, we are looking at His blessing and the grace by which He allowed us to know and supplicate to Him. We must therefore praise Him for this blessing.

The position of supplication is different from the position of attestation. From this difference, we can understand why praise is, at times, coupled with glorification, while it is separated at others.

---

[11] *Imam Sajjad, al-Sahifa al-Sajjadiya, Whispered Supplication of the Praiseful.*

Practical Praise

We can praise God in our hearts by acknowledging His ultimate goodness and perfection. We can praise Him by uttering words of praise such as "all praise belongs to God."

Praise can also be practical – praise that is translated into action. This is an important level of praise that we must aspire to. Let us look at a few examples of practical praise that we may be able to apply in our lives.

Understanding Faith. One of the thorny problems of our times is people's lack of understanding of their faith. As we read in the noble tradition:

لا تزول قدما عبد يوم القيامة حتى يُسأل عن أربع؛ عن عمره فيما أفناه، وشبابه فيما أبلاه وعن ماله أين كسبه، وفيما أنفقه، وعن حبنا أهل البيت.

The feet of a servant [of God] will not sway on the Day of Judgment [towards Hellfire] before he is asked about four – about his life, how he spent it; about his youth, how he wasted it; about his wealth, how he earned it and how he spent it; and about our love, the Holy Household.[12]

We will be asked about our wealth, how we acquired it and how we spent it. The problem is that we do not put the time and effort into learning the religious rulings that apply to our careers and our livelihoods. We work hard to earn money, and we take care to spend it in a way that will return to us the greatest value. Yet, we do not put as much effort into understanding what the divine dictates regarding these transactions.

To ask about the religious rulings surrounding our careers and livelihoods is a form of praise to God Almighty, who blessed us with everything that we have. We must praise God by seeking to better understand our faith and its rulings. We must praise Him by learning how

---

[12] Al-Majlisi, *Bihar al-Anwar*, 7:258.

we can earn and spend our wealth in this world, while maintaining His pleasure.

Paying Alms. Another way to manifest practical praise to God is to pay the alms that He made obligatory upon all of us. Abu Baseer once asked Imam al-Baqir, "who is the most expeditious in entering Hellfire?" The Imam replied,

من أكل من مال اليتيم درهماً، ونحن اليتيم.

Whoever eats a single dirham from the money of the orphans. Surely, we [the Holy Household] are the orphans![13]

To pay the obligatory alms – whether *khums* or *zakat* – is a form of praise and gratitude for the blessing of livelihood.

Imam Ali once entered the home of al-Harith ibn Ziyad. The Imam saw that the house was larger than normal. He asked al-Harith why he needed such a large home. Al-Harith grew quiet with embarrassment. The Imam did not chastise him for owning such a large estate, but rather reassured him that his house could be his ticket to Paradise. When al-Harith inquired how, the Imam replied:

تُقري فيها الضَّيفَ، وتَصِلُ فيها الرَّحِمَ، وتُطلِعُ منها الحُقوقَ مَطالِعَها، فإذا أنتَ قَد بَلَغتَ بها الآخِرَةَ

You host the guest [well], connect with your kinfolk, and pay the alms as they are due. If you do so, then you have used [this house] to reach the hereafter.[14]

God does not prohibit us from becoming wealthy. He grants wealth to us as He wishes. However, our reception of this blessing must be matched with praise. A practical method of praising God for such grace is to pay the alms as He prescribed.

Avoiding Excess and Waste. At times, we take God's blessings lightly when we spend the wealth He gave us wastefully. We plan the most

---

[13] Al-Sadouq, *Man la Yahduruh al-Faqih*, 2:42.
[14] Al-Mu'tazili, *Sharh Najul Balagha*, 2:33.

lavish of events these days – from weddings, to dinners, and even funerals sometimes. Yet, God Almighty prohibited us from being wasteful:

$$يَا بَنِي آدَمَ خُذُوا زِينَتَكُمْ عِندَ كُلِّ مَسْجِدٍ وَكُلُوا وَاشْرَبُوا وَلَا تُسْرِفُوا ۚ إِنَّهُ لَا يُحِبُّ الْمُسْرِفِينَ$$

O Children of Adam! Put on your adornments on every occasion of prayer, and eat and drink, but do not waste; indeed, He does not like the wasteful. [15]

We must spend our wealth wisely and properly. Otherwise, we are wasting one of God's great blessings upon us.

To spend wisely and properly is a form of practical praise for His blessing. God says:

$$وَضَرَبَ اللَّهُ مَثَلًا قَرْيَةً كَانَتْ آمِنَةً مُطْمَئِنَّةً يَأْتِيهَا رِزْقُهَا رَغَدًا مِّن كُلِّ مَكَانٍ فَكَفَرَتْ بِأَنْعُمِ اللَّهِ فَأَذَاقَهَا اللَّهُ لِبَاسَ الْجُوعِ وَالْخَوْفِ بِمَا كَانُوا يَصْنَعُونَ$$

Allah draws a parable: There was a town, secure and peaceful, its provision coming abundantly from every place. But it was ungrateful toward Allah's blessings. So, Allah made it taste hunger and fear because of what its people used to do. [16]

If we are ungrateful towards God's grace, we will meet a similar fate. We must maintain these blessings by always being thankful and grateful. We must be mindful of this, individually and collectively. Social policies must be instituted so that our collective and national wealth is spent wisely and apportioned justly.

O' God, allow us to be grateful for your blessings and guide us towards being praiseful. And the last of our prayers is praise be to God, Lord of the realms.

---

[15] *The Holy Quran*, 7:31.
[16] *The Holy Quran*, 16:112.

Guidance & Excellence

وَأَنْتَ مُسَدِّدٌ لِلصَّوابِ بِمَنِّكَ

You support [the believers on the path] to truth with Your grace.

Our beloved Imam taught us to recite these words after using praise to begin our supplication and exaltation of God Almighty.

What is the relationship between praise and support?

There are three possible interpretations of this relationship:

1. It could be one of causation, where divine support is the cause of praise. In other words, I would not have praised God had He not supported me in doing so.
2. Causation could also go the other way. It could be that divine support is a result of praise. It could be that as we praise God, He provides us with support.
3. It has also been said that this sentence is structured this way in order to weave a more eloquent supplication. For example, we greet the Holy Prophet at the end of our prayers by reciting, "Peace be upon you, O' Messenger of God, along with the mercy of God and His blessings!" Although this would normally be interpreted as a greeting, it is used here as an eloquent prayer for the Holy Prophet. The same is true for the verse we are speaking of. In other words, by praising God as the one who 'supports to truth' we are politely and eloquently asking for His support.

Guidance and Support

Divine support is a form of guidance by command. To understand this concept, let us look at some of the types of guidance we may encounter.

The most basic way to categorize guidance is to distinguish between the legislative and non-legislative. Legislative guidance is the task of prophets and messengers. God Almighty says,

رُسُلًا مُبَشِّرِينَ وَمُنذِرِينَ لِئَلَّا يَكُونَ لِلنَّاسِ عَلَى اللَّهِ حُجَّةٌ بَعْدَ الرُّسُلِ ۚ وَكَانَ اللَّهُ عَزِيزًا حَكِيمًا

[We have sent] apostles, as bearers of good news and warners, so that mankind may not have any argument against Allah, after the [sending of the] apostles; and Allah is all-mighty, all-wise.[1]

The warnings and glad tidings delivered by God's messengers are legislative guidance.

Non-legislative guidance is that which is delivered to God's creatures by means other than prophets and messengers. Non-legislative guidance is of two types – earned and granted.

Earned guidance is the type that God has ordained that He will provide to His servants. Of course, no one can truly earn God's guidance and blessings. No matter what we do, we do not deserve the great blessings that He bestows on us. He emanates existence and sustenance upon us through His grace. He allows us to live a safe and meaningful life in this world out of His mercy and generosity. Thus, guidance is not earned by any creature's merit, but by God's divine promise. He has promised that He will bestow His guidance upon us if we meet certain conditions. God says,

وَالَّذِينَ جَاهَدُوا فِينَا لَنَهْدِيَنَّهُمْ سُبُلَنَا ۚ وَإِنَّ اللَّهَ لَمَعَ الْمُحْسِنِينَ

As for those who strive in Us, We shall surely guide them in Our ways, and Allah is indeed with the virtuous.[2]

When God sees that a servant is being proactive and eager in worship, He provides further blessings and guidance in support of His servant's efforts. For example, God describes the Sleepers of the Cave[3] as follows:

---

[1] *The Holy Quran,* 4:165.

[2] *The Holy Quran,* 29:69.

[3] *The Sleepers of the Cave are a group of individuals who escaped religious persecution and sough refuge in a cave. They are mentioned in the Holy Quran in Chapter 18.*

نَحْنُ نَقُصُّ عَلَيْكَ نَبَأَهُم بِالْحَقِّ ۚ إِنَّهُمْ فِتْيَةٌ آمَنُوا بِرَبِّهِمْ وَزِدْنَاهُمْ هُدًى

We relate to you their account in truth. They were indeed youths who had faith in their Lord, and We had enhanced them in guidance.[4]

It was because of their faith and perseverance in God's trials that He enhanced them with guidance.

Guidance is also granted out of God's favor, without any work or effort on our part. This type of guidance can be categorized into general and particular guidance.

General guidance is provided to all of creation by the Creator. God Almighty says,

قَالَ رَبُّنَا الَّذِي أَعْطَىٰ كُلَّ شَيْءٍ خَلْقَهُ ثُمَّ هَدَىٰ

He said, 'Our Lord is He who gave everything its creation and then guided it.'[5]

Every creation is guided towards its Lord, even what we perceive to be mere inanimate objects. As we read in the Holy Quran,

وَإِن مِّن شَيْءٍ إِلَّا يُسَبِّحُ بِحَمْدِهِ وَلَٰكِن لَّا تَفْقَهُونَ تَسْبِيحَهُمْ

There is not a thing but celebrates His praise, but you do not understand their glorification.[6]

Every creation has a level of consciousness by which it praises God and receives His guidance. This is supported by a philosophical concept that states 'existence corresponds to knowledge and consciousness.' So long as a thing exists, it holds a degree of consciousness and knowledge, even though we may not be able to perceive it. Every creature knows of its limits and understands its dependence on the all-independent Lord. Because of this consciousness, even a boulder would rip asunder out of fear of God. The Holy Quran says,

---

[4] *The Holy Quran, 18:13.*
[5] *The Holy Quran, 20:50.*
[6] *The Holy Quran, 17:44.*

لَوْ أَنزَلْنَا هَٰذَا الْقُرْآنَ عَلَىٰ جَبَلٍ لَّرَأَيْتَهُ خَاشِعًا مُّتَصَدِّعًا مِّنْ خَشْيَةِ اللَّهِ ۚ وَتِلْكَ الْأَمْثَالُ نَضْرِبُهَا لِلنَّاسِ لَعَلَّهُمْ يَتَفَكَّرُونَ

Had We sent down this Quran upon a mountain, you
would have seen it humbled [and] go to pieces with the fear
of Allah. We draw such comparisons for mankind, so that
they may reflect.[7]

So long as a thing exists, it holds a degree of consciousness and receives a degree of guidance by which it praises its Lord and thanks Him for all His bounties.

Particular guidance is provided for humans as rational beings. It can be divided into guidance by creation and guidance by command.

Guidance by creation is what God provides us by way of aligning worldly causes in order to allow for the circumstances of our guidance. The most evident form of this is seen at an individual's birth. When God allows for an individual's birth within a family of believers, He sets the stage for the individual's guidance to faith. In fact, lineage plays an important role in guidance. The Holy Quran says,

إِنَّ اللَّهَ اصْطَفَىٰ آدَمَ وَنُوحًا وَآلَ إِبْرَاهِيمَ وَآلَ عِمْرَانَ عَلَى الْعَالَمِينَ ۞ ذُرِّيَّةً بَعْضُهَا مِن بَعْضٍ ۗ وَاللَّهُ سَمِيعٌ عَلِيمٌ

Indeed, Allah chose Adam and Noah, and the progeny of
Abraham and the progeny of Imran above all the nations;
some of them are descendants of the others, and Allah is
all-hearing, all-knowing.[8]

These chosen prophets are all of one lineage and heredity played its role in their selection. This is one example of how God sets the material means for the guidance of His servants.

Guidance by command is when God Almighty plants the light of guidance in the hearts of the believers. No intermediaries are used and no

---

[7] *The Holy Quran, 59:21.*

[8] *The Holy Quran, 3:33, 34.*

means of cause and effect are in play. God simply opens an individual's heart and mind to faith. He says in His Holy Book:

أَفَمَن شَرَحَ اللَّهُ صَدْرَهُ لِلْإِسْلَامِ فَهُوَ عَلَىٰ نُورٍ مِّن رَّبِّهِ ۚ فَوَيْلٌ لِّلْقَاسِيَةِ قُلُوبُهُم مِّن ذِكْرِ اللَّهِ ۚ أُولَٰئِكَ فِي ضَلَالٍ مُّبِينٍ

Is someone whose breast Allah has opened to Islam so that he follows a light from His Lord...? So, woe to those whose hearts have been hardened to the remembrance of Allah. They are in manifest error.[9]

God also says:

أَوَمَن كَانَ مَيْتًا فَأَحْيَيْنَاهُ وَجَعَلْنَا لَهُ نُورًا يَمْشِي بِهِ فِي النَّاسِ كَمَن مَّثَلُهُ فِي الظُّلُمَاتِ لَيْسَ بِخَارِجٍ مِّنْهَا ۚ كَذَٰلِكَ زُيِّنَ لِلْكَافِرِينَ مَا كَانُوا يَعْمَلُونَ

Is he who was lifeless, then We gave him life and provided him with a light by which he walks among the people, like one who dwells in a manifold darkness which he cannot leave? To the faithless is thus presented as decorous what they have been doing.[10]

The Holy Quran mentions that an Imam is able to deliver guidance by divine command. The holy verse states,

وَجَعَلْنَاهُمْ أَئِمَّةً يَهْدُونَ بِأَمْرِنَا

We made them imams, guiding by Our command....[11]

An Imam is therefore able to plant the light of guidance in the hearts of the believers, without the need for material intermediaries. The light of the Imam connects to the individual's heart, providing the guidance that they seek.

Thus, guidance by divine command is a form of non-legislative guidance that God grants out of His favor and plants in the hearts of believers.

---

[9] *The Holy Quran*, 39:22.

[10] *The Holy Quran*, 6:122.

[11] *The Holy Quran*, 21:73.

Divine Command and Immaculacy

Guidance by divine command is a grant of immaculacy. Immaculacy has levels, the lowest of which is support on the path of truth. Its highest level is safeguarding of an individual from all sin by the grace of God and light of guidance.

We supplicate to God and say, "You support [the believers on the path] to truth with Your grace." In this supplication, we are asking God Almighty to grant us immaculacy by planting the light of guidance in our hearts by His divine command.

We ask God to support us on the path to truth – both theoretical and practical. We ask for His support in achieving theoretical truth, such that we do not believe in any falsity. We ask for His support on the path of practical truth, such that all our actions align to His commands and never cross any of His boundaries.

This support on the path of truth, both theoretical and practical, is a form of immaculacy. Immaculacy is a blessing that any individual can attain, at least at its lowest levels. Our beloved Holy Prophet and the Imams from his household have achieved the highest levels of immaculacy. Immaculacy is a single light, but has multiple levels. Each of us can achieve some level of immaculacy by perseverance in God's trials and by His support.

The Imams' Supplication

If asking for support on the path of truth is equivalent to asking for immaculacy, how does the Imam ask that for himself? Is he not immaculate already? We can ask the same question about the Imam's recitation of the verse in his prayer,

اهْدِنَا الصِّرَاطَ الْمُسْتَقِيمَ

Guide us on the straight path.[12]

---

[12] *The Holy Quran*, 1:6.

Why does he ask for guidance if he is already guided? We know that our Imams would recite this verse with the utmost humility before God. Why do they pray and supplicate in this way?

As we have mentioned, immaculacy has a variety of levels. This is because immaculacy is deeply linked to knowledge. Just as knowledge has its levels – from certain knowledge, to particular certainty, to true certainty – immaculacy also has its levels.

The merit of our beloved Holy Prophet over Imam Ali in terms of knowledge dictates that he holds a higher spiritual level and a higher level of immaculacy. The merit of Imam Ali over his sons dictates that he holds a higher level of immaculacy than them. It is narrated that Imam al-Sadiq said:

نحن في الفضل سواء ولكن بعضنا أعلم من بعض.

We are all equal in virtue. However, some of us are more knowledgeable than others. [13]

Imam al-Baqir also narrates the following incident with his father, Imam al-Sajjad:

يا بني، أعطني بعض تلك الصحف التي فيها عبادة علي بن أبي طالب (ع)، فأعطيته، فقرأ فيها شيئاً يسيراً، ثم تركها من يده تضجراً، وقال: من يقوى على عبادة علي بن أبي طالب (ع)؟

'My son, give me some of the parchments in which the worships of Ali ibn Abu Talib are written.' I handed them to him. He read from them for a short while and then put them down with dismay and said, 'Who can bear the worships of Ali ibn Abu Talib?' [14]

Immaculacy has its levels. Each of our Imams was the most perfect individual in terms of knowledge and immaculacy. Yet amongst them, they held different levels of knowledge and immaculacy. Thus, they

---

[13] Al-Majlisi, *Bihar al-Anwar*, 36:409.

[14] Ibid, 46:75.

supplicate and pray to their Lord in hopes of gaining higher levels of immaculacy and growing closer to Him.

The Believer and the Holy Spirit

Another way to interpret divine support is to understand it as the strength that God gives His righteous servants through the Holy Spirit. God says in the Holy Book,

أُولَٰئِكَ كَتَبَ فِي قُلُوبِهِمُ الْإِيمَانَ وَأَيَّدَهُم بِرُوحٍ مِّنْهُ

[For] such, He has written faith into their hearts and strengthened them with a spirit from Him. [15]

The Holy Spirit is a being that God provides to support the prophets, messengers, imams, and believers. In speaking of Prophet Jesus, God says,

وَآتَيْنَا عِيسَى ابْنَ مَرْيَمَ الْبَيِّنَاتِ وَأَيَّدْنَاهُ بِرُوحِ الْقُدُسِ

We gave Jesus, the son of Mary, manifest proofs and confirmed him with the Holy Spirit. [16]

According to the noble traditions, the Holy Spirit is not Archangel Gabriel. It is a being of a higher status and greater influence than the archangels. God makes the distinction between the two in the Holy Quran when He says,

تَنَزَّلُ الْمَلَائِكَةُ وَالرُّوحُ فِيهَا بِإِذْنِ رَبِّهِم مِّن كُلِّ أَمْرٍ

In it the angels and the Spirit descend, by the leave of their Lord, with every command. [17]

The Holy Spirit is thus not amongst the angels, but is a being distinct from them. It is the creature that God appoints to support His chosen servants.

---

[15] *The Holy Quran*, 58:22.
[16] *The Holy Quran*, 2:87.
[17] *The Holy Quran*, 97:4.

Immaculacy and Free Will

The late Sheikh Muhammad Jawad Mughnia argued that God's prophets and messengers do not possess free will when it comes to delivering their divine message. In other words, they perform the duties of delivering the message mechanically, without any ability or possibility of error. He understood this from the following Quranic verses:

عَالِمُ الْغَيْبِ فَلَا يُظْهِرُ عَلَىٰ غَيْبِهِ أَحَدًا ۞ إِلَّا مَنِ ارْتَضَىٰ مِن رَّسُولٍ فَإِنَّهُ يَسْلُكُ مِن بَيْنِ يَدَيْهِ وَمِنْ خَلْفِهِ رَصَدًا ۞ لِيَعْلَمَ أَن قَدْ أَبْلَغُوا رِسَالَاتِ رَبِّهِمْ وَأَحَاطَ بِمَا لَدَيْهِمْ وَأَحْصَىٰ كُلَّ شَيْءٍ عَدَدًا

Knower of the Unseen, He does not disclose His [knowledge of the] Unseen to anyone, except to an apostle He approves of. Then He dispatches a sentinel before and behind him so that He may ascertain that they have communicated the messages of their Lord, and He encompasses all that is with them, and He keeps a count of all things.[18]

The verse says that each prophet is surrounded by an escort of angels who are sent to ensure his complete performance of his duties. Delivery of the divine message becomes mechanical, with no room for fault.

This opinion is in error. Delivery of the divine message is an action like any other action of the prophets and messengers. It does not differ from their other actions and duties, and is therefore subject to their free will. They are immaculate in their delivery of the message, just as they are immaculate in all their other actions.

It is out of their beauty and enlightenment that they do not commit any sin or mistake. They do not add, subtract, err, neglect, forget, or deviate from any portion of their message. If they had done, their punishment would have been most severe, due to their high status and great responsibility. As God says in the Holy Quran,

---

[18] *The Holy Quran*, 72:26-28.

لَوْ تَقَوَّلَ عَلَيْنَا بَعْضَ الْأَقَاوِيلِ ◆ لَأَخَذْنَا مِنْهُ بِالْيَمِينِ ◆ ثُمَّ لَقَطَعْنَا مِنْهُ الْوَتِينَ

Had he faked any sayings in Our name, We would have
surely seized him by the right hand and then cut off his
aorta.[19]

If the prophets and messengers had no free will, this verse would be
void of meaning. What good is a promise of punishment if the subject
has no capacity to disobey to begin with? Since God does not speak
frivolously, we know that He promises His punishment because His
messengers have the capacity to disobey – although they do not out of
their free will and volition. They deliver the message exactly as they
were tasked. God speaks of our Holy Prophet and says,

وَمَا يَنطِقُ عَنِ الْهَوَىٰ ◆ إِنْ هُوَ إِلَّا وَحْيٌ يُوحَىٰ

Nor does he speak out of [his own] desire: it is just a
revelation that is revealed [to him].[20]

The verse that was used to argue for the messengers' supposed lack of
free will is not speaking of immaculacy. Rather, it is a description of
God's support for His chosen servant through the Holy Spirit, which
always accompanies them. The Holy Spirit is their sentinel.

فَإِنَّهُ يَسْلُكُ مِن بَيْنِ يَدَيْهِ وَمِنْ خَلْفِهِ رَصَدًا ۞ لِيَعْلَمَ أَن قَدْ أَبْلَغُوا رِسَالَاتِ رَبِّهِمْ

Then He dispatches a sentinel before and behind him so
that He may ascertain that they have communicated the
messages of their Lord.[21]

These verses explain to us that the messengers are not only immaculate,
but are also supported with the Holy Spirit. God granted them immaculacy by purifying their hearts and enlightening their souls. He provided them with the Holy Spirit, which was further support for them
in fulfilling their divine duties.

---

[19] *The Holy Quran*, 69:44-46.

[20] *The Holy Quran*, 53:3, 4.

[21] *The Holy Quran*, 72:27, 28.

Additional evidence of the messengers' free will in delivering their message is found in the following verse:

وَلَا تَعْجَلْ بِالْقُرْآنِ مِن قَبْلِ أَن يُقْضَىٰ إِلَيْكَ وَحْيُهُ

Do not hasten with the Quran before its revelation is completed for you. [22]

God also says in the Holy Quran:

لَا تُحَرِّكْ بِهِ لِسَانَكَ لِتَعْجَلَ بِهِ ❀ إِنَّ عَلَيْنَا جَمْعَهُ وَقُرْآنَهُ ❀ فَإِذَا قَرَأْنَاهُ فَاتَّبِعْ قُرْآنَهُ ❀ ثُمَّ إِنَّ عَلَيْنَا بَيَانَهُ

Do not move your tongue with it to hasten it. Indeed, it is up to Us to put it together and to recite it. And when We have recited it, follow its recitation. Then, its exposition [also] lies with Us. [23]

Thus, we see that there are two ways to understand this verse of the supplication.

وأنت مسدد للصواب بمنك

You support [the believers on the path] to truth with Your grace.

First, we can understand it as a prayer for immaculacy, which God grants by His favor and through His command.

Second, it can be understood as a request for support through the Holy Spirit, which God appoints to His righteous servants so long as they remain faithful and humble supplicants.

O' God, make us amongst those who You support on the path of truth.

---

[22] *The Holy Quran*, 20:114.

[23] *The Holy Quran*, 75:16-19.

The Oasis of
Supplication

وَأَيْقَنْتُ أَنَّكَ أَنْتَ أَرْحَمُ الرَّاحِمِينَ فِي مَوْضِعِ الْعَفْوِ وَالرَّحْمَةِ

**And I have come to know with certainty that You are the
most merciful in disposition of forgiveness and clemency!**

Scholars say that mercy is an attribute of God's divine actions, and not
an attribute of His essence. His mercy is to emanate goodness and
blessing. His emanation of existence, sustenance, and guidance is what
we call 'mercy.' Let us first address the distinction between attributes
of essence and action before we delve deeper into understanding His
mercy.

Attributes of God's essence are those attributes which are indistin-
guishable from Him. They do not lag behind Him in any way, nor do
they depend on anything outside of Him. For example, His omnipotence, omniscience, and omnibenevolence are of His essence.

Attributes of God's actions are those that are not realized without an
object outside of Him. Such attributes include creation and blessing.
He is the creator because He emanates existence to His creations. He is
the sustainer because He emanates blessings to those creations. These
attributes are unlike the attributes of His essence. They are seen
through His actions and are not distinguishable without a view to His
creatures.

Beneficence and Mercy

God's beneficence encompasses all things. It reaches the most minute
subatomic particle and envelops the largest galaxies. He says in His
Holy Book,

وَرَحْمَتِي وَسِعَتْ كُلَّ شَيْءٍ

My mercy embraces all things.[1]

---

[1] *The Holy Quran*, 7:156.

Everything in existence is a recipient of His divine mercy and beneficence. His mercy is also deeply connected to His power. The Holy
Quran says,

الرَّحْمَنُ عَلَى الْعَرْشِ اسْتَوَى

The All-beneficent, settled on the Throne. [2]

Exegetes say that whoever controls the Throne controls all of creation.
Everything has a center, and the center of creation is at the divine
Throne. It is the center of all commands and the source of all directives.
This blessed verse is referring to God's absolute control and power over
His creation. The Throne is not a physical place where He sits, but a
denotation of His supreme authority over all things.

Why does the above verse refer to God as the All-beneficent? Because
He is at the center of control over all things, He is the source of emanation of blessing and mercy to all things. Thus, His mercy embraces
all things.

God Almighty is also the most merciful when it comes to the believers.
He refers to this in the blessed verse,

فَمَن يُرِدِ اللَّهُ أَن يَهْدِيَهُ يَشْرَحْ صَدْرَهُ لِلْإِسْلَامِ

*Whomever Allah desires to guide, He opens his breast to
Islam.* [3]

He also says,

أَفَمَن شَرَحَ اللَّهُ صَدْرَهُ لِلْإِسْلَامِ فَهُوَ عَلَى نُورٍ مِّن رَّبِّهِ

*Is someone whose breast Allah has opened to Islam so that
he follows a light from His Lord...?* [4]

Emphasis on Mercy

Why did the Holy Imam focus on the trait of mercy in this segment of
the supplication?

---

[2] *The Holy Quran, 20:5.*
[3] *The Holy Quran, 6:125.*
[4] *The Holy Quran, 39:22.*

First, supplication is a request for God's beneficence and mercy. When we supplicate and ask God for forgiveness, blessings, guidance, or health, we are asking Him to emanate His mercy and beneficence on us. As such, it was fitting for the Imam to start the supplication beseeching God by His mercy.

Second, the Imam wanted to show us that supplication itself is a grand mercy. In addressing this idea, we will go over two points:(1) the Holy Imam's emphasis on the trait of mercy, and (2) the ethical impact of supplication.

The Imam places an emphasis on supplication as a mode of divine mercy. The fact that an individual is blessed to supplicate and pray before the Almighty Lord is a mercy of itself. The facets of mercy seen in supplication can be summarized as follows:

First, supplication brings peace and tranquility, and lifts the specter of worry and sorry from the soul.

An individual might go through difficult times in their life. They may not find an escape from these troubles and worries. A believer might be tried with sins and disobedience, which bring great worry and grief over the heart.

A believer may fall victim to sin. Yet unlike a hypocrite or disbeliever, their sins weigh heavy on their heart. As we are told in the noble tradition:

إذا أذنب المنافق كان ذنبه كذبابة طارت أمام عينه، أما المؤمن إذا أذنب كان ذنبه كالجبل على صدره

When a hypocrite sins, his sin is [as insignificant to him] as a fly which flew in front of his eyes. However, if a believer sins, his sin would be like a mountain on his chest.

A believer is so connected to God that any form of disobedience or shortcoming leaves a heavy psychological toll and creates a cloud of sorrow and guilt that will weigh heavy on him.

If a believer cannot express this guilt and sorrow, it would continue to suffocate them and lead them to despair.

There is one tried and true cure for this despair, a method to remove the clouds of guilt – supplication. Supplication allows us to express our guilt and seek refuge from their ill outcomes. Supplication is a mercy in itself, because of the peace and tranquility it brings to the supplicant. As God says in His Holy Book:

قُلْ يَا عِبَادِيَ الَّذِينَ أَسْرَفُوا عَلَى أَنْفُسِهِمْ لَا تَقْنَطُوا مِن رَّحْمَةِ اللَّهِ ۚ إِنَّ اللَّهَ يَغْفِرُ الذُّنُوبَ جَمِيعًا ۚ إِنَّهُ هُوَ الْغَفُورُ الرَّحِيمُ

Say [that Allah declares,] 'O My servants who have committed excesses against their own souls, do not despair of the mercy of Allah. Indeed, Allah will forgive all sins. Indeed, He is the All-forgiving, the All-merciful.[5]

Second, supplication is a cure to the disease of hardheartedness. God says,

ثُمَّ قَسَتْ قُلُوبُكُم مِّن بَعْدِ ذَٰلِكَ فَهِيَ كَالْحِجَارَةِ أَوْ أَشَدُّ قَسْوَةً

Then your hearts hardened after that, so they are like stones, or even harder.[6]

If callousness grows to control an individual's heart due to their deviance and excess in disobedience, they will grow further and further away from the grazing grounds of God's select flock. As Imam al-Sadiq is narrated to have said:

إذا أذنب الرجل خرج من قلبه نكتة سوداء، فإن تاب انمحت وإن زاد حتى تغلب على قلبه فلا يفلح بعدها أبداً.

If a man sins, a black speck appears in his heart. If he repents, it is erased. If he persists, it will grow until it overtakes his heart, so that he will never succeed.[7]

---

[5] *The Holy Quran*, 39:53.

[6] *The Holy Quran*, 2:74.

[7] Al-Kulayni, *al-Kafi*, 2:271.

Excess in committing sins and disobeying God's commands creates a dark shadow that overtakes an individual's soul. The Holy Quran says,

كَلَّا بَلْ رَانَ عَلَى قُلُوبِهِم مَّا كَانُوا يَكْسِبُونَ

No, that is not the case! Rather, their hearts have been sullied by what they have been earning.[8]

An individual who allows themself to fall prey to their base desires – chasing after their beastly inclinations – will develop the illness of hard-heartedness. The symptoms of this disease are an inability to listen to sound advice, and a repulsion at the mention of death and the afterlife.

What is the cure to this illness?

Supplication is the cure that can soften a hard heart. It is the panacea that brings back tenderness, kindness, and sympathy to the heart. Make it a habit to cry and weep with guilt! To habituate the self to weeping and supplication removes the hard crust that begins to build up over time with sin and disobedience.

We can see the beauty of this in the supplications of the Master of Prostrators, Imam al-Sajjad. He teaches us to supplicate and say,

وَمَا لِي لَا أَبْكِي وَلَا أَدْرِي إِلَى مَا يَكُونُ مَصِيرِي وَأَرَىٰ نَفْسِي تُخَادِعُنِي وَأَيَّامِي تُخَاتِلُنِي وَقَدْ خَفَقَتْ عِنْدَ رَأْسِي أَجْنِحَةُ الْمَوْتِ

And why would I not weep while I have no knowledge of my fate and I observe my soul deceiving itself and my days are fading away and the wings of death have flapped close by?

Why do I not weep? Am I a hard rock that refuses to feel guilt? Have I fallen so far away from God's mercy that I do cannot taste the sublime sweetness of supplication?

---

[8] *The Holy Quran, 83:14.*

فَمَا لِي لاَ أَبْكِي أَبْكِي لِخُرُوجِ نَفْسِي أَبْكِي لِظُلْمَةِ قَبْرِي أَبْكِي لِضِيقِ لَحْدِي أَبْكِي
لِسُؤَالِ مُنْكَرٍ وَنَكِيرٍ إِقَّايَ أَبْكِي لِخُرُوجِي مِنْ قَبْرِي عُرْيَاناً ذَلِيلاً حَامِلاً ثِقْلِي عَلَى
ظَهْرِي

So why would I not weep? I weep for my soul departing my body. I weep for the darkness of my grave. I weep for the narrowness of my tomb. I weep for the questioning of [the angels] Munkar and Nakeer of me [in my grave]. I weep for my coming out of my grave [on the Day of Resurrection] naked, humiliated, and carrying my book [of deeds] on my back.

Who will aid me on that day? Who can I count on? Who will stand by my side at all these trials?

أَنْظُرُ مَرَّةً عَنْ يَمِينِي وَأُخْرَى عَنْ شِمَالِي إِذِ الْخَلاَئِقُ فِي شَأْنٍ غَيْرِ شَأْنِي لِكُلِّ امْرِئٍ
مِنْهُمْ يَوْمَئِذٍ شَأْنٌ يُغْنِيهِ وُجُوهٌ يَوْمَئِذٍ مُسْفِرَةٌ ضَاحِكَةٌ مُسْتَبْشِرَةٌ وَوُجُوهٌ يَوْمَئِذٍ عَلَيْهَا
غَبَرَةٌ تَرْهَقُهَا قَتَرَةٌ وَذِلَّةٌ

I look to the right once and to the left once. Behold! The creatures will each be engaged with matters other than mine. Every person that day has a concern of his own. Many faces on that day shall be bright, laughing, joyous. And many faces on that day, on them shall be dust. Darkness, and humiliation shall cover them. [9]

It is narrated that Imam al-Hassan – an immaculate Imam – would be seen weeping on his deathbed. He would be asked why he weeps when he is the grandson of the Holy Prophet, and an individual heavily praised by God's Messenger. Imam al-Hassan was said to have performed Hajj twenty times. On three different occasions, he would give away half of his wealth for the sake of God. When he was asked why he wept, he said,

---

إنما أبكي لخصلتين: هول المطلع وفراق الأحبة

I weep for two things: the terror seen [on Resurrection] and departing my loved ones.[10]

Imam al-Hassan would weep for the terror seen when he remembered the difficulties of ascension and descension of the soul to reach its final abode.

Supplication is the cure that brings tenderness to the heart and removes the callousness built by sin and disobedience. It is therefore a great instance of God's mercy and beneficence that every believer would do well to take advantage of.

The Ethics of Supplication

Supplication is a great method we can use to develop in ourselves some of the most significant ethical principles that our faith teaches us.

Accountability. Supplication teaches us to be accountable to ourselves, and to judge ourselves before we are judged. The Holy Prophet is narrated to have said:

حاسبوا أنفسكم قبل أن تحاسبوا وزنوها قبل أن توزنوا، وتجهزوا للعرض الأكبر

Judge yourself before you are judged. Weigh [your deeds] before you are weighed. Prepare yourself for the grand trial![11]

We have before us a great opportunity that we must reap. We have the opportunity of life. We must use its limited hours and days to better ourselves and reach our highest goal. This cannot happen without holding ourselves accountable before we are held to account by our Lord. The Messenger of God explained to his close companion:

---

[10] *Al-Kulayni, al-Kafi,* 1:461.

[11] *Al-'Amili, Wasa'el al-Shi'a,* 16:99.

يا أبا ذر: إذا أصبحت فلا تحدّث نفسك بالمساء، وإذا أمسيت فلا تحدّث
نفسك بالصباح، وخذ من صحتك قبل سقمك، ومن حياتك قبل موتك، فإنك
لا تدري ما اسمك غداً. يا أبا ذر: كن على عمرك أشحّ منك على درهمك ودينارك.

*O' Aba Thar, if you awaken in the morning, do not think
to yourself of the night. If you go to sleep, do not think to
yourself of the morning. Make use of your health before you
grow ill, and of your life before your death. Surely, you will
not know what your name will be tomorrow! O' Aba Thar,
be more concerned with your time than your Dirham and
Dinar.*[12]

Reap the opportunity of life! Invest your time in this world! Unfortunately, many of us are infected with the disease of heedlessness. We walk the road of life without knowing where our steps are taking us. We do not look at the road we have taken. We do not see where it is taking us. As the Holy Quran says:

وَلَقَدْ ذَرَأْنَا لِجَهَنَّمَ كَثِيرًا مِنَ الْجِنِّ وَالْإِنسِ ۖ لَهُمْ قُلُوبٌ لَا يَفْقَهُونَ بِهَا وَلَهُمْ أَعْيُنٌ لَا
يُبْصِرُونَ بِهَا وَلَهُمْ آذَانٌ لَا يَسْمَعُونَ بِهَا ۚ أُولَٰئِكَ كَالْأَنْعَامِ بَلْ هُمْ أَضَلُّ ۚ أُولَٰئِكَ هُمُ
الْغَافِلُونَ

*Certainly, We have winnowed out for Hell many of the jinn
and humans: they have hearts with which they do not
understand, they have eyes with which they do not see, they
have ears with which they do not hear. They are like cattle;
indeed, they are more astray. It is they who are the
heedless.*[13]

Can anyone run a business without accounting their profits and losses? If a person does not keep a balance sheet, would they not be mismanaging their business? In the same sense, we are blameworthy when we live our lives without taking account of our victories and losses, our achievements and shortcomings.

[12] Al-Majlisi, *Bihar al-Anwar*, 74:75.
[13] *The Holy Quran*, 7:179.

We spend our lives worrying about our livelihoods, careers, spouses, families, and friends. What about ourselves? What is the self's place and when will it be judged? When will we spend the time to reform, train, and purify it?

The Commander of the Faithful says,

إِنَّمَا هِيَ نَفْسِي أُرُوضُهَا بِالتَّقْوَى لِتَأْتِي آمِنَةً يَوْمَ الخَوْفِ الأَكْبَرِ

Rather, it is my self which I tame with piety so that it may come forward in peace on the Grand Day of Fear [i.e., the Day of Judgment]. [14]

The Holy Prophet would say to a group of his companions after arriving back from battle,

أفضل الجهاد من جاهد نفسه التي بين جنبيه

The greatest struggle is to struggle against an individual's self which he holds between his sidearms. [15]

Hisham ibn al-Hakam also narrates that Imam al-Kadhim would say,

يا هشام ليس منا من لم يحاسب نفسه كل يوم فإن عمل حسنة إستزاد منه وإن عمل سيئا استغفر الله منه وتاب

O' Hisham, an individual is not of us if he does not hold himself to account every day – so that if he did a good deed, he [asks God] for more, and if he did ill, he would seek forgiveness from God and repent. [16]

The followers of the Imams must possess a long-term vision and an ability to think beyond the present. A long-term vision is not only about social, political, and scientific analyses. It is about looking at where we came from and understanding our ultimate destination. It is about understanding how every step could change your path. It is about recognizing when you have slipped and getting back to God's ordained path.

---

[14] *Al-Radi, Nahj al-Balagha, Letter 45.*

[15] *Al-'Amili, Wasa'el al-Shi'a, 15:163.*

[16] *Al-Nouri, Mustadrak al-Wasa'el, 12:153.*

Take five minutes of your time before you sleep or when you wake up. Spend that time with yourself. Review the past 24 hours of your life. If you see any shortcoming, seek repentance and resolve not to make the same mistake. If there was an achievement and improvement, ask God to continue His blessings so that you can sustain it.

Know that holding yourself accountable is the means by which you can better yourself. God says,

إِنَّ اللَّهَ لَا يُغَيِّرُ مَا بِقَوْمٍ حَتَّى يُغَيِّرُوا مَا بِأَنْفُسِهِمْ

Indeed, Allah does not change a people's lot, unless they change what is in their souls.[17]

Supplication gives us the opportunity to judge ourselves and trains us to be self-accountable. It is therefore a mode of God's mercy and beneficence in this world, by which He guides us toward Him.

Love. Supplication plants the love of God in the individual's heart. Which of us can claim that we do not need God's love to fill their heart and soul?

Excess love for one thing surely leads to neglect of another. Someone who excessively loves luxury and wealth will end up neglecting their spouse and family. An individual who excessively loves his wife may end up neglecting his social duties. This is due to the imbalance that excess creates in the individual's life.

However, there can be no limit to an individual's love for God. There is no such thing as excessive love in this regard. Instead, greater love for God will reflect in greater appreciation and love for family, society, and all other matters. Greater love for God creates greater good in the individual's life.

The Holy Quran categorizes people into two groups – those who exceed in their love of this world and those who exceed in divine love.

As for those who are excessive in love of this temporal world, the Holy Quran describes them as follows:

---

[17] *The Holy Quran, 13:11.*

نُيِّنَ لِلنَّاسِ حُبُّ الشَّهَوَاتِ مِنَ النِّسَاءِ وَالْبَنِينَ وَالْقَنَاطِيرِ الْمُقَنْطَرَةِ مِنَ الذَّهَبِ وَالْفِضَّةِ وَالْخَيْلِ الْمُسَوَّمَةِ وَالْأَنْعَامِ وَالْحَرْثِ ۗ ذَٰلِكَ مَتَاعُ الْحَيَاةِ الدُّنْيَا

The love of [worldly] allures, including women and children, accumulated piles of gold and silver, adorned horses, livestock, and farms has been made to seem decorous to mankind. Those are the wares of the life of this world....[18]

The love of this world places the individual's desires at the center of their worldview, such that they would place value only in whatever they find pleasurable.

Those who choose God as the object of their love experience a much more sublime emotion. God says in the Holy Quran,

وَالَّذِينَ آمَنُوا أَشَدُّ حُبًّا لِّلَّهِ

Surely, the faithful have a more ardent love for Allah![19]

The believers are those who allow themselves to melt in the love of God. They hold the greatest love, awe, respect, and trust in Him. They are in complete contrast with those who anchor their hearts to this world. As our beloved Imams teach us,

حب الدنيا رأس كل خطيئة ورأس العبادة حسن الظن بالله

Love of this world is at the helm of every ill action, and at the helm of worship is trust in God.[20]

Scholars of ethics list two important effects of divine love. First, love for Him brings peace and tranquility to the heart. The love of any object is naturally accompanied by fear and anxiety. If you love someone, you fear that you might lose them. An individual's love for their wealth is ridden with anxiety over how they might squander it. The only love that plants peace and tranquility in the heart of a lover is the love of the Almighty.

---

[18] *The Holy Quran*, 3:14.

[19] *The Holy Quran*, 2:165.

[20] *Al-Nouri, Mustadrak al-Wasa'el*, 12:40.

أَلَا بِذِكْرِ اللّهِ تَطْمَئِنُّ الْقُلُوبُ

Behold! The hearts find rest in Allah's remembrance![21]

Second, love of God will never lead to grief and sorrow. An individual who loves this fleeting world will always be in a state of grief. An individual who is attached to their wealth will doubtlessly lose some of it at some point.

Those who direct their love solely to God know that He never forgets them and will always emanate His beneficence unto them. He will never leave our side. He will never neglect us. We must never fear or grieve, knowing that He is by our side.

أَلَا إِنَّ أَوْلِيَاءَ اللّهِ لَا خَوْفٌ عَلَيْهِمْ وَلَا هُمْ يَحْزَنُونَ

Look! The friends of Allah will indeed have no fear, nor will they grieve.[22]

We must always be glad and joyous, trusting in our beloved who promised us an eternal life by His side,

لَا خَوْفٌ عَلَيْهِمْ وَلَا هُمْ يَحْزَنُونَ ❀ الَّذِينَ آمَنُوا وَكَانُوا يَتَّقُونَ

[They shall] have no fear nor will they grieve – those who have faith and are Godwary.[23]

Supplication plants and fosters the love of God in the believer's heart. We should strive to supplicate and pray to Him so that we can strengthen this spiritual connection. We must seek humility and servility before our Almighty Lord in order to prepare ourselves for more of His mercy and beneficence.

Charity. Supplication teaches us to be charitable and supplants any selfish tendencies within us. Many of us suffice ourselves to focus on our desires – our bellies, wallets, and comforts. The days come and go, while our only thought is about our own pleasure.

---

[21] *The Holy Quran, 13:28.*

[22] *The Holy Quran, 10:62.*

[23] *The Holy Quran, 10:63.*

This is either a result of a mistake in upbringing, a reflection of the individual's developed habits, or a result of ill company and bad friends who egg the individual on in their selfishness. How can an individual escape from the shackles of selfishness? How can we get past ourselves to see others? How can we forget the 'I' and remember the 'you'?

We must teach ourselves to think of others – to think of the disadvantaged, poor, and oppressed. We teach ourselves to think of others through following the examples of our beloved Imams and reciting the supplications that they taught us. Imam al-Sajjad teaches us to pray and say:

اللَّهُمَّ إِنِّي أَعْتَذِرُ إِلَيْكَ مِنْ مَظْلُومٍ ظُلِمَ بِحَضْرَتِي فَلَمْ أَنْصُرْهُ، وَمِنْ مَعْرُوفٍ أُسْدِيَ إِلَيَّ فَلَمْ أَشْكُرْهُ، وَمِنْ مُسِيءٍ اعْتَذَرَ إِلَيَّ فَلَمْ أَغْذِرْهُ، وَمِنْ ذِي فَاقَةٍ سَأَلَنِي فَلَمْ أُوثِرْهُ، وَمِنْ حَقِّ ذِي حَقٍّ لَزِمَنِي لِمُؤْمِنٍ فَلَمْ أُوَفِّرْهُ، وَمِنْ عَيْبِ مُؤْمِنٍ ظَهَرَ لِي فَلَمْ أَسْتُرْهُ، وَمِنْ كُلِّ إِثْمٍ عَرَضَ لِي فَلَمْ أَهْجُرْهُ.

O' God, I ask Your pardon for the person wronged in my presence whom I did not help, the favor conferred upon me for which I returned no thanks, the wrongdoer who asked pardon from me and whom I did not pardon, the needy person who asked from me and whom I did not prefer over myself, the right of a believer who possesses a right incumbent upon me which I did not fulfil, the fault of a believer which became evident to me and which I did not conceal, and every sin which presented itself to me and which I failed to avoid.

اللهم وَسَدِّدْنِي لِأَنْ أُعَارِضَ مَنْ غَشَّنِي بِالنُّصْحِ، وَأَجْزِيَ مَنْ هَجَرَنِي بِالْبِرِّ، وَأُثِيبَ مَنْ حَرَمَنِي بِالْبَذْلِ، وَأُكَافِيَ مَنْ قَطَعَنِي بِالصِّلَةِ، وَأُخَالِفَ مَنِ اغْتَابَنِي إِلَى حُسْنِ الذِّكْرِ، وَأَنْ أَشْكُرَ الْحَسَنَةَ، وَأُغْضِيَ عَنِ السَّيِّئَةِ.

O' God, support me to repay whomever is dishonest toward me with good counsel, compensate whomever estranges from me with benevolence, reward whomever deprives me with charity, recompense whomever cuts me off with affection, oppose whomever slanders me with good mention, and give thanks for good while shutting my eyes to evil![24]

We see the same thing when we turn to the life of our dear Lady Fatima. Imam al-Hassan would say,

ما كان في الدنيا أعبد من فاطمة (ع).

There was none in this world greater in worship than Fatima.[25]

One night, Imam al-Hassan stayed awake to observe his mother, Lady Fatima, in prayer. She prayed from nightfall until dawn and Imam al-Hassan watched her throughout. When she finally finished her prayers at dawn, he approached to ask a question. The hours that he spent watching and listening to her prayers, he only heard her ask God to help the poor, the sick, the needy, her neighbors, her community, and all of those she knew. Not once did he hear her ask of something for herself. He asked his mother,

يا أمّاه! لَم تدعي لنفسِكِ كما تدعين لغيرِكِ!

O' mother! You have not prayed for yourself as you prayed for others!

Lady Fatima replied,

يا بُنيّ، الجار، قبل الدار.

My Son, [put] your neighbor before your household.[26]

The progeny of our Holy Prophet Muhammad were dedicated to their societies. The community lived in their hearts and prayers. A true vision for their Muslim brothers and sisters lived in their actions and teachings. God Almighty praised them in His Holy Book, saying:

---

[24] Abtahi, al-Sahifa al-Sajjadiya, 166.

[25] Al-Majlisi, Bihar al-Anwar, 43:76.

[26] Al-'Amili, Wasa'el al-Shi'a, 4:150.

وَيُطْعِمُونَ الطَّعَامَ عَلَى حُبِّهِ مِسْكِينًا وَيَتِيمًا وَأَسِيرًا ✦ إِنَّمَا نُطْعِمُكُمْ لِوَجْهِ اللّٰهِ لَا نُرِيدُ مِنكُمْ جَزَاءً وَلَا شُكُورًا

For the love of Him, they feed the needy, the orphan and the prisoner, [saying,] 'We feed you only for the sake of Allah. We desire no reward from you, nor thanks.[27]

This is our role models' way of life.

Supplication brings forth the manifestations of God's mercy and is an ethical wellspring for the believer. The fact that we are blessed to supplicate is one of God's greatest mercies upon us.

We ask God to allow us to thank Him for His boundless mercy.

---

[27] *The Holy Quran,* 76:9.

Divine Wisdom

وَأَيْقَنْتُ أَنَّكَ أَنْتَ أَرْحَمُ الرَّاحِمِينَ فِي مَوْضِعِ الْعَفْوِ وَالرَّحْمَةِ، وَأَشَدُّ الْمُعَاقِبِينَ فِي مَوْضِعِ النَّكَالِ وَالنِّقْمَةِ، وَأَعْظَمُ الْمُتَجَبِّرِينَ فِي مَوْضِعِ الْكِبْرِيَاءِ وَالْعَظَمَةِ

And I have come to know with certainty that You are the most merciful in disposition of forgiveness and clemency! [Still, You] are the sternest exactor at the time of exemplary punishment and chastisement, and the most dominant [Lord] in the domain of majesty and greatness.

This listing of God's divine attributes aims to convey a particular understanding of God's wisdom. God's mercy is deeply intertwined with His wisdom. Wisdom dictates that mercy and punishment be put in its proper place. God's dominance is deeply intertwined with His wisdom, dictating that His majesty and greatness be put in the right place. Thus, the placement of His attributes and actions in their rightful place is an indication of His absolute wisdom.

What is the standard for where mercy and chastisement should be placed?

Scholars of ethics tell us that there is a single standard in this regard – the standard of worship or insolence. Worship and obedience of God makes a servant a proper recipient of His mercy. On the other hand, disobedience and insolence in the face of God's commands and blessings makes a servant a proper recipient of His chastisement.

To better understand this concept, let us contemplate on the following tradition. It is narrated that Imam al-Sadiq said:

خِفِ اللهَ كَأَنَّكَ تَرَاهُ، وَإِنْ كُنْتَ لا تَرَاهُ فَإِنَّهُ يَرَاكَ، فَإِنْ كُنْتَ تَرَى أَنَّهُ لا يَرَاكَ فَقَدْ كَفَرْتَ، وَإِنْ كُنْتَ تَعْلَمُ أَنَّهُ يَرَاكَ ثُمَّ بَرَزْتَ لَهُ بِالْمَعْصِيَةِ فَقَدْ جَعَلْتَهُ مِنْ أَهْوَنِ النَّاظِرِينَ عَلَيْكَ

Fear God as if you see Him. Surely, even if you do not see Him, He sees you. If you think that He does not see you, then you have disbelieved. If you know that He sees you and

you face Him with disobedience, then you have made Him
the least significant of your observers. [1]

An individual who does not think that God sees has rejected God's omniscience and omnipotence, thus disbelieving in Him. An individual may acknowledge God's omniscience and omnipotence, yet insolently disobey His commands. Such an individual would be trivializing God's words and scorning His commands. This is a form of insolent rebellion against the Almighty, making the individual a proper recipient of His wrath.

This is why Imam al-Sajjad taught his companion Abu Hamza to supplicate to God, saying:

ما عصيتك إذ عصيتك وأنا بك شاكٌ ولا بنكالك جاهل ولا لعقوبتك متعرض
ولا بأمرك مستخف ولكن سولت لي نفسي وأعانني عليها شقوتي.

I did not disobey You - when I disobeyed You - with doubt
in You, ignorant of Your punishment, provoking Your
retribution, or belittling Your commands. However, my
soul prompted me and I was aided by my deviance. [2]

Our disobedience is not out of doubt in Him. We are not ignorant of His punishment and retribution. Our sins are not because we belittle His commands.

Whatever sin we may commit is not out of disbelief in Him. It is out of our carnal desires and whims, which prompt us to do disobedience. The Holy Quran says,

وَمَا أُبَرِّئُ نَفْسِي ۚ إِنَّ النَّفْسَ لَأَمَّارَةٌ بِالسُّوءِ إِلَّا مَا رَحِمَ رَبِّي

Yet I do not absolve my [own carnal] soul, for the [carnal]
soul indeed prompts [men] to evil, except in as much as my
Lord has mercy. [3]

An individual who disobeys God knowing His commands, knowledge, and power is insolently rebelling against His divine will. However, an

---

[1] Al-Kulayni, al-Kafi, 2:68.

[2] Al-Majlisi, Bihar al-Anwar, 46:81.

[3] The Holy Quran, 12:53.

individual who is overcome by desire and whim into disobedience is still a proper recipient of divine mercy.

Thus, the standard in receiving God's mercy or wrath is based on an individual's worship or insolence. Worship of God may sometimes be accompanied by a few sins here and there – given that those sins were the result of being overwhelmed by desire and whim, and not out of rebellion against the Almighty's commands. In that case, the individual will feel regret and remorse for their sins, and will seek God's forgiveness and clemency. Such an individual will remain a proper recipient of God's mercy. When that individual sins as a form of rebellion, rejection, and insolence against God, they become a proper recipient of divine wrath and chastisement.

Understanding Divine Wisdom

There is a misconception that has been posed regarding God's divine wisdom. The proponents of this misconception claim that it is impossible for us to understand whether God's actions are wise or unwise.

A wise individual is one whose actions are in line with the best interests of the whole. When we see an individual whose actions comply with the best interest of their community, we recognize that they are a wise individual. The premise here is that for an individual's actions to be wise, they must conform to some pre-existing notion of best interest. If an action does not comply in this way, it is not the wisest option.

The question is this: 'What if there is no best interest to be identified?' When God acts in a certain way, how can we identify what the underlying interests are and if His actions advance them in the best way? Is there even any underlying interest that we can ask about?

This is an intricate theological study, which we will attempt to elucidate in this chapter. Namely, how can we understand God's divine wisdom? To reach this understanding, we must seek to first understand the meaning of human wisdom. We will then see if we can find a way to understand God's sublime wisdom by analogy and rational reasoning.

Human Wisdom

Every voluntary action is linked to two primary components. The first component is the cause and reason behind the action. The second is the correspondence between the cause and the underlying interests.

Cause. Philosophers say that every action has four causes: a material cause, a formal cause, an efficient cause, and a final cause. To understand this concept, let us ask ourselves how a house is built.

To build a house, we must first seek its *material cause* – wood, drywall, concrete, steel, and the like. If we do not have these materials, we cannot build a house.

We also need a *formal cause* – the form in which we must place these materials in order to build the house. You cannot build a house without blueprints of some sort.

Next, we need an *efficient cause* – things outside the components which act on them to create the final product. In our example of the house, we need an architect, carpenter, engineer, electrician, plumber, and the like. We also need saws, hammers, and whatever other tools may be needed for these builders to take the materials and fashion them into a house.

Lastly, we need a *final cause* – a purpose. A house is built so that a family can take it as their home.

Is purpose necessary for a voluntary action? A voluntary action cannot be undertaken without will. Will is comprised of four factors – conception, belief, desire, and intent.

For example, let us ask how an individual might develop the will to pray. First, they must conceive of and understand what prayer is. Next, they must believe in prayer's benefits and effects. After belief, the individual must desire to pray and reap those benefits. Finally, there must be an intention to actually expend the effort to pray.

It is not possible for an individual to undertake a voluntary action without first conceiving and believing in its purpose – even if that purpose was futile or whimsical. For example, an individual may waste hours every day watching television or playing video games. What is the purpose behind this voluntary action? Probably entertainment. It might be a whimsical and unwise purpose, but it's a purpose nonetheless.

Thus, a voluntary action cannot exist based on material, formal, and efficient causes alone. There must be a purpose for which that action is undertaken.

Correspondence. To judge whether or not an action is wise, we must measure the degree of correspondence between its purpose and general best fundamental interests. For example, action may be undertaken for the purpose of 'killing time'. Such an action is clearly futile, because there is no fundamental interest that it corresponds to. Futility is a shortcoming and would not be a pursuit of a rational and wise individual.

Human actions are thus linked to their causes and corresponding fundamental interests. If there is no corresponding interest, then the action is unwise. We can therefore understand human wisdom by corresponding the purpose behind an action with its underlying fundamental interests.

Meanings of Divine Wisdom

As we have outlined at the outset of this chapter, God's mercy and chastisement are always in sync with His divine wisdom. We reached this understanding through a reading of the verses of the supplication that we laid out at the beginning of the chapter.

To better understand divine wisdom, let us answer a misconception that some philosophers have posed against it.

The misconception says that for God's actions to be wise, they must have a purpose that corresponds to some underlying fundamental interests. The claim is that there is no purpose behind God's actions because He is the ultimate cause and purpose. There is nothing distinct from Him that we can attribute to be a purpose behind His actions.

Even if His actions did have purpose, there is no evidence that they correspond to some underlying fundamental interest.

Muslim philosophers say that 'a deficient actor is perfected by his purpose; a perfect actor has no purpose – his purpose is himself.'

To illustrate, imagine a miser who has come to his senses and wants to become generous and charitable. To do so, he begins to give out his wealth and never turns away a person who is in need, as a way of habituating himself to generosity. The personal purpose behind his actions is to better himself by attaining this particular character trait.

A deficient actor is thus perfected through a purpose. In other words, the purpose behind a deficient individual's actions is always to better themselves and cure their deficiencies. Another example of this can be seen in a cowardly individual. Will they succumb to their fears or confront them? If they runs away from what they fear, then it is for the purpose of maintaining their own safety and wellbeing – a form of betterment in itself. If they do face their fears, then it is for the sake of strengthening their will and gaining courage. As the Commander of the Faithful says:

إذا هبت أمراً فقع فيه، فإن شدة توقيه أعظم مما تخاف منه.

If you fear something, pursue it. Surely, excess precaution
is greater than what you fear. [4]

But what about an individual who is generous or brave? There is no personal purpose behind an individual who has reached each form of excellence. A generous individual does not give for a purpose, but because their generous character dictates that they give. A courageous individual does not face their fears for a purpose, but it comes naturally to them out of the excellence of their character.

---

[4] Al-Radi, *Nahj al-Balagha, Short Saying #175.*

Thus, a perfect actor has no personal purpose for his or her actions. Rather, causation and purpose stems from their nature. A deficient actor may thus be asked about their purpose, while a perfect actor has no purpose other than their character.

God Almighty is perfection itself. He is perfect in every way. He is not deficient in any way. Thus, asking for a purpose behind His actions is nonsensical. His very nature dictates that He acts in the most perfect form.

God's divine nature dictates that He emanates beneficence. His divine nature dictates that He emanates life and blessings to His creatures. As the holy verse declares,

لَا يُسْأَلُ عَمَّا يَفْعَلُ وَهُمْ يُسْأَلُونَ

He is not questioned concerning what He does, but they are questioned.[5]

Therefore, we cannot define God's divine wisdom by reference to a personal purpose. As the all-perfect Creator, He has no personal purpose and His actions bring no benefit to Him.

Now let us turn to the misconception that God's actions cannot be identified as wise, because there is no evidence that they correspond to an underlying fundamental interest.

The proponents of this misconception claim that we cannot identify God's actions as wise, because our experience in this world does not provide evidence that His actions correspond to an underlying fundamental interest.

Sure, if we look at the sun, we can tell that its existence is necessary to the support of life on Earth. But why did He create Satan and what fundamental interests does that serve? Why did He create illness, disease, and birth defects? Why did He create a world full of natural disasters like hurricanes, earthquakes, and droughts? What are the underlying fundamental interests behind all this?

---

[5] *The Holy Quran*, 21:23.

If wisdom means the correspondence between actions and underlying interests, then we cannot prove His wisdom, because we cannot understand the interests underlying all His actions. If we cannot understand the underlying interests, then we cannot identify whether or not His actions actually correspond to and advance those interests in the best possible way. Therefore, we cannot tell whether His actions are wise or futile.

The answer to this misconception is that God's wisdom does in fact mean that His actions correspond to an underlying fundamental interest. However, we understand that His actions are indeed wise, not through empirical analysis, but through rational proof.

Why might anyone act unwisely? Why might they do something that is futile or whimsical? The reason behind an unwise action is one of three things – either ignorance, need, or inability. We cannot think of a fourth reason why someone might act unwisely.

God is much more sublime than to have such deficiencies attributed to Him.

A person might act unwisely because they do not understand the circumstances of their actions and their possible outcomes. However, we cannot ascribe any ignorance to God, the omniscient. He says in His Holy Book,

وَمَا يَعْزُبُ عَن رَّبِّكَ مِن مِّثْقَالِ ذَرَّةٍ فِي الْأَرْضِ وَلَا فِي السَّمَاءِ وَلَا أَصْغَرَ مِن ذَٰلِكَ وَلَا أَكْبَرَ إِلَّا فِي كِتَابٍ مُّبِينٍ

Not an atom's weight escapes your Lord in the Earth or in the sky, nor [is there] anything smaller than that nor bigger, but it is in a manifest Book.[6]

A person might know what the wisest action is, but they might be unable to undertake it. An unwise act might thus be the product of the individual's inability. Again, this defect cannot be ascribed to God the omnipotent.

---

[6] *The Holy Quran, 10:61.*

An individual might also act unwisely because of their individual needs. People might waste their time with useless banter and gossip, because they need to entertain themselves. This is also a deficiency that cannot be ascribed to God, the all-sufficient. He says:

يَا أَيُّهَا النَّاسُ أَنتُمُ الْفُقَرَاءُ إِلَى اللَّهِ ۖ وَاللَّهُ هُوَ الْغَنِيُّ الْحَمِيدُ

O mankind! You are the ones who stand in need of Allah,
and Allah—He is the All-sufficient, the All-laudable. [7]

All-sufficiency – as theologians and philosophers explain – is the attribute of His infinite existence. His infinite nature dictates that He is all-sufficient. Being all-sufficient dictates that He is in no need for entertainment, diversion, or play.

Therefore, understanding God's omniscience, omnipotence, and all-sufficiency leads us to understand that He is all-wise.

Divine Wisdom and Will

God's dominance means that His will is always done. Nothing can contradict His will or be in any way that is not conforming to it. He says in His Holy Book,

إِنَّمَا أَمْرُهُ إِذَا أَرَادَ شَيْئًا أَن يَقُولَ لَهُ كُن فَيَكُونُ

All His command, when He wills something, is to say to it
'Be,' and it is. [8]

His majesty means that all perfections belong to Him. This is because existence is the source of all perfection, and He is the source of all existence.

His greatness means that His authority and ownership over all things are evident to those who are willing to see.

To better understand His greatness, let us delve a little deeper into the idea of ownership. Philosophers categorize ownership into three categories – legal, real, and true ownership.

---

[7] *The Holy Quran, 35:15.*

[8] *The Holy Quran, 36:82.*

Legal ownership is often evidenced through paperwork or legal principle. I legally own a piece of land if I hold its title. I am presumed to legally own a ring if it is in my possession.

Real ownership is evidenced by control. I own myself, because I control my senses and my actions.

True ownership is evidenced by the ability to bring things into and out of existence. True ownership is reserved to God Almighty, as He is the one who emanates existence and can take anything out of existence whenever He wills. He emanates existence to all beings, and their continued existence is conditioned on His will. This is the meaning of His true ownership of all things.

Our beloved Imam al-Mahdi teaches us that God's wisdom dictates the exemplification of His dominance in the domain of His majesty and greatness.

وَأَعْظَمَ الْمُتَجَبِّرِينَ فِي مَوْضِعِ الْكِبْرِيَاءِ وَالْعَظَمَةِ.

[You are] the most dominant [Lord] in the domain of majesty and greatness.

For example, God's wisdom dictates that His dominance is exemplified in the determination of each individual's lifespan. God says,

فَإِذَا جَاءَ أَجَلُهُمْ لَا يَسْتَأْخِرُونَ سَاعَةً ۖ وَلَا يَسْتَقْدِمُونَ

When their time comes, they shall not defer it by a single hour, nor shall they advance it.[9]

God Almighty exemplifies His dominance by implementing His will and exercising His ownership over all things. Even in a safe and prosperous land, a disaster might strike without warning. These are all exemplifications of His dominance, majesty, and greatness. He says,

فَسُبْحَانَ الَّذِي بِيَدِهِ مَلَكُوتُ كُلِّ شَيْءٍ وَإِلَيْهِ تُرْجَعُونَ

So immaculate is He in whose hand is the dominion of all things, and to whom you shall be brought back.[10]

---

[9] *The Holy Quran, 7:34.*
[10] *The Holy Quran, 36:83.*

In one tradition God is narrated as saying,

من لم يرض بقضائي، ولم يصبر على بلائي، ولم يشكر على نعمائي، فليعبد رباً
سوائي، وليخرج من أرضي وسمائي.

*Whoever does not accept My judgement, is not patient with
My trials, and does not thank Me for My blessings, let them
worship a lord other than Me and let them escape from My
Earth and My heavens.*[11]

If we can find any place where God does not dominate and where His
majesty and greatness are not present, then we can take refuge from
His chastisement there and feel free to sin against Him as we please.
However, so long as we are in His dominion – so long as we cannot
even extend our lives for a second beyond what He wills – then we
should abide by His commands.

God Almighty's wisdom dictates that He exemplifies his dominance
and ownership of all things, without allowing us to contravene or contradict His will.

We ask Him by His wisdom to keep us in the domain of His mercy and
blessings.

---

[11] *Al-Mazandarani, Sharh Usool al-Kafi,* 1:222.

Divine Support

اللَّهُمَّ أَذِنْتَ لِي فِي دُعَائِكَ وَمَسْأَلَتِكَ، فَاسْمَعْ يَا سَمِيعُ مِدْحَتِي، وَأَجِبْ يَا
رَحِيمُ دَعْوَتِي، وَأَقِلْ يَا غَفُورُ عَثْرَتِي، فَكَمْ يَا إِلَهِي مِنْ كُرْبَةٍ قَدْ فَرَّجْتَهَا،
وَهُمُومٍ قَدْ كَشَفْتَهَا، وَعَثْرَةٍ قَدْ أَقَلْتَهَا، وَرَحْمَةٍ قَدْ نَشَرْتَهَا، وَحَلْقَةٍ بَلَاءٍ قَدْ
فَكَكْتَهَا

O' God, You have given me permission to invoke and ask
of You. So, listen, O' all-Hearing, to my praise. Accept, O'
all-Beneficent, my supplication. Discount, O' most-Clement, my shortcoming. O' God, how many a difficulty have
You removed? How many a sorrow have You dispelled?
How many a shortcoming have You discounted? How
many a mercy have You spread? How many a woesome
shackle have you unraveled?

A person may object to our beloved Imam asking God to accept his
supplication and hear his praise. God has already promised that He will
listen and answer so long as we supplicate to Him. He says in His Holy
Book:

وَقَالَ رَبُّكُمُ ادْعُونِي أَسْتَجِبْ لَكُمْ إِنَّ الَّذِينَ يَسْتَكْبِرُونَ عَنْ عِبَادَتِي سَيَدْخُلُونَ
جَهَنَّمَ دَاخِرِينَ

Your Lord has said, 'Call Me, and I will hear you!' Indeed,
those who are disdainful of My worship will enter Hell in
utter humiliation.[1]

He also says,

وَإِذَا سَأَلَكَ عِبَادِي عَنِّي فَإِنِّي قَرِيبٌ أُجِيبُ دَعْوَةَ الدَّاعِ إِذَا دَعَانِ

When My servants ask you about Me, [tell them that] I am
indeed nearmost. I answer the supplicant's call when he
calls Me.[2]

---

[1] The Holy Quran, 40:60.
[2] The Holy Quran, 2:186.

What does the Imam mean when he says that God has given permission for him to supplicate? What does it mean when he asks for God to listen and answer?

God's permission can be understood in two ways – legislative and creational.

Legislative permission simply means that God did not forbid a particular action. For example, God gave us permission to sleep, eat, and drink – it is not haram to do so.

Creational permission means that God has allowed the proper causes to take effect. He has created this world and willed for it to be organized in a system of cause and effect. For example, His system dictates that fire cannot exist without creating the effect of burning. His system dictates that a human child cannot be conceived without a mother and a father.

This does not mean that He has completely delegated this world to its causal system and lifted the hands of His dominance and control. Causes cannot create their effects independent of God's will and permission. Fire cannot burn without God's will and permission. If He wills for fire not to burn, then it will not. He says,

تَبَارَكَ الَّذِي بِيَدِهِ الْمُلْكُ وَهُوَ عَلَىٰ كُلِّ شَيْءٍ قَدِيرٌ

Blessed is He in whose hands is all sovereignty, and He has power over all things.[3]

In the case of fire creating its effect, He says,

قُلْنَا يَا نَارُ كُونِي بَرْدًا وَسَلَامًا عَلَىٰ إِبْرَاهِيمَ

We said, 'O fire! Be cool and safe for Abraham!'[4]

A cause creating its effect is therefore contingent on God's will and permission. This is the permission that God grants when He says,

---

[3] *The Holy Quran*, 67:1.

[4] *The Holy Quran*, 21:69.

مَا أَصَابَ مِن مُّصِيبَةٍ إِلَّا بِإِذْنِ اللَّهِ

No affliction visits [anyone] except by Allah's leave.[5]

Speaking of Prophet Jesus's ability to heal the blind and revive the dead, the Holy Quran says,

وَأُبْرِئُ الْأَكْمَهَ وَالْأَبْرَصَ وَأُحْيِ الْمَوْتَى بِإِذْنِ اللَّهِ

I heal the blind and the leper and I revive the dead by Allah's leave.[6]

Therefore, God granting us permission to supplicate can be interpreted in one of two ways.

Firstly, God has blessed us with the ability to supplicate and guided us toward it. He inspired our hearts with the desire to supplicate. This is a grant of permission for us to supplicate. Thus, the meaning of the Imam's words in the supplication could be the creational permission to supplicate.

Secondly, the Imam could be referring to the Quranic verses we mentioned earlier. In those verses, God gave us permission to supplicate and promised to answer. The Imam's mention of this permission would thus be a reference to those verses, and showing proper manners in speaking to the Almighty.

We turn to God and ask him permission to supplicate to Him. Yes, He has already granted permission to all His servants. Still, my calls are coming from a sinful soul. My voice is that of an individual who has disobeyed God's commands. O' God, will You please hear my cries? Will You overlook my disobedience and answer my pleas?

This is the proper etiquettes of servitude and servility that we must use in speaking to the Almighty Lord.

---

[5] *The Holy Quran*, 64:11.
[6] *The Holy Quran*, 3:49.

Beseeching God

The Imam said, "O' God, You have given me permission to invoke and ask of You." What is the difference between invocation and asking? A person may invoke God simply be admitting servitude to Him and acknowledging shortcomings in serving Him. A person who invokes God does not necessarily need to ask for something specific.

To ask is to make a request, whether or not it comes with servitude and servility. That is why you ask a question when you are requesting an answer – it does not necessarily indicate a position of servitude.

Invocation and asking are like means and ends. You invoke someone to gain their attention, so that you may ask and make your request.

A person might ask, 'Why do you need to get God's attention? Is He not omniscient and attentive at all times?' God Almighty says,

وَإِن تَجْهَرْ بِالْقَوْلِ فَإِنَّهُ يَعْلَمُ السِّرَّ وَأَخْفَى

Whether you speak loudly [or in secret tones,] He indeed knows the secret and what is still more hidden.[7]

He also says,

وَإِن تُبْدُوا مَا فِي أَنفُسِكُمْ أَوْ تُخْفُوهُ يُحَاسِبْكُم بِهِ اللَّهُ

Whether you disclose what is in your hearts or hide it, Allah will bring you to account for it.[8]

However, what is meant by gaining God's attention is to elicit a merciful look from Him. Yes, God knows and is always attentive, but is He looking at us mercifully? His mercy is what we are trying to elicit by invoking Him.

God has given us permission to stand before Him and supplicate. We must invoke Him by showing our servitude and servility, thereby gaining a merciful look from Him. We can then ask and beseech Him for all our needs.

---

[7] *The Holy Quran*, 20:7.

[8] *The Holy Quran*, 2:284.

The Foundations of Supplication

A reader may look at some of the verses of the Holy Quran or the supplications and think that there's a degree of redundancy. Take the following verse:

وَإِذَا سَأَلَكَ عِبَادِي عَنِّي فَإِنِّي قَرِيبٌ ۖ أُجِيبُ دَعْوَةَ الدَّاعِ إِذَا دَعَانِ ۖ فَلْيَسْتَجِيبُوا لِي وَلْيُؤْمِنُوا بِي لَعَلَّهُمْ يَرْشُدُونَ

When My servants ask you about Me, [tell them that] I am indeed nearmost. I answer the supplicant's call when he calls Me. So let them respond to Me, and let them have faith in Me, so that they may fare rightly. [9]

Why does God say, "I answer the supplicant's call when he calls Me"? Why not stop at, "I answer the supplicant's call"?

The answer lies in the fact that not every supplication is a true call to God. So, what is a true call? A true call is that which satisfies two conditions.

First, it must come from the heart and not be a mere movement of the tongue. We often pray to God with our tongues, but how often do we pray with our hearts? A heartfelt prayer must come with an eagerness to meet God and with an awe of His majesty. As the Holy Quran describes,

إِنَّهُمْ كَانُوا يُسَارِعُونَ فِي الْخَيْرَاتِ وَيَدْعُونَنَا رَغَبًا وَرَهَبًا ۖ وَكَانُوا لَنَا خَاشِعِينَ

Indeed, they were active in [performing] good works, and they would supplicate Us with eagerness and awe and were humble before Us. [10]

A heartfelt supplication comes with fear of God's chastisement and punishment.

---

[9] *The Holy Quran*, 2:186.
[10] *The Holy Quran*, 21:90.

إِنَّمَا الْمُؤْمِنُونَ الَّذِينَ إِذَا ذُكِرَ اللَّهُ وَجِلَتْ قُلُوبُهُمْ

*The faithful are only those whose hearts tremble [with awe]
when Allah is mentioned.*[11]

At the same time, a heartfelt supplication comes with immense hope
and understanding of God's boundless mercy. As God says,

وَرَحْمَتِي وَسِعَتْ كُلَّ شَيْءٍ

My mercy embraces all things.[12]

A true supplication to God Almighty is thus characterized by eagerness, awe, fear, and hope – emotions that come with a true understanding of servitude to the Almighty.

Second, a true call to God comes with absolute devotion to Him.

God Almighty created this world within a system of cause and effect.
God blesses us with sustenance, but requires us to put forth the work
and effort to achieve it. He cures the ill, but asks us to seek medicine
and nurse our diseases. A believer will put forward the effort to earn a
living, and will seek the aid of a doctor to cure their illness. However,
they do so with absolute conviction that true sustenance and health are
in the hands of the Almighty.

This is the meaning of the verse where God states, "I answer the supplicant's call when he calls Me." He does not answer any call, but only
the true calls of His devoted servants.

Based on this understanding, our scholars have interpreted the "distressed" who is answered by God as the devoted servant – one who
knows that none can answer his prayers but the Almighty. God says in
the Holy Quran,

أَمَّنْ يُجِيبُ الْمُضْطَرَّ إِذَا دَعَاهُ وَيَكْشِفُ السُّوءَ

*Is it He who answers the call of the distressed [person] when
he invokes Him and removes his distress...?*[13]

---

[11] *The Holy Quran*, 8:2.
[12] *The Holy Quran*, 7:156.
[13] *The Holy Quran*, 27:62.

In the same vein, the Imam teaches us to supplicate to God with the true calls of a devoted servant.

اللَّهُمَّ أَذِنْتَ لِي فِي دُعائِكَ وَمَسْأَلَتِكَ، فَاسْمَعْ يا سَمِيعُ مِدْحَتِي، وَأَجِبْ يا رَحِيمُ دَعْوَتِي، وَأَقِلْ يا غَفُورُ عَثْرَتِي

O' God, You have given me permission to invoke and ask of You. So listen, O' all-Hearing, to my praise. Accept, O' all-Beneficent, my supplication. Discount, O' most-Clement, my shortcoming.

Levels of Proximity

These verses of the supplication could also be a reference to the levels of proximity to God Almighty. Scholars of ethics say that there are levels and degrees of proximity.

So listen, O' all-Hearing, to my praise. The first level of proximity is that of approach – God Almighty approaches the individual, so that the individual may approach and be devoted to Him. As such, the individual becomes a proper recipient of divine mercy – a position we discussed in the previous chapter.

Accept, O' all-Beneficent, my supplication. The second level is that of emanation of God's mercy, so that the individual becomes free of the shackles of the world. Mankind is made of two components – the physical component made of the realm of divine sovereignty, and a metaphysical component made of the realm of divine dominion. God Almighty says,

تَبَارَكَ الَّذِي بِيَدِهِ الْمُلْكُ وَهُوَ عَلَى كُلِّ شَيْءٍ قَدِيرٌ

Blessed is He in whose hands is all sovereignty, and He has power over all things. [14]

He also says,

---

[14] *The Holy Quran*, 67:1.

فَسُبْحَانَ الَّذِي بِيَدِهِ مَلَكُوتُ كُلِّ شَيْءٍ وَإِلَيْهِ تُرْجَعُونَ

So immaculate is He in whose hand is the dominion of all
things, and to whom you shall be brought back.[15]

This second level of proximity is expressed in the call of "Accept, O'
all-Beneficent, my supplication." In other words, we ask God to free us
from the realm of sovereignty and take us into the realm of dominion.
We ask Him to take us from our physical prison to the courtyard of
sublime devotion and servility. This level cannot be reached without
the proper emanations of divine mercy.

There are many believers who say, "Why is it that we supplicate to God
but our prayers are not answered? We call him with true devotion and
flowing tears, yet our calls are not answered!"

Such prayers are indeed answered, but at times the supplicant does not
pay attention to God's answer. The answer comes in the level of spirituality that God grants you – where your tears flow out of longing, awe,
fear, and hope. God answers His servants' calls by allowing them to
ascend to the courtyard of divinity and swim in the sea of His love and
majesty.

Discount, O' most-Clement, my shortcoming. The third level of is
that of purification. Every individual is liable to slip and sin. Even God's
prophets would say,

وَمَا أُبَرِّئُ نَفْسِي ۚ إِنَّ النَّفْسَ لَأَمَّارَةٌ بِالسُّوءِ إِلَّا مَا رَحِمَ رَبِّي

Yet I do not absolve my [own carnal] soul, for the [carnal]
soul indeed prompts [men] to evil, except inasmuch as my
Lord has mercy.[16]

We ask our Lord to have mercy on us and purify us from our carnal
desires that constantly prompt us toward evil.

---

[15] *The Holy Quran, 36:83.*
[16] *The Holy Quran, 12:53.*

Divine Blessings

The Imam mentions numerous divine blessings in the supplication, which include either the emanation of good or protection from evil.

فَكَمْ يَا إِلهِي مِنْ كُرْبَةٍ قَدْ فَرَّجْتَهَا، وَهُمُومٍ قَدْ كَشَفْتَهَا، وَعَثْرَةٍ قَدْ أَقَلْتَهَا، وَرَحْمَةٍ قَدْ نَشَرْتَهَا، وَحَلْقَةِ بَلَاءٍ قَدْ فَكَكْتَهَا

O' God, how many a difficulty have You removed? How many a sorrow have You dispelled? How many a shortcoming have You discounted? How many a mercy have You spread? How many a woesome shackle have You unraveled?

How many a mercy have You spread?

How many a disobedient servant have You forgiven? How many an obedient servant have You honored? How many a creation have You blessed with sustenance? These are all emanations of good that God grants to His creatures.

God also protects His creatures from evil. These evils can either be internal or external to the creature, and may either be voluntary or involuntary.

How many a sorrow have You dispelled?

God Almighty protects us from the sorrows and psychological illnesses of the world. Our hope in Him grants us refuge from our anxieties, fears, and hesitations.

How many a shortcoming have You discounted? Our all-merciful Lord protects us from the evils that we bring unto ourselves. He protects us from our own shortcomings through His boundless love and grace. He says:

قُلْ يَا عِبَادِيَ الَّذِينَ أَسْرَفُوا عَلَى أَنْفُسِهِمْ لَا تَقْنَطُوا مِن رَّحْمَةِ اللَّهِ ۚ إِنَّ اللَّهَ يَغْفِرُ
الذُّنُوبَ جَمِيعًا ۚ إِنَّهُ هُوَ الْغَفُورُ الرَّحِيمُ

Say [that Allah declares,] 'O My servants who have committed excesses against their own souls, do not despair of the mercy of Allah. Indeed, Allah will forgive all sins. Indeed, He is the All-forgiving, the All-merciful.[17]

How many a woesome shackle have You unraveled?

At times we find ourselves shackled in the woes of this world. We may not be able to see a way out from these shackles. They may weigh so heavily on us that we begin to reach a point of despair. In those dark moments, the only glimmer of light comes from our hope in our wise and capable Lord.

Our noble traditions tell us that as Prophet Abraham was being thrown into the fire, he was intercepted by several of the highest angels. Yet when each of those angels offered him help, he refused. He simply said, "My request is with my Lord!" God answered his request.

قُلْنَا يَا نَارُ كُونِي بَرْدًا وَسَلَامًا عَلَى إِبْرَاهِيمَ

We said, 'O fire! Be cool and safe for Abraham!'[18]

Even in the darkest of times, Prophet Abraham did not lose hope in his Lord. As the Holy Quran teaches us,

وَمَن يَتَوَكَّلْ عَلَى اللَّهِ فَهُوَ حَسْبُهُ

And whoever puts his trust in Allah, He will suffice him.[19]

A beautiful tradition attributed to Imam al-Sadiq explains God's divine promise to answer His servants:

---

[17] *The Holy Quran, 39:53.*
[18] *The Holy Quran, 21:69.*
[19] *The Holy Quran, 65:3.*

من أعطي ثلاثا لم يمنع ثلاثا: من أعطي الدعاء أعطي الإجابة ومن أعطي الشكر
أعطي الزيادة ومن أعطي التوكل أعطي الكفاية،

ثم قال: أتلوت كتاب الله عز وجل وَمَن يَتَوَكَّلْ عَلَى اللّهِ فَهُوَ حَسْبُهُ

وقال: لَئِن شَكَرْتُمْ لَأَزِيدَنَّكُمْ

وقال: ادْعُونِي أَسْتَجِبْ لَكُمْ.

*Whoever is granted three is not deprived from another
three. Whoever is granted [the blessing of] supplication is
also granted acceptance. Whoever is granted thankfulness
is granted an increase [in blessings]. Whoever is granted
trust [in God] is granted that which suffices him. Have you
not read the words of God?*

*'And whoever puts his trust in Allah, He will provide for
him,'*

'If you are grateful, I will surely enhance you [in blessing],'
and

'Call Me, and I will hear you!'[20]

How can we ever lose hope in God when we are given such a promise?!

How many a difficulty have You removed?

Even when the calamities of this world get the better of us, God is there
to remove those difficulties. Whether it is illness, financial difficulties,
the loss of a loved one, or any other adversity – we can gain the strength
to overcome through reliance on the Almighty.

Enumerating God's Blessings

Why did the Imam enumerate all these blessings that God has granted
us? Why not simply say, "How many blessings have You granted?"
Why does he go into this detail?

---

[20] *Al-Mazandarani, Sharh Usool al-Kafi,* 8:211; citing: *The Holy Quran,* 65:3, 14:7, and 40:60.

To enumerate God's blessings is a form of appreciation and thankfulness. When you want to thank a person who did you a favor, you start by recalling what they did. That is a form of thankfulness for their kindness. If you speak to your mother and say, "You carried me for nine months where no one else would! You fed me even when you were hungry! You comforted me even when you were troubled!" That is a form of thanks and appreciation for nurturing and raising you.

One of our noble traditions recalls the following conversation between God and Prophet Moses:

فيما أوحى الله عز وجل إلى موسى عليه السلام يا موسى اشكرني حق شكري، قال: كيف أشكرك حق شكرك، وكلما وصلت الى شكر علمت أنه نعمة منك تستحق الشكر عليها؟

قال: الآن شكرتني حق شكري حيث علمتَ أن ذلك مني

Amongst what God Almighty revealed to Moses, He said, 'O' Moses, thank Me as is rightfully due to Me.' He asked, 'How do I thank You as is rightfully due to You? Especially that whenever I thank You, I know that it is a blessing from You that You deserve to be thanked for!' God said, 'Now you have thanked Me as is rightfully due to Me, as you have come to know that all of that is from Me.'[21]

We ask God by all His blessings to continue to support and bless us along our path toward proximity to Him.

---

[21] *Al-Kulayni, al-Kafi, 2:92.*

Oneness of God

الحَمْدُ للهِ الَّذِي لَمْ يَتَّخِذْ صاحِبَةً وَلا وَلَدًا، وَلَمْ يَكُنْ لَهُ شَرِيكٌ فِي المُلْكِ
وَلَمْ يَكُنْ لَهُ وَلِيٌّ مِنَ الذُّلِّ وَكَبِّرْهُ تَكْبِيرًا.

**All praise be to God, who has not taken unto Himself a
wife, nor a son, and who has no partner in sovereignty,
nor any protecting friend through dependence. Magnify
Him with all magnificence.**

After recounting God's endless blessings, the natural progression is to
praise and thank Him for those blessings. The Imam proceeds to praise
God by emphasizing the most fundamental principle of faith – oneness
of God (tawheed).

Here, we encounter a theological discussion about whether or not there
can be a son to God. Our respected scholars tell us that the label of
'child of God' cannot apply to any individual in the real sense. Neither
can it apply to anyone in the metaphorical sense. Let us address these
points one by one.

No Real Child

There can be no real child to God, because an offspring is a derivative
of its parents in its existence. This means that the offspring shares in
the qualities of its parent.

A human child necessarily shares in the qualities of its parents. The
child of two human parents is a human. On a biological level, a child
shares their parents' DNA. The offspring of a human cannot be a horse
or a cat. This is a basic understanding of derivation – a concept which
extends further than this example. This is why Imam al-Sajjad teaches
us that our fathers are our roots. He says in his treatise on rights,

وأما حق أبيك فأن تعلم أنه أصلك.

As for the right of your father, it is that you know that he is your root.[1]

If God had a true child, that would mean that the child shares in the attributes of divinity. Just as God is omniscient and omnipotent, the child would also be omniscient and omnipotent. Just as God is eternal and infinite, the child would also be eternal and infinite. However, sharing necessarily requires limits. If God had a child, where would His limits end and where would the limits of the child begin?

In other words, we believe that God Almighty is a being of boundless knowledge, power, and life. However, the mere existence of another being with supposed boundless knowledge, power, and life necessitates that both beings have boundaries.

The existence of God and a being like God – a child of God, for example – means that each of them must have their boundaries and limits. Thus, the existence of a hypothetical being like God is impossible, as it would be a limit on the limitless Lord. This contradicts the belief in God's infinite nature. Thus, a real child would be a limit on God's infinite existence and attributes, and is therefore impossible.

We also know that an individual takes on a spouse and begets a child for specific needs, biological or otherwise. Yet God Almighty is greater than having any sort of need. So why would He take up a child? If no reason exists for Him taking a child, then that action would be arbitrary and futile – yet God is sublime above any such description.

No Adopted Child

Does God take up 'metaphorical children'? Would He adopt anyone to be His child? God Almighty takes up some of His servants as prophets, messengers, and imams. Why would He not take any of them up as children?

---

[1] *Al-Sadouq, Man la Yahdaruh al-Faqih, 2:622.*

No one can become an adopted child of God, as it would also be a limit on God's supreme nature. His supreme nature dictates that He has absolute control over all His creation. He can raise whomever He likes and demote whomever He likes.

If any creature becomes God's adoptive child, they will gain a great honor through that special relationship. Such an honor is contradictory to God's supreme nature. God Almighty says in the Holy Book,

لَّوۡ أَرَادَ اللَّهُ أَن يَتَّخِذَ وَلَدًا لَّاصۡطَفَىٰ مِمَّا يَخۡلُقُ مَا يَشَاءُ ۚ سُبۡحَانَهُ ۖ هُوَ اللَّهُ الۡوَاحِدُ الۡقَهَّارُ

Had Allah intended to take a son, He could have chosen from those He has created whatever He wished. Immaculate is He! He is Allah, the One, the All-paramount.[2]

Finally, what would it mean for God's divine justice if He were to adopt one of His creatures as a child? Parents have a natural and rational tendency to favor their children. Adopting a child would put God's justice and impartiality into question. There is no familial relationship between God and any of His creatures – a fact that our Imams would emphasize in teaching their followers about the importance of good works. Imam al-Rida would say:

مَنْ أَعَانَ ظَالِماً فَهُوَ ظَالِمٌ، وَمَنْ خَذَلَ ظَالِماً فَهُوَ عَادِلٌ. إنَّهُ لَيْسَ بَيْنَ اللهِ وَبَيْنَ أَحَدٍ قَرَابَةٌ، وَلاَ تُنَالُ وِلاَيَتُنَا إِلاَّ بِالطَّاعَةِ.

Whoever helps an oppressor is himself an oppressor. Whoever abandons an oppressor is just. Indeed, there is no kinship between God and any [of His creations]. Indeed, [affiliation with us] is attained only through obedience [to God].[3]

---

[2] *The Holy Quran*, 39:4.

[3] Al-Sadouq, *'Uyun Akhbar al-Ridha*, 1:260.

God's Oneness

God is one. That is the basis of our monotheistic belief in God. But what does 'oneness' mean? Our scholars tell us that when we describe God, oneness is an essential trait and not a numerical trait.

What is numerical oneness? Numerical oneness applies to a thing when it possesses a quality different from others. For example, when you say 'one cup of water' you ascribe numerical oneness to the cup. It possesses water, where as other cups may possess other drinks or be empty.

Numerical oneness is not an affirmative description of an object. It is a negation of other possibilities. There could very well have been another cup of water on the table – at which point you would have said 'two cups of water.'

Many people incorrectly understood God's oneness as numerical oneness. That is why some objected to the message of the Holy Prophet:

وَقَالَ الْكَافِرُونَ هَٰذَا سَاحِرٌ كَذَّابٌ ✦ أَجَعَلَ الْآلِهَةَ إِلَٰهًا وَاحِدًا إِنَّ هَٰذَا لَشَيْءٌ عُجَابٌ

The faithless say, 'This is a magician, a mendacious liar.'
'Has he reduced the gods to one god? This is indeed an odd thing!'[4]

Numerical oneness would indeed be an odd belief. It would be a simple negation of other gods, without any affirmative claim about the one. In this sense, numerical oneness is actually an unjustified limit on God's infinite nature. It would negate the existence of other deities, but keep them within the realm of possibility. In reality, God's oneness dictates that a second is an absolute impossibility.

God Almighty's oneness is not numerical, but essential. When we describe God as one, we make an affirmative statement about His unique and infinite nature.

To better understand the concept, imagine a one-dimensional space – what we normally call a number line. In this one-dimensional plane,

---

[4] *The Holy Quran, 38:4-5.*

draw a line. The line should have arrows on both ends to indicate that it has no beginning point and no end point. Within this one-dimensional plane, our one line is both unique and infinite. Whatever line segment or ray you draw in that plane, it is encompassed by the line. You cannot draw a second line that is distinct from the first. The line is one in essence – at all times both infinite and unique.

Therefore, a correct understanding of God's oneness is one that not only negates others, but one that affirms His unique and infinite nature.

Reading the Holy Quran, we find that God is at times described as *wahid,* and at other times as *ahad.* Both of these words mean 'one,' but scholars draw an important distinction between the two. For example, God says in the Holy Book,

قُلْ هُوَ اللَّهُ أَحَدٌ

Say, 'He is Allah, the One.'[5]

God describes Himself as *ahad* to convey the meaning of essential oneness. He is the one who is unique and infinite in every way. That is why He follows up on that verse and says,

قُلْ هُوَ اللَّهُ أَحَدٌ ◆ اللَّهُ الصَّمَدُ

Say, 'He is Allah, the One. Allah is the All-embracing.'[6]

Because His oneness is essential, there can be nothing beside Him. He has no boundary, so there is nothing that He does not embrace. He who has no boundaries and nothing alike Him, is truly one. He is the self-sufficient who suffices everything else in existence through His boundless emanation. God continues to say,

لَمْ يَلِدْ وَلَمْ يُولَدْ ◆ وَلَمْ يَكُنْ لَهُ كُفُوًا أَحَدٌ

'He neither begat, nor was begotten, nor has He any equal.'[7]

---

[5] *The Holy Quran, 112:1.*
[6] *The Holy Quran, 112:1-2.*
[7] *The Holy Quran, 112:3-4.*

If He was begotten, He would not be absolute. If He begat, He would be limited, as we discussed above. Rather, His oneness dictates that there is no second and nothing alike to Him.

In other verses, God describes Himself as *wahid*. He says,

$$\text{لِّمَنِ الْمُلْكُ الْيَوْمَ ۖ لِلَّهِ الْوَاحِدِ الْقَهَّارِ}$$

'To whom does the sovereignty belong today?' 'To Allah, the One, the All-paramount!'[8]

He also says,

$$\text{أَأَرْبَابٌ مُّتَفَرِّقُونَ خَيْرٌ أَمِ اللَّهُ الْوَاحِدُ الْقَهَّارُ}$$

Are different masters better, or Allah, the One, the All-paramount?[9]

The reader will notice that whenever God uses the term *wahid*, He couples it with a description of His supreme and paramount nature. This is so that the reader will not think that He is speaking of numerical oneness. In other words, even if there is any being other than Him, its existence is ultimately by Him and through Him. Thus, the fact that there are beings other than Him does not limit Him in any way.

This is why the Imam teaches us to recite in the supplication:

$$\text{الْحَمْدُ لِلَّهِ الَّذِي لَمْ يَتَّخِذْ صَاحِبَةً وَلَا وَلَدًا، وَلَمْ يَكُنْ لَّهُ شَرِيكٌ فِي الْمُلْكِ وَلَمْ يَكُنْ}$$
$$\text{لَّهُ وَلِيٌّ مِنَ الذُّلِّ وَكَبِّرْهُ تَكْبِيرًا.}$$

All praise be to God, who has not taken unto Himself a wife, nor a son, and who has no partner in sovereignty, nor any protecting friend through dependence. Magnify Him with all magnificence.

The being that possesses the quality of essential oneness is indeed magnificent. There is nothing which can rival His greatness. As such, a true understanding of God's oneness naturally leads us to glorify God for His peerless magnificence.

---

[8] *The Holy Quran*, 40:16.

[9] *The Holy Quran*, 12:39.

Thankfulness

الْحَمْدُ للهِ بِجَمِيعِ مَحَامِدِهِ كُلِّهَا عَلَى جَمِيعِ نَعَمِهِ كُلِّهَا

All praise be to God, with the entirety of all praise for the entirety of all His bounties.

When we read this verse, a few questions come to mind. What does the Imam mean by "the entirety of all praise"? Why the emphasis on all of God's bounties? Can we truly understand the magnitude of His bounties so that we can properly thank Him for them? To answer these questions, we will address three points.

Causation

What is causation?

A cause is something that "gives rise to an action, phenomenon, or condition."[1] Causation is the relationship between the cause and the effect it gives rise to.

Causation is not just an observed phenomenon in this world. It is a law of reality that flows throughout the universe. God Almighty made fire a cause for burning, while making burning its necessary effect. There is an existential link between fire and burning. This existential link exists between every cause and its effect.

God created this system of interdependency between His creations. He willed for a tree to need its causes – a root, soil, water, sunlight, and the like. He willed for the tree to become firewood and be the cause for fire. Without this system of interdependencies, the universe would not flow and change in this beautiful way.

Thus, change is a result of dependency. If there was no dependency, there would be no change in the world. Therefore, God's wisdom dictated that the world be built on a system of dependency – the system of cause and effect.

---

[1] *Oxford*

In this system of dependency, we see that there are many creations that are placed directly at mankind's service. For example, we use agriculture to grow crops that we consume to continue our existence and survival.

At the same time, there are many creations that serve these plants. The soil gives them nutrients. Insects and fungi break down material to enrich the soil. The cycle continues, and everything in the realm of creation is interconnected in this way. The result is that everything in this world is at the control and service of mankind, either directly or indirectly.

Using the aforementioned premises, we can conclude that everything in the realm of creation was made to serve mankind. God said,

$$\text{أَلَمْ تَرَوْا أَنَّ اللَّهَ سَخَّرَ لَكُمْ مَّا فِي السَّمَاوَاتِ وَمَا فِي الْأَرْضِ}$$

Do you not see that Allah has disposed for you whatever there is in the heavens and whatever there is in the Earth...?[2]

This interconnected and interdependent world is a source of continuous divine blessings unto mankind. As we read in the Holy Quran,

$$\text{كُلًّا نُّمِدُّ هَٰؤُلَاءِ وَهَٰؤُلَاءِ مِنْ عَطَاءِ رَبِّكَ ۚ وَمَا كَانَ عَطَاءُ رَبِّكَ مَحْظُورًا}$$

To these and to those—to all We extend the bounty of your Lord, and the bounty of your Lord is not confined.[3]

This interdependent world has all been placed under mankind's dominion. It is a blessing that continues to give to mankind generation after generation. Can we even count the many blessings that God has bestowed on us in this world? We cannot. The Almighty says in the Holy Quran,

---

[2] *The Holy Quran, 31:20.*
[3] *The Holy Quran, 17:20.*

وَإِن تَعُدُّوا نِعْمَةَ اللَّهِ لَا تُحْصُوهَا

If you enumerate Allah's blessings, you will not be able to count them.[4]

How could we possibly count His blessings, knowing that He created the entire world for us? We have yet to fully understand our world, let alone count its many advantages. We must therefore acquiesce to the Quranic declaration:

وَآتَاكُم مِّن كُلِّ مَا سَأَلْتُمُوهُ وَإِن تَعُدُّوا نِعْمَتَ اللَّهِ لَا تُحْصُوهَا إِنَّ الْإِنسَانَ لَظَلُومٌ كَفَّارٌ

He gave you all that you had asked Him. If you enumerate Allah's blessings, you will not be able to count them. Indeed, man is most unfair and ungrateful![5]

Even if we cannot easily identify and count all of His blessings, we must thank Him with full understanding of that fact. He says,

وَأَسْبَغَ عَلَيْكُمْ نِعَمَهُ ظَاهِرَةً وَبَاطِنَةً

He has showered upon you His blessings, the outward, and the inward.[6]

He showered us with His outward blessings – life, sustenance, limbs, and the like. He has also showered us with inward blessings, such as guidance and forgiveness. He says:

وَالَّذِينَ جَاهَدُوا فِينَا لَنَهْدِيَنَّهُمْ سُبُلَنَا

As for those who strive in Us, We shall surely guide them in Our ways.[7]

إِنَّا هَدَيْنَاهُ السَّبِيلَ إِمَّا شَاكِرًا وَإِمَّا كَفُورًا

Indeed, We have guided him to the way, be he grateful or ungrateful.[8]

---

[4] *The Holy Quran*, 16:18.
[5] *The Holy Quran*, 14:34.
[6] *The Holy Quran*, 31:20.
[7] *The Holy Quran*, 29:69.
[8] *The Holy Quran*, 76:3.

This is why the Imam places such an emphasis in the supplication on the "entirety of all His bounties." We are not able to understand, number, and recount all His blessings. We must thank and praise Him with full recognition of that fact.

The Problem of Evil

Our scholars tell us that everything in creation is a blessing of God Almighty. There is therefore no such thing as 'evil' amongst creation. How can this be when we see evil unfold before our eyes every day? What about sin, illnesses, war, and natural disasters?

The Holy Quran speaks of God's making and perfecting of everything in the realm of creation. It says,

ذَٰلِكُمُ اللَّهُ رَبُّكُمْ خَالِقُ كُلِّ شَيْءٍ

That is Allah, your Lord, the creator of all things.[9]

Our belief is that God Almighty created everything. We also believe that He is perfect in every way, and that He perfected His creation. The Holy Quran says,

الَّذِي أَحْسَنَ كُلَّ شَيْءٍ خَلَقَهُ

[It is God] who perfected everything that He created.[10]

Therefore, we believe that everything in creation is perfect, from the largest galaxy down to every subatomic particle. How can we reconcile this belief with the evil we see around us every day?

Our scholars tell us that everything is perfect when seen in the lens of its relationship with God. God brought everything into existence and out of the abyss of nothingness. That itself is a perfection. It is objectively better to exist than to not exist.

---

[9] *The Holy Quran, 40:62.*
[10] *The Holy Quran, 32:6.*

Evil is not a trait of creation and existence. Rather, it comes out of some artificial or subjective understanding of an object or situation. Existence in itself is good, but it may be seen as evil when seen through a subjective lens of its relationship to another creation.

For example, we know that water is the basis of all life. We cannot doubt the perfection of its existence. Each of us needs to drink water to stay hydrated and alive. However, if a person drinks too much water, it will negatively affect their body. Water can even become a poison if consumed at a high enough level. God gave life to things through water, yet a person can drown and end their life with water. No one can claim that water is evil because of this. Instead, it is only seen as evil when seen through the subjective lens of its negative effect in a particular situation.

Understanding the fact that there is no evil in creation allows us to better comprehend the perspective that the Imam is conveying through the supplication. The emphasis on praising God for the "entirety of all His bounties" is because all of His creation is perfection and a blessing.

Existence and Awareness

Muslim philosophers say that existence and awareness are interconnected, such that anything in existence has some degree of awareness. This is a concept emphasized by the Holy Quran in the following verse:

وَإِن مِّن شَيْءٍ إِلَّا يُسَبِّحُ بِحَمْدِهِ وَلَٰكِن لَّا تَفْقَهُونَ تَسْبِيحَهُمْ

There is not a thing but celebrates His praise, but you do not understand their glorification. [11]

---

[11] *The Holy Quran, 17:44.*

وَإِنَّ مِنَ الْحِجَارَةِ لَمَا يَتَفَجَّرُ مِنْهُ الْأَنْهَارُ ۚ وَإِنَّ مِنْهَا لَمَا يَشَّقَّقُ فَيَخْرُجُ مِنْهُ الْمَاءُ ۚ وَإِنَّ مِنْهَا لَمَا يَهْبِطُ مِنْ خَشْيَةِ اللَّهِ

For there are some stones from which streams gush forth, and there are some of them that split, and water issues from them, and there are some that fall for the fear of Allah. [12]

لَوْ أَنزَلْنَا هَٰذَا الْقُرْآنَ عَلَىٰ جَبَلٍ لَّرَأَيْتَهُ خَاشِعًا مُّتَصَدِّعًا مِّنْ خَشْيَةِ اللَّهِ

Had We sent down this Quran upon a mountain, you would have seen it humbled [and] go to pieces with the fear of Allah. [13]

God describes boulders and mountains – things we see as insentient – as being aware and knowing of Him. Everything in creation has a degree of sentience and is continuously praising and glorifying the Almighty.

Everything in existence is aware of itself from a positive and a negative aspect. From a positive aspect, a being is aware of its existence and capabilities. A human individual knows that they are alive, and that they can think and move. This positive awareness of the beauty in our own creation leads us to a question: where did we get this ability and beauty from? Certainly, we did not give it to ourselves. There must be a limitless well of beauty that gave us this beauty. By realizing our own existence, we come to realize the existence of the Almighty. God says in the Holy Quran,

سَنُرِيهِمْ آيَاتِنَا فِي الْآفَاقِ وَفِي أَنفُسِهِمْ حَتَّىٰ يَتَبَيَّنَ لَهُمْ أَنَّهُ الْحَقُّ

Soon We shall show them Our signs in the horizons and in their own souls, until it becomes clear to them that He is the Truth. [14]

Just as we have a positive awareness, we also have a negative awareness. Just as we understand our ability, we also understand our limits. We

---

are aware of our own weakness and ignorance. Yet, these limits cannot bind the limitless wellspring of existence. We therefore move from understanding our own limits to glorifying the majestic and limitless Almighty.

This applies to us humans as well as to every other creation. As we mentioned, every creation has some level of sentience, and can therefore understand the beauty and majesty of its creator.[15]

Every being is aware of God's beauty and majesty. Every being thanks and praises God based on that awareness. It follows that the degree of awareness results in differing degrees of praise and thanks. A being that is more aware of God's beauty and majesty will be more thankful and praising. The Immaculate Imam's understanding of God's beauty is greater than mine, and therefore his praise of the Almighty is at a higher level. The Holy Prophet's praise and thankfulness to God is the greatest amongst all creation.

We ask God Almighty by His limitless bounties to keep us amongst the thankful.

---

[15] See: The Holy Quran, 17:44.

Divine Majesty

الحَمْدُ لِلهِ الَّذِي لا مُضادَّ لَهُ في مُلْكِهِ وَلا مُنازِعَ لَهُ في أَمْرِهِ، الحَمْدُ لِلهِ الَّذِي لا شَرِيكَ لَهُ في خَلْقِهِ وَلا شَبِيهَ لَهُ في عَظَمَتِهِ

All praise be to God, who has no opposition to His sovereignty, nor any challenge to His commands, nor a partner in His creation, nor is there anything similar to Him in His greatness.

God Almighty is the Lord of command and creation. What is the difference between the two?

God emanates existence to all creation, thereby giving every creation its ability to be. However, His emanation is either immediate or delayed. For example, when He says to a thing "be," it comes into being immediately without any intermediate cause. This is what we refer to as God's command. As the Holy Quran says,

إِنَّما أَمْرُهُ إِذا أَرادَ شَيْئًا أَنْ يَقُولَ لَهُ كُنْ فَيَكُونُ

All His command, when He wills something, is to say to it 'Be,' and it is.[1]

God may also emanate existence through an intermediary. This delayed emanation is what we call creation. For example, God creates a tree through allowing it to grow from a seed in the worldly system of cause and effect.

Thus, command and creation are two different methods of emanating existence. The Holy Quran says,

أَلا لَهُ الخَلْقُ وَالأَمْرُ

Look! All creation and command belong to Him.[2]

Creation is the emanation of existence through some delay or intermediary. That is why God speaks of His creation of the world and says,

---

[1] *The Holy Quran, 36:82.*

[2] *The Holy Quran, 7:54.*

هُوَ الَّذِي خَلَقَ السَّمَاوَاتِ وَالْأَرْضَ فِي سِتَّةِ أَيَّامٍ

It is He who created the heavens and the Earth in six days.[3]

God also says:

وَلَقَدْ خَلَقْنَا الْإِنسَانَ مِن سُلَالَةٍ مِّن طِينٍ ● ثُمَّ جَعَلْنَاهُ نُطْفَةً فِي قَرَارٍ مَّكِينٍ ● ثُمَّ
خَلَقْنَا النُّطْفَةَ عَلَقَةً فَخَلَقْنَا الْعَلَقَةَ مُضْغَةً فَخَلَقْنَا الْمُضْغَةَ عِظَامًا فَكَسَوْنَا الْعِظَامَ لَحْمًا

*Certainly, We created man from an extract of clay. Then
We made him a drop of [seminal] fluid [lodged] in a secure
abode. Then We created the drop of fluid as a clinging
mass. Then We created the clinging mass as a fleshy tissue.
Then We created the fleshy tissue as bones. Then We
clothed the bones with flesh.*[4]

Command is God's emanation of existence without any delay or intermediary. As such, it is instantaneous, like the blink of an eye. God says,

وَمَا أَمْرُنَا إِلَّا وَاحِدَةٌ كَلَمْحٍ بِالْبَصَرِ

*Our command is but a single [word], like the twinkling of
an eye.*[5]

When emanation of existence is delayed, God refers to it as creation.
That is the case with the creation of the body in the verse referenced
above. When emanation of existence is instantaneous, God refers to it
as command. The example of that is the soul, which God says is of His
command. This understanding is taken directly from Quranic verses.
God says,

إِنَّ مَثَلَ عِيسَىٰ عِندَ اللَّهِ كَمَثَلِ آدَمَ خَلَقَهُ مِن تُرَابٍ ثُمَّ قَالَ لَهُ كُن فَيَكُونُ

*Indeed, the case of Jesus with Allah is like the case of Adam:
He created him from dust, then said to him, 'Be,' and he
was.*[6]

---

[3] *The Holy Quran*, 57:4.

[4] *The Holy Quran*, 23:12-14.

[5] *The Holy Quran*, 54:50.

[6] *The Holy Quran*, 3:59.

In other words, God created the body, then commanded a soul into it. When God says 'be,' it is a matter of His command. He says,

إِنَّمَا أَمْرُهُ إِذَا أَرَادَ شَيْئًا أَن يَقُولَ لَهُ كُن فَيَكُونُ

All His command, when He wills something, is to say to it 'Be,' and it is.[7]

God also says:

وَيَسْأَلُونَكَ عَنِ الرُّوحِ قُلِ الرُّوحُ مِنْ أَمْرِ رَبِّي وَمَا أُوتِيتُم مِّنَ الْعِلْمِ إِلَّا قَلِيلًا

[When] they question you concerning the Spirit, say: 'The Spirit is of the command of my Lord, and you have not been given of the knowledge, except a few [of you].'[8]

God does not say that the soul is of His 'creation,' but of His 'command.'

Sovereignty and Dominion

Everything in this world is brought into existence by God Almighty. Nothing can ever leave His control. Everything is directly linked to Him through His continuous emanation of existence.

Everything in this world is linked to Him – He creates, sustains, and may end any existence. This control is often categorized into two types: sovereignty and dominion. What is the difference between the two types of divine control?

Everything in this world has observable and unseen aspects. God Almighty says that He is:

عَالِمُ الْغَيْبِ وَالشَّهَادَةِ

The Knower of the sensible and the unseen.[9]

The observable aspects of this universe are referred to as the realm of sovereignty. This includes the forms of existence that we can sense. On the other hand, the realm of the unseen cannot be reached by our

---

[7] *The Holy Quran, 36:82.*

[8] *The Holy Quran, 17:85.*

[9] *The Holy Quran, 23:92.*

senses. It includes the linkage between the observable world and the Almighty. This is the realm of God's dominion.

The Holy Quran emphasized God's control over both sovereignty and dominion. It says,

تَبَارَكَ الَّذِي بِيَدِهِ الْمُلْكُ

Blessed is He in whose hands is all sovereignty. [10]

The Holy Quran also says,

فَسُبْحَانَ الَّذِي بِيَدِهِ مَلَكُوتُ كُلِّ شَيْءٍ وَإِلَيْهِ تُرْجَعُونَ

So immaculate is He in whose hand is the dominion of all things, and to whom you shall be brought back. [11]

Human beings generally do not see farther than the observable universe. We are thus limited in our senses to the realm of sovereignty. However, there are individuals who can see beyond the material world and witness God's dominion. God says,

وَكَذَلِكَ نُرِي إِبْرَاهِيمَ مَلَكُوتَ السَّمَاوَاتِ وَالْأَرْضِ وَلِيَكُونَ مِنَ الْمُوقِنِينَ

Thus, did We show Abraham the dominions of the heavens and the Earth, that he might be of those who possess certitude. [12]

Abraham did not reach certainty until he was shown the dominions of the heavens and the Earth. At that point, he saw the deep connection between this world and its Creator.

This is why scholars of ethics say that this world we live in is itself Hellfire and Paradise. These are not places beyond our material world, but are a label for the reality of our existence in this world. However, we only see this world from the perspective of divine sovereignty. We do not see Hellfire and Paradise in this world, because we have not been shown the dominions of the heavens and the Earth.

---

[10] *The Holy Quran, 67:1.*

[11] *The Holy Quran, 36:83.*

[12] *The Holy Quran, 6:75.*

There are individuals who are able to see the realm of dominion, and therefore see Paradise and Hellfire in this world. The Holy Quran refers to this idea and says:

كَلَّا إِنَّ كِتَابَ الْأَبْرَارِ لَفِي عِلِّيِّينَ ❖ وَمَا أَدْرَاكَ مَا عِلِّيُّونَ ❖ كِتَابٌ مَّرْقُومٌ ❖ يَشْهَدُهُ الْمُقَرَّبُونَ

Indeed, the record of the pious is in Illeeyun. And what will show you what is Illeeyun? It is a written record, witnessed by those brought near [to Allah]. [13]

Those who are brought near to God can therefore see the place of the pious in Paradise. This is not a reference to the hereafter, as everyone can see the place of the pious in the hereafter. Rather, it is a vision that God allows them in this world. God also says:

كَلَّا لَوْ تَعْلَمُونَ عِلْمَ الْيَقِينِ ❖ لَتَرَوُنَّ الْجَحِيمَ ❖ ثُمَّ لَتَرَوُنَّهَا عَيْنَ الْيَقِينِ

Indeed, were you to know with certain knowledge, you would have surely seen Hell [in this very life]. Afterward you will surely see it with the eye of certainty. [14]

If we had reached a level of certainty, we would have seen Paradise and Hellfire in this life.

It is narrated that Imam Ali would say,

لو كشف لي الغطاء ما ازددت يقينا

If the veil were to be removed for me, I would not increase in certainty. [15]

The lifting of the veil is a reference to death. God says,

فَكَشَفْنَا عَنكَ غِطَاءَكَ فَبَصَرُكَ الْيَوْمَ حَدِيدٌ

We have removed your veil from you, and so today your eyesight is acute. [16]

---

[13] *The Holy Quran,* 83:18-21.

[14] *The Holy Quran,* 102:5-7.

[15] Ibn Tawus, 'Ayn al-'Aabra, 22.

[16] *The Holy Quran,* 50:22.

The Imam's words mean that, for him, there is no difference between what he sees in life and in death. For us, we will see the reality of everything once we pass away and the veil is lifted. The Imam has seen the realm of dominion and the lifting of the veil would do nothing for him.

Rejecting Partners

We can now turn back to the verses of the supplication and provide a better understanding in light of the above information. The Imam said,

الْحَمْدُ لِلَّهِ الَّذِي لَا مُضَادَّ لَهُ فِي مُلْكِهِ وَلَا مُنَازِعَ لَهُ فِي أَمْرِهِ، الْحَمْدُ لِلَّهِ الَّذِي لَا شَرِيكَ لَهُ فِي خَلْقِهِ وَلَا شَبِيهَ لَهُ فِي عَظَمَتِهِ

All praise be to God, who has no opposition to His sovereignty, nor any challenge to His commands, nor a partner in His creation, nor is there anything similar to Him in His greatness.

Everything in existence is brought to be through His emanations. Everything is under His sovereignty. How can He ever have any opposition in His sovereignty?

God's command is instantaneous. It is only a matter of Him willing 'be' and it is. How can anyone challenge His command? Even if someone wished to oppose His commands, there would be no chance to do so.

Neither can there be any partner to Him. That is because partnership is the result of one of two things, either need or defeat.

A person would need a partner if they are not able to finish a task alone. If I am not able to start a business by myself, I would need to find a partner to help me in the endeavor. We take partners through marriage because of our physical and emotional needs for partnership.

A person may also take a partner if they are defeated and forced into partnership. If two forces are vying for different outcomes, the result will either be the victory of one over the other, or a partnership reached through compromise.

Neither of these two reasons apply to God Almighty. He is the one who sustains all other things. He has no need, but fulfills the needs of His creations. Neither can He be overtaken or overpowered by anyone. After all, He is the one who "has no opposition to His sovereignty, nor any challenge to His commands." There's no other imaginable reason for an individual to take a partner.

This is all an aspect of God's greatness. What would make a lord great in power? A great lord must be sovereign over his realm, his commands must be without opposition, and he must hold this power exclusively. God is the one who has no opposition in His sovereignty. He is the one whose commands cannot be challenged. He is the one Lord who has no partner. He is therefore the great Lord and there is nothing similar to Him in His greatness.

We ask Him by His greatness to envelop us in His boundless mercy and grace.

The Wellspring of Generosity

الحَمْدُ للهِ الفَاشِي في الخَلْقِ أَمْرُهُ وَحَمْدُهُ، الظَّاهِرِ بالكَرَمِ مَجْدُهُ، الباسِطِ بالجُودِ يَدَهُ، الَّذِي لا تَنْقُصُ خَزائِنُهُ، وَلا يَزِيدُهُ كَثْرَةُ العَطاءِ إلاَّ جُوداً وَكَرَماً، إنَّهُ هُوَ العَزِيزُ الوَهَّابُ.

> **All praise be to God, whose command and praise have**
> **proliferated throughout creation. His glory is evident**
> **through His magnanimity. His hands are open and over-**
> **flowing with generosity. His vaults never diminish. His**
> **great bounties do not increase Him in anything but mani-**
> **festations of His generosity and magnanimity. Surely, He**
> **is the mighty and the provider for all things.**

When speaking of God's command, there are two ways of understanding the term. The first is God's command as opposed to His creation – a topic we addressed in a previous chapter.

The second meaning of divine command is God's lordship, control, and administration of the world. He says in His Holy Book:

إنَّ رَبَّكُمُ اللَّهُ الَّذِي خَلَقَ السَّمَاوَاتِ وَالأَرْضَ في سِتَّةِ أَيَّامٍ ثُمَّ اسْتَوَى عَلَى العَرْشِ يُدَبِّرُ الأَمْرَ

Indeed, your Lord is Allah, who created the heavens and
the Earth in six days, and then settled on the Throne,
directing the command.[1]

وَسَخَّرَ لَكُمُ الفُلْكَ لِتَجْرِيَ في البَحْرِ بِأَمْرِهِ

He disposed the ships for you[r benefit] so that they may
sail at sea by His command.[2]

God's command over His creation is a reference to His lordship. Everything in this world came to be and continues to exist by His permission. Nothing can take place without His will. Nothing in this world can escape His control and lordship.

---

[1] *The Holy Quran, 10:3.*

[2] *The Holy Quran, 14:32.*

We have also mentioned in previous chapters that there is an inherent link between existence and awareness. Everything in this world has some degree of sentience and understands its own existence. Just as His command is enveloping of the entirety of everything, so does His praise. Everything in existence praises Him out of awareness of His beauty and majesty.[3]

Divine Manifestation

Our scholars say that God has three types of manifestation. First, He manifests to Himself. In other words, He has perfect knowledge of Himself.

Second, God manifests through His attributes. The attributes of power, knowledge, and life are manifestations of His divine essence.

Third, He manifests through His actions. He creates and sustains. He gives life and takes it away. His actions are a type of manifestation of His divine essence. This is referenced in the following verse of the Holy Quran:

اللَّهُ نُورُ السَّمَاوَاتِ وَالْأَرْضِ ۚ مَثَلُ نُورِهِ كَمِشْكَاةٍ فِيهَا مِصْبَاحٌ ۖ الْمِصْبَاحُ فِي زُجَاجَةٍ ۖ الزُّجَاجَةُ كَأَنَّهَا كَوْكَبٌ دُرِّيٌّ يُوقَدُ مِن شَجَرَةٍ مُّبَارَكَةٍ زَيْتُونَةٍ لَّا شَرْقِيَّةٍ وَلَا غَرْبِيَّةٍ يَكَادُ زَيْتُهَا يُضِيءُ وَلَوْ لَمْ تَمْسَسْهُ نَارٌ

Allah is the Light of the heavens and the Earth. The parable of His Light is a niche wherein there is a lamp—the lamp is in a glass; the glass is as it were a glittering star, lit from a blessed olive tree, neither eastern nor western, whose oil almost lights up, though fire should not touch it.[4]

The very existence of the heavens and the Earth is a manifestation of His divine essence. God's actions are a method by which He appears to His creatures.

---

[3] *See: The Holy Quran, 17:44.*
[4] *The Holy Quran, 24:35.*

The reader should take note that when we speak of manifestation, we do not mean transfiguration. We do not mean that God Almighty takes the form of His creation. He is sublime above any such claim! However, He shows us a glimpse of His divine essence by exercising His power, knowledge, and wisdom. If we take the time to ponder on the creation of the heavens and the Earth, we would clearly see that they are the making of a magnificent Lord.

By pondering on all the blessings that God has given us, we come to a better understanding of His attributes. "His glory is evident through His magnanimity."

Divine Generosity

A reference to God's hands is either an indication of His power or generosity. He says in His Holy Book,

يَدُ اللّٰهِ فَوۡقَ أَيۡدِيۡهِمۡ

The hand of Allah is above their hands.[5]

This means His power controls any authority that we may have. In another verse, a reference to God's hands is made in describing His limitless giving. He says,

أَوَلَمۡ يَرَوۡا أَنَّا خَلَقۡنَا لَهُم مِّمَّا عَمِلَتۡ أَيۡدِينَا أَنۡعَامًا فَهُمۡ لَهَا مَالِكُونَ

Have they not seen that We have created for them—of what Our hands have worked—cattle, so they have become their masters?[6]

The reference to His hands is actually one to His giving of boundless blessings and bounties. The Imam is thus speaking about God's innumerable blessings.

---

[5] The Holy Quran, 48:10.
[6] The Holy Quran, 36:71.

وَإِن تَعُدُّوا نِعْمَةَ اللّٰهِ لَا تُحْصُوهَا

If you enumerate Allah's blessings, you will not be able to count them. [7]

God Almighty gives out His undiminishable sources and treasuries. He says,

وَإِن مِّن شَيْءٍ إِلَّا عِندَنَا خَزَائِنُهُ وَمَا نُنَزِّلُهُ إِلَّا بِقَدَرٍ مَّعْلُومٍ

There is not a thing but that its sources are with Us, and We do not send it down except in a known measure. [8]

There are two possible understandings of God's treasuries. It may be a reference to the means that He provides for the sustenance of His creatures. For example, a plant cannot live without proper soil, water, air, and sunlight. God continues to give these sources of sustenance. The reference to His treasuries can therefore be understood as His continuous sustenance of His creatures through providing these necessary means.

Philosophers propose another possible meaning. They say that every creation has a limited and an unlimited existence. Its limited existence is its presence in this material world. My body is a limited, material existence. It exists within a limited space and time. For my body to come about, I needed parents who begot and nurtured me.

Every creation also has an unlimited, abstract existence. This abstract form is stored in God's treasuries, and He gives of it to bring everything into existence.

The Imam is describing God's undiminishable giving. Some might think that if God opens His hands with giving, that might diminish what He holds. The Imam is clarifying that misconception, teachings us that God's treasures can never be diminished – not in the slightest. As we read in the supplication,

---

[7] *The Holy Quran, 16:18.*

[8] *The Holy Quran, 15:21.*

الباسطِ بالجُودِ يَدَهُ، الَّذِي لا تَنْقُصُ خَزائِنُهُ

His hands are open and overflowing with generosity. His vaults never diminish.

The Imam is clarifying the difference between our generosity and divine generosity. If we are generous and giving, that will diminish from what we have. The fear of this diminishment might cause us to be less generous. This is not the case with the Almighty. He gives freely and His treasures never diminish. As He says in His Holy Book,

كُلًّا نُمِدُّ هَٰؤُلَاءِ وَهَٰؤُلَاءِ مِنْ عَطَاءِ رَبِّكَ ۚ وَمَا كَانَ عَطَاءُ رَبِّكَ مَحْظُورًا

To these and to those—to all We extend the bounty of your Lord, and the bounty of your Lord is not confined.[9]

No matter how much He gives, there can be no end to His blessings. He says,

قُل لَّوْ كَانَ الْبَحْرُ مِدَادًا لِّكَلِمَاتِ رَبِّي لَنَفِدَ الْبَحْرُ قَبْلَ أَن تَنفَدَ كَلِمَاتُ رَبِّي وَلَوْ جِئْنَا بِمِثْلِهِ مَدَدًا

Say, 'If the sea were ink for the words of my Lord, the sea would be spent before the words of my Lord are finished, though We replenish it with another like it.'[10]

His word is not what we understand of written letters. It is the wellspring of existence that He gives to His creatures. He says,

إِنَّمَا الْمَسِيحُ عِيسَى ابْنُ مَرْيَمَ رَسُولُ اللَّهِ وَكَلِمَتُهُ أَلْقَاهَا إِلَىٰ مَرْيَمَ

The Messiah, Jesus, son of Mary, was only an apostle of Allah, and His Word that He cast toward Mary.[11]

God Almighty is the necessary existence. His being is boundless and infinite. He is not limited in any way. Because He is infinite, His creation must also be infinite. This is based on the philosophical principle of homogeneity of cause and effect. A seed grows into a tree of the same kind. An animal is born of a fertilized egg from the same species. The

---

[9] *The Holy Quran*, 17:20.

[10] *The Holy Quran*, 18:109.

[11] *The Holy Quran*, 4:171.

effect does not deviate from its cause in this sense. You cannot grow a human from an acorn.[12]

The principle of homogeneity of cause and effect tells us that since God Almighty is limitless, His bounties and giving must also be limitless. As such, "His vaults never diminish."

The Imam continues in the supplication,

وَلَا يَزِيدُهُ كَثْرَةُ الْعَطَاءِ إِلَّا جُوداً وَكَرَما، إِنَّهُ هُوَ الْعَزِيزُ الْوَهَّابُ.

His great bounties do not increase Him in anything but manifestations of His generosity and magnanimity. Surely, He is the mighty and the provider for all things.

This verse of the supplication acts as a reminder of His absolute self-sufficiency. Just as His giving does not diminish Him any way, it does not benefit Him in any way either. His infinite and absolute nature means that He is not lacking in any way. If He is without need, there can be nothing that can benefit Him in any way.

His giving neither adds nor takes away anything from Him. It is only a reflection of His generous and magnanimous essence. It is a reflection of His might that He provides for all things, without that having any effect on Him.

We ask Him by His boundless generosity to continue to give us from His undiminishable treasuries.

---

[12] The principle of homogeneity of cause and effect (*al-sinkhiyyah bayn al-'illah wa'l-ma'lul*) states that: a cause gives rise to an effect based on the specific properties of the cause, such that an effect cannot be the result of any cause.

If we see that our neighbor has a new kitten, we will not assume that it hatched from a chicken egg. Neither would we think that a chicken egg was laid by a cat.

There must be a relationship between cause and effect. If we observe the presence of rust (iron oxide) on a surface, we can conclude that there was a chemical reaction that included iron and oxygen. Iron oxide could not have arisen out of a mingling of gold and helium, or any other combination of elements except for iron and oxygen.

The applications of this principle have been given detailed study in the books of theology and philosophy; the reader can look there for further elucidation.

Grace

اللَّهُمَّ إِنِّي أَسْأَلُكَ قَلِيلاً مِنْ كَثِيرٍ، مَعَ حَاجَةٍ بِي إِلَيْهِ عَظِيمَةٍ وَغِنَاكَ عَنْهُ قَدِيمٌ، وَهُوَ عِنْدِي كَثِيرٌ وَهُوَ عَلَيْكَ سَهْلٌ يَسِيرٌ.

**O God, I ask for so little from so much [that You have] –
while my need for it is so great, You have always been the
self-sufficient [without need for anything]. To me, it is so
great, while to You it is simple and effortless.**

How should we approach the Almighty in our supplications? Reciting
the Holy Quran gives us an idea of how we should approach speaking
to our Lord.

The holy verses state,

إِنَّهُمْ كَانُوا يُسَارِعُونَ فِي الْخَيْرَاتِ وَيَدْعُونَنَا رَغَبًا وَرَهَبًا

*Indeed, they were active in [performing] good works, and
they would supplicate Us with eagerness and awe.*[1]

وَادْعُوهُ خَوْفًا وَطَمَعًا ۚ إِنَّ رَحْمَتَ اللَّهِ قَرِيبٌ مِّنَ الْمُحْسِنِينَ

*Supplicate Him with fear and hope: indeed, Allah's mercy
is close to the virtuous.*[2]

The Holy Quran praises the believers who supplicate to the Almighty
with fear and hope, eagerness and awe.

In this verse of the supplication, our Imam is teaching us how to supplicate to God with eagerness and hope. He does so by highlighting the
absolute dependency of creation to the all-independent and self-sufficient Lord.

---

[1] *The Holy Quran, 21:90.*
[2] *The Holy Quran, 7:56.*

112

Obedience

There is a theological discussion about the meaning of disobedience; is it one and the same as injustice or a different concept?

To understand the idea of disobedience, we must first explain the concept of lordship. Lordship can be categorized into two types: legal and real.

A prime example of legal lordship is that of a king or emperor. A king's authority over the citizens of a country comes from the political and legal structure of the country. A teacher has a degree of legal lordship in the classroom that allows them to run the class. This type of lordship is not based on any real source of authority, but on social, political, and legal structures put in place by a community.

True lordship is reserved for God Almighty. His lordship stems from the fact that He is the creator and sustainer of everything in this universe. He says in His Holy Book,

ذَٰلِكُمُ اللَّهُ رَبُّكُمْ خَالِقُ كُلِّ شَيْءٍ لَّا إِلَٰهَ إِلَّا هُوَ

That is Allah, your Lord, the creator of all things; there is no god except Him.[3]

His lordship stems from His creatorship. The fact that He is our Lord necessitates our obedience to Him. He is our creator and sustainer. He is the Almighty and most majestic. It is His right to be obeyed.

Therefore, a servant's disobedience is an injustice. To act justly is to give everyone their due right. To know someone's right but not give it to them is injustice. When a servant obeys their Lord, they have given Him His due right. To disobey God is to oppress Him – it is denial of His right of obedience. This is the opinion of most theologians.

Some theologians have disagreed with this opinion. They say that it is impossible for anyone to oppress God. To oppress someone is to cause

---

[3] *The Holy Quran, 40:62.*

some reduction or deficiency in the oppressed, either tangibly or intangibly.

A person may transgress against another individual or their property. If I cause someone physical harm, I have oppressed them by causing them pain and taking away their health. If I destroy someone's property, I have oppressed them by creating a deficiency in their holdings.

Oppression may also be intangible. If a system discriminates against a group of people for the color of their skin, then the system is oppressive, whether or not it causes any tangible harm. Requiring people of a particular color to sit in the back of the bus may not cause tangible harm to someone's person or property, but is a derogation of their worth and character.

It is unimaginable for anyone to oppress God in any way. Who can cause any deficiency in God's lordship and ownership over His creation? In this vast world of endless space and numerous galaxies, how can something as small as a human take anything away from Him? He is the self-sufficient and all-independent creator and sustainer of this world. Nothing can harm Him in any way. Nothing can cause the slightest inconvenience or affect Him in any way.

Neither can anyone cause Him any intangible oppression. God's lordship, glory, and majesty do not come from an outside source. Whereas our respect and dignity come from how others treat us, the same is not true for God Almighty. Whereas we rely on social and legal constructs to assess our social value, God's majesty and grandeur are attributes of His essence. Nothing we do can ever take away from God's majesty because it is a description of who He is, not of how people treat Him.

Therefore, we cannot say that a person oppresses God when they disobey Him. This understanding is supported by a number of Quranic verses. God Almighty tells us that our disobedience is not a wrong done toward Him. We only oppress ourselves when we disobey His commands. He says,

وَمَا ظَلَمُونَا وَلَكِن كَانُوا أَنفُسَهُمْ يَظْلِمُونَ

They did not wrong Us, but they used to wrong [only] themselves.[4]

Divine Independence

This is why Imam al-Sajjad teaches us to stand before our Lord and say:

إِلَهِي لَمْ أَعْصِكَ حِينَ عَصَيْتُكَ وَأَنَا بِرُبُوبِيَّتِكَ جَاحِدٌ وَلاَ بِأَمْرِكَ مُسْتَخِفٌّ وَلاَ لِعُقُوبَتِكَ مُتَعَرِّضٌ وَلاَ لِوَعِيدِكَ مُتَهَاوِنٌ لَكِنْ خَطِيئَةٌ عَرَضَتْ سَوَّلَتْ لِي نَفْسِي وَغَلَبَنِي هَوَايَ وَأَعَانَتِي عَلَيْهَا شِقْوَتِي وَغَرَّنِي سِتْرُكَ الْمُرْخَى عَلَيَّ

O' my Lord! I did not disobey You when I did because I rejected Your divinity, because I belittled Your commands, that I was daringly challenging Your punishment, or that I did not appreciate Your forewarning. Yet, the mistake has occurred, and my self misled me, my sinful desires won over me, my misery helped me to it, and Your protective veil over my sins lured me.

How many sins do we commit out of our sinful desires? Yet, how can any of them ever harm our Almighty Lord in any way? How can they affect His lordship, sovereignty, and dominion in any way?

Even if I were disobeying Him out of rebellion, even if I were belittling His commands, even if I were challenging Him, my actions would not be any greater than the steps of an ant on a mighty mountain. I cannot take away from His sovereignty and dominion. His boundless mercy and forgiveness – despite humanity's great and repeated sins – is an indication of the fact that our disobedience takes nothing away from His authority.

And what would it harm Him if He is to have mercy on His servants? It is His character to have clemency and envelop His creatures in mercy. The vaults of His blessings are never diminished and His majesty is not derogated by His boundless giving and mercy.

---

[4] *The Holy Quran*, 2:57.

اللّٰهُمَّ إِنِّي أَسْأَلُكَ قَلِيلاً مِنْ كَثِيرٍ، مَعَ حَاجَةٍ بِي إِلَيْهِ عَظِيمَةٍ وَغِنَاكَ عَنْهُ قَدِيمٌ، وَهُوَ عِنْدِي كَثِيرٌ وَهُوَ عَلَيْكَ سَهْلٌ يَسِيرٌ.

O God, I ask for so little from so much [that You have] –
while my need for it is so great, You have always been the
self-sufficient [without need for anything]. To me, it is so
great while to You it is simple and effortless.

Without His mercy, we would all be liable to suffer the fires of punishment – a punishment which the heavens and the Earth would not be able to stand. My need for safety from this punishment is so great! My need for the provisions of the afterlife is so great! You are the self-sufficient who has no need to punish His servants!

The Imam places special emphasis in describing God's self-sufficiency as an eternal trait. Oftentimes, we may give something away when we feel like we do not need it anymore. We donate used clothing to the poor, thinking that we are doing them a great favor. God Almighty's giving is not of this kind. He was never in need of anything and His giving has always been out of His favor.

In other words, had God been in need of punishing us at any point in time and then that need was somehow alleviated, His forgiveness would not be out of favor and mercy, but simply out of self-sufficiency. This would be contradictory to the Almighty's immense wisdom, which dictates that He exercise His clemency and mercy in the position of forgiveness.

We ask Him by His boundless wisdom to envelop us in His limitless mercy.

Perils of Sin

اللَّهُمَّ إِنَّ عَفْوَكَ عَنْ ذَنْبِي، وَتَجَاوُزَكَ عَنْ خَطِيئَتِي، وَصَفْحَكَ عَنْ ظُلْمِي، وَسَتْرَكَ عَلَى قَبِيحِ عَمَلِي، وَحِلْمَكَ عَنْ كَثِيرِ جُرْمِي عِنْدَمَا كَانَ مِنْ خَطَائِي وَعَمْدِي، أَطْمَعَنِي فِي أَنْ أَسْأَلَكَ مَا لَا اسْتَوْجِبُهُ مِنْكَ، الَّذِي رَزَقْتَنِي مِنْ رَحْمَتِكَ، وَأَرَيْتَنِي مِنْ قُدْرَتِكَ، وَعَرَّفْتَنِي مِنْ إِجَابَتِكَ

O' God, truly, when You forgive my sins, overlook my mistakes, pardon my transgressions, cover up my foul actions, and show forbearance in spite of my many crimes committed both negligently and intently, I am tempted to ask for that which I do not deserve from You. You have blessed me through Your mercy, shown me Your omnipotence, and acquainted me with Your answers [for my prayers].

This portion of the supplication addresses the perils of sin. Unfortunately, many people fall into sin, as if their obedience or disobedience has no value to them. In reality, our sins should weigh significantly on our minds.

The noble tradition says:

المنافق إذا أذنب كان ذنبه كذبابة مرت على وجهه، والمؤمن إذا أذنب كان ذنبه على صدره كالصخرة الثقيلة

When a hypocrite sins, his sin is [as insignificant to him] as a fly that passed by his face. When a believer sins, his sin weighs like a heavy boulder on his chest.

A believer's sins weigh heavily on their chest because they understand their perils. This segment of the supplication addresses five of these perils.

First, the supplication addresses **the peril of punishment**. Disobedience to God makes the individual a proper recipient of divine punishment. In fact, according to Quranic theory, the sin itself manifests into punishment. As God Almighty says,

إِنَّمَا تُجْزَوْنَ مَا كُنتُمْ تَعْمَلُونَ

You are only being requited for what you used to do.[1]

In other words, your punishment is a manifestation of the misdeeds you committed in your worldly life.

Thus, if you turn to your actions and deeds, you will see what you have prepared for your hereafter. You live your hereafter in this world, but in a different manifestation. Your worships and supplications are themselves the paradise that you will experience in the hereafter.

Second, the Imam addresses **the peril of corruption**. Disobedience to God's commands corrupts the soul. As Imam al-Baqir said:

ما من عبد إلا وفي قلبه نكتة بيضاء، فإذا أذنب ذنبا خرج في النكتة نكتة سوداء، فإن تاب ذهب ذلك السواد وإن تمادى في الذنوب زاد ذلك السواد حتى يغطي البياض فإذا غطى البياض لم يرجع صاحبه إلى خير أبدا وهو قول الله عز وجل (كلا بل ران على قلوبهم ما كانوا يكسبون)

Every servant has a light speck in his heart. Whenever he transgresses with a sin, a dark spot will emerge out of the light spot. If he repents, that darkness will recede. If he continues to transgress with sin, the darkness will expand until it covers the light. Once the light has been covered, the individual will never turn back. That is the word of God Almighty, 'No, that is not the case! Rather, their hearts have been sullied by what they have been earning.'[2]

Third, **disobedience distances the individual from their Lord**. Some people think that as long as we have the intercession of the Holy Prophet and his Progeny, sin is not very consequential. Sure, divine mercy and the intercession of the Holy Household provide a haven from God's punishment. However, distance away from the Almighty is not cured through mercy and intercession.

---

[1] The Holy Quran, 52:16.
[2] Al-Majlisi, Bihar al-Anwar, 70:332. Citing: The Holy Quran, 83:14.

Closeness to God requires active effort and sustained obedience to His commands. In order to overcome our sins and begin to grow closer to God, we must seek His complete pardon.

Fourth, **evil deeds imperil the individual's stature in the eyes of any witness**. The first and greatest witness is God Almighty. But there are also other witnesses that will look down on an individual for their wicked behavior. The first of these witnesses is angels. Imam Ali teaches us in the supplication:

الَّذِينَ وَكَّلْتَهُم بِحِفْظِ مَا يَكُونُ مِنِّي وَجَعَلْتَهُمْ شُهُوداً عَلَيَّ مَعَ جَوَارِحِي، وَكُنتَ أَنتَ الرَّقِيبَ عَلَيَّ مِن وَرَائِهِمْ، وَالشَّاهِدَ لِمَا خَفِيَ عَنْهُمْ

Those [angels] whom You have appointed to watch over what appears from me and whom You have made, along with my bodily members, witness against me. Still, You are the Watcher over me from behind them, and the Witness of what is hidden from them.[3]

The other witness is our beloved Holy Prophet. As we read in the Holy Quran,

وَكَذَلِكَ جَعَلْنَاكُمْ أُمَّةً وَسَطًا لِتَكُونُوا شُهَدَاءَ عَلَى النَّاسِ وَيَكُونَ الرَّسُولُ عَلَيْكُمْ شَهِيدًا

Thus, We have made you a middle nation that you may be witnesses to the people, and that the Apostle may be a witness to you.[4]

Even if we are to attain the mercy of our Lord and the intercession of the Immaculate Holy Household, that would save us from punishment, but would not rectify our image in the eyes of witnesses. Will we be happy with the disappointment of these witnesses in us? Will we be content with being known as deviants by God Almighty, the Holy Prophet, the Immaculate Progeny, and the noble angels?

---

[3] *Al-Qummi, Mafateeh al-Jinan, 100.*
[4] *The Holy Quran, 2:143.*

Finally, **disobedience fosters audacity**. When a person has the audacity to disobey God in one thing, they will more easily disobey Him elsewhere as well. A second sin will lead to a third. As Imam al-Sajjad is narrated to have said:

اتقوا الكذب الصغير منه والكبير في كل جد وهزل فإن الرجل إذا كذب في الصغير اجترى على الكبير

Beware of lying, whether small or big, serious or in jest. Surely, if a man lies on a small matter, he will dare to do so over what is greater.[5]

In addition, The Commander of the Faithful states,

أشد الذنوب ما استهان به صاحبه

The greatest of sins is the one that is belittled by the one who commits it.[6]

The supplication treats these perils one by one. The Imam is teaching us about these perils and how we should beseech God to save us from them. The supplication says,

اللّهُمَّ إِنَّ عَفْوَكَ عَنْ ذَنْبِي، وَتَجَاوُزَكَ عَنْ خَطِيئَتِي، وَصَفْحَكَ عَنْ ظُلْمِي، وَسِتْرَكَ عَلَى قَبِيحِ عَمَلِي، وَحِلْمَكَ عَنْ كَثِيرِ جُرْمِي عِنْدَماكَانَ مِنْ خَطَأِي وَعَمْدِي، أَطْمَعَنِي فِي أَنْ أَسْأَلَكَ ما لا اسْتَوْجِبُهُ مِنْكَ

O' God, truly, when You forgive my sins, overlook my mistakes, pardon my transgressions, cover up my foul actions, and show forbearance in spite of my many crimes committed both negligently and intently, I am tempted to ask for that which I do not deserve from You.

O' God, "forgive my sins" and save me from the peril of punishment through Your forgiveness.

"Overlook my mistakes" and save me from the peril of corruption. As You have said,

---

[5] Al-Kulayni, al-Kafi, 2:338.
[6] Al-'Amili, Wasa'el al-Shi'a, 15:312.

أَفَمَن شَرَحَ اللَّهُ صَدْرَهُ لِلْإِسْلَامِ فَهُوَ عَلَىٰ نُورٍ مِّن رَّبِّهِ

Is someone whose breast Allah has opened to Islam so that he follows a light from His Lord...?[7]

Lift any darkness from my heart and allow me to remain obedient to Your commands. "Pardon my transgressions" and save me from the peril of distance from You. Allow me to be a proper recipient of Your blessings and mercy.

"Cover up my foul actions" and save me from the peril of disappointing those who You have made witnesses against me. Save me from the peril of disappointing the Holy Prophet and his Immaculate Progeny.

"Show forbearance in spite of my many crimes" and save me from the peril of audacity against Your commands. Guide me with the light of repentance. Allow my guilt to be my penance.

اللهم إن كان الندم على الذنب توبة فإني وعزتك من النادمين

O' God, if remorse over sin is repentance, then by Your Honor, I am of the remorseful![8]

O' God, You show forbearance while I show audacity! But no matter how audacious I have become in transgressing against Your commands, I ask Your continued forbearance! Bring me toward You with the guiding light of repentance. I know I do not deserve any of this, but I am "tempted to ask for that which I do not deserve from You" – due to Your continued forgiveness, pardon, and forbearance.

Divine Favor

This segment of the supplication leads us to a question – are divine rewards a favor or an entitlement?

The majority of our scholars say that rewards are a divine favor. No matter what we can do, we never deserve God's great rewards. All the

---

[7] *The Holy Quran*, 39:22.

[8] Al-Majlisi, *Bihar al-Anwar*, 91:142.

rewards that we may receive are out of His favor and not an entitlement.

There is no contract between God and His creatures that necessitates reward. When you enter a contract with another individual, there is an offer and an acceptance. One party pays a price to receive a product or service from the other. If a party performs its obligations as described in the contract, the other party must also perform its obligations.

There is no contract between God and His servants. Our worships and good deeds do not constitute performance on a contract. In fact, if a person worships God with this mentality, their rituals would be invalid. Our worships must be performed with the intent of seeking closeness to God, not bartering with Him.

A person should worship God either as obedience to His commands, out of thankfulness for His blessings, or out of recognition that He is worthy of being worshipped. Worship cannot be approached like a deal or contract. It must be approached with a reverent heart and the intention of growing closer to the Almighty.

Moreover, how can anyone claim that they deserve a reward when they were merely returning things to their rightful owner? Is a debtor entitled to a prize for repaying their debts?

God Almighty is the true owner of all things. He brought us into existence, sustained us throughout our lives, allowed us to worship and praise Him, and taught us to be good to one another. Everything we do is contingent on the life and ability that He gave us. All our actions are out of His favor. How can we ever claim entitlement to anything?

This is true of divine rewards. So, what about everything that God gives us without us asking or putting forth any effort? What about His bringing us into existence and sustaining us throughout our lives? What about the forgiveness and forbearance that He gives to so many sinners? It is all out of His boundless favor.

Identifying Divine Favors

The next segment of the supplication reads,

الَّذِي رَزَقْتَنِي مِنْ رَحْمَتِكَ، وَأَرَيْتَنِي مِنْ قُدْرَتِكَ، وَعَرَّفْتَنِي مِنْ إِجَابَتِكَ

You have blessed me through Your mercy, shown me Your
omnipotence, and acquainted me with Your answers [for
my prayers].

God's bestowal of favors on His creatures can be categorized into three types.

God's favors start with His constant giving of blessings. He gives us our existence and sustains us throughout our lives. He gives us our livelihoods, skills, knowledge, and wealth. These blessings are a type of mercy that He continuously grants His creatures.

God Almighty also bestows the favor of repelling troubles and misfortune away from His servants. Even when the troubles of this world drive us to the point of despair, He is there to alleviate our pains and fulfill our hopes. As we recite in one supplication:

يا من تحل به عقد المكاره، ويا من يفثأ به حد الشدائد

O' You by whom the knots of adversity are resolved. O' You
by whom the severity of difficulties is assuaged.[9]

When He repels troubles and misfortune, God is showcasing His divine omnipotence to His servants.

Finally, God bestows His favor through answering His servants' supplications. This type of divine favor is different in that it is a sign of divine love. His answers to our prayers are a sign of His love.

We are not entitled to any of this. His bestowal of blessings, repelling of misfortune, and answering of prayers are all gifts that He gives us out of His favor.

We only ask Him to continue to shower us with His boundless favors.

---

[9] *Al-Qummi, Mafateeh al-Jinan, 162.*

Safety in
Supplication

فَصِرْتُ أَدْعُوكَ آمِناً، وَأَسْأَلُكَ مُسْتَأْنِساً، لا خَائِفاً وَلا وَجِلاً، مُدِلاً عَلَيْكَ فِيَا قَصَدْتُ فِيهِ إِلَيْكَ

So I persist in calling out, believing in You. I invoke You, talking familiarly, not afraid nor shy, but assured of Your love and kindness whenever I turn to You.

When God Almighty sees His servants in a position of servility and reverence, He will shower them with His love and affection.

There is no greater joy than a servant experiencing their Lord's affection. He is so close to His servants and so willing to shower them with His love.

وَقَالَ رَبُّكُمُ ادْعُونِي أَسْتَجِبْ لَكُمْ إِنَّ الَّذِينَ يَسْتَكْبِرُونَ عَنْ عِبَادَتِي سَيَدْخُلُونَ جَهَنَّمَ دَاخِرِينَ

Your Lord has said, 'Call Me, and I will hear you!' Indeed, those who are disdainful of My worship will enter Hell in utter humiliation.[1]

وَإِذَا سَأَلَكَ عِبَادِي عَنِّي فَإِنِّي قَرِيبٌ أُجِيبُ دَعْوَةَ الدَّاعِ إِذَا دَعَانِ

When My servants ask you about Me, [tell them that] I am indeed nearmost. I answer the supplicant's call when he calls Me.[2]

When a servant experiences the love and affection of his Lord, he will feel driven to seek to grow closer to that love. He will beg and beseech his Lord not to turn away and abandon him. This is the feeling of a servant who is opening the gates of supplication, like a child begging their father not to leave their side.

The supplication also speaks of supplicating to God in safety. The Holy Quran supports the idea that a believer should find safety by the side of his Lord. It says,

---

[1] *The Holy Quran, 40:60.*
[2] *The Holy Quran, 2:186.*

أَلَا إِنَّ أَوْلِيَاءَ اللَّهِ لَا خَوْفٌ عَلَيْهِمْ وَلَا هُمْ يَحْزَنُونَ

Look! The friends of Allah will indeed have no fear nor will they grieve.[3]

The believer should not have any anxiety or fear about his Lord. Instead, he should feel safe and at peace.

يَا أَيَّتُهَا النَّفْسُ الْمُطْمَئِنَّةُ ✦ ارْجِعِي إِلَى رَبِّكِ رَاضِيَةً مَّرْضِيَّةً

'O soul at peace! Return to your Lord, pleased and pleasing![4]

الَّذِينَ آمَنُوا وَتَطْمَئِنُّ قُلُوبُهُم بِذِكْرِ اللَّهِ ۗ أَلَا بِذِكْرِ اللَّهِ تَطْمَئِنُّ الْقُلُوبُ

'... those who have faith and whose hearts find rest in the remembrance of Allah.' Behold! The hearts find rest in Allah's remembrance![5]

However, there are other verses in the Holy Quran that describe the believers as the most fearful of God. How do we reconcile between these two types of verses? Take these verses, for example:

إِنَّمَا الْمُؤْمِنُونَ الَّذِينَ إِذَا ذُكِرَ اللَّهُ وَجِلَتْ قُلُوبُهُمْ وَإِذَا تُلِيَتْ عَلَيْهِمْ آيَاتُهُ زَادَتْهُمْ إِيمَانًا وَعَلَى رَبِّهِمْ يَتَوَكَّلُونَ

The faithful are only those whose hearts tremble [with awe] when Allah is mentioned, and when His signs are recited to them, they increase their faith, and who put their trust in their Lord.[6]

إِنَّمَا يَخْشَى اللَّهَ مِنْ عِبَادِهِ الْعُلَمَاءُ ۗ إِنَّ اللَّهَ عَزِيزٌ غَفُورٌ

Only those of Allah's servants having knowledge fear Him. Indeed, Allah is all-mighty, all-forgiving.[7]

---

[3] The Holy Quran, 10:62.
[4] The Holy Quran, 89:27-28.
[5] The Holy Quran, 13:28.
[6] The Holy Quran, 8:2.
[7] The Holy Quran, 35:28.

وَأَمَّا مَنْ خَافَ مَقَامَ رَبِّهِ وَنَهَى النَّفْسَ عَنِ الْهَوَى ۞ فَإِنَّ الْجَنَّةَ هِيَ الْمَأْوَى

But as for him who is awed by the position of his Lord and restrains his soul from [following] desires, his refuge will indeed be Paradise.[8]

وَلِمَنْ خَافَ مَقَامَ رَبِّهِ جَنَّتَانِ

For him who stands in awe of the position of his Lord will be two gardens.[9]

The believers who know God are the most fearful of Him. How do we reconcile that with the verses that describe the believers as having no fear and finding rest in the remembrance of God?

There are three ways to answer this question.

First, each of us has two distinct types of relationships – our relationship with God Almighty, and our relationship with all of His creatures. When we think of our relationship with God, we feel fear and anxiety for not properly thanking and praising Him for all the blessing that He bestowed on us. When we think of our relationship to His creatures, we feel safety and comfort in knowing that He is our guardian and protector.

Second, there are two levels for our relationship to God. At the first level, we acknowledge that divine will controls our lives, and we are subject to the consequences of His pleasure and displeasure. Remembering God at this level should invoke fear and anxiety in us, as we do not know whether or not we have attained His pleasure. At the second level, a believer realizes that everything that God commands and creates are in fact blessings. Even if we do not see them as such at first glance, we will see the hidden blessing behind everything if we simply take the time to ponder. At this level, remembrance of God becomes a source of peace and tranquility for the believer.

---

[8] *The Holy Quran,* 79:40-41.

[9] *The Holy Quran,* 55:46.

Finally, fear and safety are reflective of the believer's state of mind. In other words, the believer will at times go through a state of fear when thinking of their Lord, while at other times they will feel safety and tranquility. The state of fear or safety is dependent on the believer's state of mind.

A believer feels fear and anxiety when they think about God and how He holds the reigns of mercy in His hands. God says in His Holy Book,

$$مَّا يَفْتَحِ اللَّهُ لِلنَّاسِ مِن رَّحْمَةٍ فَلَا مُمْسِكَ لَهَا ۖ وَمَا يُمْسِكْ فَلَا مُرْسِلَ لَهُ مِن بَعْدِهِ ۚ وَهُوَ الْعَزِيزُ الْحَكِيمُ$$

Whatever mercy Allah unfolds for the people, no one can withhold it, and whatever He withholds, no one can release it except Him, and He is the All-mighty, the All-wise. [10]

This is the meaning of the verses that speak of the believers being in awe of the 'position of their Lord.' The believer is anxious because they understand the majesty and grandeur of God. Our Lord is in the position of spreading and withholding mercy. A believer will understand this and be in awe of that position.

A believer will feel safety and tranquility when they understand that God is the only path to happiness.

Money might buy happiness sometimes, but it also brings about trouble and misfortune. The same is true of everything in this world – family, career, and so forth. There is nothing in this world that brings absolute happiness – nothing save God Almighty.

Every cause in creation is given its causality by God. Nothing can bring about happiness if it were not for God allowing it to do so. A believer realizes this fact and finds peace in knowing that all happiness comes from his Lord.

The following Quranic verse describes the states of fear and tranquility that a believer goes through. God says:

---

[10] *The Holy Quran*, 35:2.

اللَّهُ نَزَّلَ أَحْسَنَ الْحَدِيثِ كِتَابًا مُتَشَابِهًا مَثَانِيَ تَقْشَعِرُّ مِنْهُ جُلُودُ الَّذِينَ يَخْشَوْنَ
رَبَّهُمْ ثُمَّ تَلِينُ جُلُودُهُمْ وَقُلُوبُهُمْ إِلَى ذِكْرِ اللَّهِ ۚ ذَٰلِكَ هُدَى اللَّهِ يَهْدِي بِهِ مَن
يَشَاءُ ۚ وَمَن يُضْلِلِ اللَّهُ فَمَا لَهُ مِنْ هَادٍ

*Allah has sent down the best of discourses, a scripture
[composed] of similar motifs, whereat shiver the skins of
those who fear their Lord, then their skins and hearts relax
at Allah's remembrance. That is Allah's guidance, by
which He guides whomever He wishes; and whomever
Allah leads astray, has no guide.*[11]

In other words, the believer will tremble when thinking of the position
of their Lord, then feel safety in knowing that He is their guide and
protector.

---

[11] *The Holy Quran, 39:23.*

Answered
Supplication

فَإِنْ أَبْطَأَ عَنِّي عَتَبْتُ بِجَهْلِي عَلَيْكَ، وَلَعَلَّ الَّذِي أَبْطَأَ عَنِّي هُوَ خَيْرٌ لِي لِعِلْمِكَ بِعَاقِبَةِ الْأُمُورِ

Yet, when [Your answer] is delayed for me, I blame You out of my ignorance – although perhaps the delay is a blessing for me. Surely, You alone know the consequence of all things.

The segment of the supplication leads us to a question. Oftentimes, we hear people complain that despite their sincere and devoted supplications to God, they do not find any answer to their prayers.

If our prayers are not being answered, what is the meaning of the following verse?

وَقَالَ رَبُّكُمُ ادْعُونِي أَسْتَجِبْ لَكُمْ ۚ إِنَّ الَّذِينَ يَسْتَكْبِرُونَ عَنْ عِبَادَتِي سَيَدْخُلُونَ جَهَنَّمَ دَاخِرِينَ

Your Lord has said, 'Call Me, and I will hear you!' Indeed, those who are disdainful of My worship will enter Hell in utter humiliation.[1]

What does it mean when God says the following verse?

وَإِذَا سَأَلَكَ عِبَادِي عَنِّي فَإِنِّي قَرِيبٌ ۖ أُجِيبُ دَعْوَةَ الدَّاعِ إِذَا دَعَانِ

When My servants ask you about Me, [tell them that] I am indeed nearmost. I answer the supplicant's call when he calls Me.[2]

There are two primary factors for an answered supplication.

Trust in God

First, a supplicant must call God with full faith and trust in Him. In one narration, God Almighty is reported to say:

---

[1] *The Holy Quran, 40:60.*
[2] *The Holy Quran, 2:186.*

132

أنا عند ظن عبدي، فلا يظن بي إلا خيرا

I am at the expectations of My servant. Surely, he should expect nothing of Me but good.[3]

To have faith and trust in God means that we should not pray to Him thinking that our supplications are meaningless. Many people think that their supplications are ineffective and meaningless because God Almighty has predetermined how blessings will be apportioned among His servants.

For example, we may supplicate to God, asking Him for sustenance or forgiveness. If He has determined that He will grant us those things, then our prayers are meaningless, because we would have received those blessings even without prayer. If God had determined not to give us those blessings, no prayer can contradict His will and we will not receive those blessings, no matter how much we supplicate.

Therefore, the claim is that prayer is meaningless because anything that we ask is predetermined either to occur or not to occur.

This misconception is especially prevalent among those who believe in the idea of predetermination – that human beings have no free will, but are predestined to choose and act as they do. In fact, this misconception is a specific application of that broader concept of predetermination to our supplications.

In general, the answer to this misconception lies in the fact that God Almighty created this world as a system of cause and effect. He determined that when a cause exists, its effect will exist as well. It is not predetermined that things will burn, but that they can burn if touched by fire.

We are not predetermined to act as we do. Instead, we are given the ability to choose between alternative courses of action. The consequences of our actions are determined based on our actions. In other

---

[3] *Al-Majlisi, Bihar al-Anwar, 90:305.*

words, the outcomes are determined by their proper causes, which include human will in choosing one path or the other.

Apply this concept to the process of supplication. God created this world as a system of causes and effects. One of those causes is supplication itself. Each of us is given the option to supplicate or not to supplicate, and each of those alternatives results in a different consequence. In other words, God Almighty determined my sustenance since the beginning of time. However, part of that sustenance is conditional, to be granted only when the proper causes are set in place. Those causes include supplication, as well as hard work, dedication, truthfulness, and other human choices.

Our supplications are not meaningless, because God Almighty allowed us to gain His conditional blessings based on our free choice to supplicate. Supplication is one amongst many natural causes that combine to bring about certain consequences.

The Reality of Badaa'

We might hear the concept of *badaa'* being attributed to the Holy Household and their school of thought. It is a complex topic that is often misunderstood. It is important to properly understand this concept, as it is closely linked to our understanding of divine omniscience and justice.

Simply put, badaa' is the belief that voluntary actions carry consequences. A person who does not believe in badaa' might say, "If God knows that I will obey Him, then I am bound to obey Him." This is true, because if God knows that a person will obey, then disobedience would turn God's knowledge into ignorance. And since this is an impossibility, then everything that God knows is bound to happen.

This argument is used to support belief in the idea of predestination. The answer to this misconception lies in the belief of badaa'. We believe that God not only knows of our actions, but that our actions are undertaken out of our free will. He knows that we pray out of our own volition. He knows that we will be cured when we drink our medicine.

For example, God knows that person A will live 70 years – conditioned on person A keeping his connection with his relatives, giving charitably, and supplicating to God for a long life. God provides person A with the choice to either undertake these acts and live 70 years, or forgo them and live 40 years. God knows what person A will choose, yet person A's choices are consequential and undertaken by free will.

When I know that my actions can lengthen my life and preserve my health, I will voluntarily undertake those acts. God Almighty gave us the choice. His knowledge of our choices cannot be equated to predetermination of our actions.

The bottom line is that badaa' is the belief that voluntary actions carry consequences, and that not all things in this world are predetermined. When you know that your actions carry consequences, you will make an effort to reach the best consequences by making the wisest decisions. That is why some narrations say,

ما عبد الله بشيء مثل البداء.

God is not worshipped with anything like Badaa'.[4]

Another narration says,

الدعاء مخ العبادة.

Supplication is the core of worship.[5]

If you believe that your actions are voluntary and have their consequences, you will know that your supplication is a choice that has its consequences as well. To have faith and trust in God is to believe that your supplications have their consequences – that God hears your calls and answers your prayers. To think that your supplications are meaningless is to lose trust and faith in the Almighty.

---

[4] Al-Kulayni, al-Kafi, 1:146.

[5] Al-'Amili, Wasa'el al-Shi'a, 7:27.

Natural Causes and Supplication

*How do we reconcile between trusting in the power of
supplication and seeking natural causes for our needs? Can I
rely on supplication to cure my illness, or do I need to see a
physician and take my medication? Why do we need to seek a
livelihood if we can simply supplicate to God for sustenance
and wealth?*

Supplication is not a sufficient condition for all intended consequences. If it were a sufficient condition, then it would make sense to
leave all other causes and rely solely on supplication.

For anything to take place in this world, it may need a number of conditions to be met. To build a house, you need a blueprint, building material, and builders. If you do not have building materials, you cannot
build the house.

The same is true with our relationship with God. He emanates His
blessings to all His creations. Yet He willed for this world to flow in the
system of cause and effect. There are conditions that must be met for
His emanations to be properly received in this world.

This is why our scholars say that the Holy Prophet and his Immaculate
Progeny are a condition to the entire universe. God Almighty is the
source of emanation and the creator of all things. He willed for His
most magnificent creations to be the condition for all others. Just as He
willed for medicine to be a condition for health, and effort a condition
for the blessing of livelihood – He willed for the Holy Prophet and his
Immaculate Household to be the condition for the existence and sustenance of all other creatures.

This is why we read in *al-Ziyara al-Jami'a al-Kabeera*,

بكم فتح الله وبكم يختم، وبكم ينزل الغيث، وبكم يمسك السماء أن تقع على الأرض
إلا بإذنه.

*With you, God began creation, and with you, He shall seal
it. For your sake does He pour down rain, for your sake*

does He withhold the heavens from falling on the Earth,
except by His permission.[6]

We know that God Almighty is the source of all blessings. We also acknowledge that He willed for this world to be a system of causes and means. We therefore pursue those means, while at the same time supplicating for Him to ease our journey and deliver us to our intended consequences.

Seeking the Best Outcome

When we supplicate to God and ask Him for our needs, what
are we really asking Him for? Are we asking Him to grant us
the things we ask for simply for those things' sake? Or are we
asking Him for the best of outcomes?

God answers our prayers when we ask Him for things that are not detrimental to us. A person in a moment of despair might ask God to end their life. God knows the full and beautiful life that person can lead, and the opportunities they have to grow closer toward perfection. God's wisdom and mercy dictate that a prayer like this is not granted.

Take the time to ponder on that person's supplication. Are they really asking for death? Or are they asking for a better life? And if they were given those two alternative outcomes, which would they choose?

When we supplicate to God, we are not only asking Him for all the things we enumerate. We are asking Him to give us the best of lives and lead us to the best of outcomes. If I pray for something that will be of detriment to me, God's wisdom and mercy dictate that I do not receive that detriment.

With all of this, we can better understand this segment of the supplication:

---

[6] Al-Sadouq, al-Faqeeh, 2:594.

فَإِنْ أَبْطَأَ عَنِّي عَتِبْتُ بِجَهْلِي عَلَيْكَ، وَلَعَلَّ الَّذِي أَبْطَأَ عَنِّي هُوَ خَيْرٌ لِي لِعِلْمِكَ بِعَاقِبَةِ الْأُمُورِ

Yet, when [Your answer] is delayed for me, I blame You out of my ignorance – although perhaps the delay is a blessing for me. Surely, You alone know the consequence of all things.

We ask God Almighty by His infinite mercy and wisdom to grant us the best of consequences in all things.

Divine Love

فَلَمْ أَرَ مَوْلًى كَرِيمًا أَصْبَرَ عَلَى عَبْدٍ لَئِيمٍ مِنْكَ عَلَيَّ يَا رَبِّ، إِنَّكَ تَدْعُونِي فَأُوَلِّي عَنْكَ، وَتَتَحَبَّبُ إِلَيَّ فَأَتَبَغَّضُ إِلَيْكَ، وَتَتَوَدَّدُ إِلَيَّ فَلَا أَقْبَلُ مِنْكَ، كَأَنَّ لِي التَّطَوُّلَ عَلَيْكَ، فَلَمْ يَمْنَعْكَ ذَلِكَ مِنَ الرَّحْمَةِ لِي وَالْإِحْسَانِ إِلَيَّ، وَالتَّفَضُّلِ عَلَيَّ بِجُودِكَ وَكَرَمِكَ. فَارْحَمْ عَبْدَكَ الْجَاهِلَ، وَجُدْ عَلَيْهِ بِفَضْلِ إِحْسَانِكَ إِنَّكَ جَوَادٌ كَرِيمٌ.

I know no generous master who is more forbearing to a miscreant servant than You are to me. O' Lord, You continue to invite me, but I continue to turn You down. You seek my love, while I seek Your displeasure. You show me affection, but I do not accept it from You. As if I have the right to be insolent towards You! Yet this did not stop You from having mercy on me, being benevolent toward me, and favoring me with Your mercy and generosity. So have mercy on Your ignorant servant and be generous to him with Your favors and kindness, surely You are generous and kind.

In this segment, the Imam describes the extent of God's forbearance and mercy towards His creatures. No matter how much an individual insists on disobedience and delves into wretchedness, God turns towards us with mercy, continued blessings, and opportunities to change. As the Imam describes, "I know no generous master who is more forbearing to a miscreant servant than You are to me."

God Almighty gave us internal and external signs that lead us to Him. His internal signs include our reason, which we can use to ponder on ourselves and the rest of creation. His external signs include the prophets and messengers that He sent to us.

Both types of signs call on us to be steadfast. God says in the Holy Quran:

140

فَاسْتَقِمْ كَمَا أُمِرْتَ

So be steadfast, just as you have been commanded.[1]

فَاسْتَقِيمَا وَلَا تَتَّبِعَانِّ سَبِيلَ الَّذِينَ لَا يَعْلَمُونَ

*So be steadfast, and do not follow the way of those who do
not know.*[2]

Yet, the calls of these signs can be drowned by the calls of desire:

وَمَا أُبَرِّئُ نَفْسِي ۚ إِنَّ النَّفْسَ لَأَمَّارَةٌ بِالسُّوءِ إِلَّا مَا رَحِمَ رَبِّي

*Yet I do not absolve my [own carnal] soul, for the [carnal]
soul indeed prompts [men] to evil, except inasmuch as my
Lord has mercy.*[3]

Despite God's repeated calls, we turn Him down. He seeks our love
while we seek His displeasure. He shows us affection, but we do not
accept it from Him.

Love and Affection

What is the difference between love and affection?

Love is an emotion felt in the heart. Affection is the act of showing love.
Affection is love in action.

God Almighty shows us love and affection, and inspires our hearts with
love. There are times where we find ourselves longing for repentance
and guidance. There are days where we find our hearts longing to pray,
supplicate, and recite the Holy Quran. We remember our beloved Holy
Prophet and his Immaculate Household, longing to live by their example.

These moments, whether long or fleeting, He inspires this love in us so
that we can grow closer to Him.

---

[1] *The Holy Quran*, 11:112.

[2] *The Holy Quran*, 10:89.

[3] *The Holy Quran*, 12:53.

Still, we reject His overtures and reply with disobedience. The darkness of sin and desire is stronger than the light of these passing moments. Our ears seem to prefer the whispers of Satan over the calls of God. We find ourselves driven by our carnal desires that prompt us toward evil.

Sin piles up over sin. Our continued disobedience darkens our souls so that we start to feel repulsion at our prayers, supplications, mosques, and anything that connects us with God. We must turn to God and admit, "You seek my love while I seek Your displeasure. You show me affection, but I do not accept it from You."

God doesn't just give us these passing moments of love. He puts His love into action. Day after day, He continues to sustain us out of His blessings. No matter how much we insist on sin, He continues to grant us boon after boon. I continue to sin, but He allows me to graduate at the top of my class. I disobey so many of His commands, but He gives me the best job.

No matter how many times He closes the door of sin for me, I find a way to pry it open.

This is true for most people. We are given blessing after blessing, yet we reject His love and affection. We act as if we have a right to be insolent in the face of our Lord!

Still, none of this stops Him from continuing to shower us with His blessings. As we read in the supplication:

كَأَنَّ لِيَ التَّطَوُّلَ عَلَيْكَ، فَلَمْ يَمْنَعْكَ ذلِكَ مِنَ الرَّحْمَةِ لِي وَالإِحْسانِ إِلَيَّ، وَالتَّفَضُّلِ عَلَيَّ بِجُودِكَ وَكَرَمِكَ

As if I have the right to be insolent towards You! Yet this did not stop You from having mercy on me, being benevolent toward me, and favoring me with Your mercy and generosity.

Here, the Imam addresses three things in regards to God's gifts to His creatures.

He gives to us out of His boundless mercy, which He grants to all creatures. Whether animate or inanimate, believer or not, God showers everything with His mercy.

He rewards us with His benevolence. When He sees any virtuous trait in His servants, He is quick to shower them with His rewards.

He also favors His servants with greater blessings than He grants to others. He has favored us with better health, greater knowledge, and so forth.

This segment of the supplication is evident of the Almighty's boundless forbearance and magnanimity towards His servants, even though we continue to sin and disobey.

Why the Details?

A question might cross the reader's mind when reading these segments of the supplication: why all this detail?

There are three explanations that can be provided here.

First, an individual might detail their misdeeds to prepare themself for repentance. If we want to truly repent from our sins, we must feel the gravity of our actions. This allows us to feel the guilt and remorse required for true repentance. In order to invoke this remorse in us, the Imam helps us in detailing our sins.

The Imam is helping me to remember that when I sinned, I was rewarded with forgiveness. When I disobeyed, I was rewarded with forbearance. When I rebelled, I was rewarded with mercy. I begin to ponder on all my misdeeds and all of God's benevolence toward me. I feel remorse not only for my misdeed, but for having disobeyed such an honorable and merciful Lord.

Detailing our sins allows us to feel the remorse needed for true repentance. Remorse allows us to repent a sincere repentance, after which we will not return to sin. God says,

يَا أَيُّهَا الَّذِينَ آمَنُوا تُوبُوا إِلَى اللَّهِ تَوْبَةً نَّصُوحًا

O you who have faith! Repent to Allah with sincere repentance![4]

Second, the Imam is teaching us self-critique as a method of self-development. Each of us must critique ourselves before critiquing others. We cannot blame everything on our society and circumstances. We must judge ourselves for every action we take and every word we speak.

The Imam goes through all these details to guide us through the process of self-critique. It is not enough to say, 'I sinned, and God forgave.' We must stop at every one of our misdeeds and judge ourselves for our ill actions. Our Imams emphasized self-critique and its importance in our journey toward our Lord. Imam Ali said:

حاسبوا أنفسكم قبل أن تحاسبوا وزنوها قبل أن توزنوا، وتجهزوا للعرض الأكبر

Judge yourself before you are judged. Weigh [your deeds] before you are weighed. Prepare yourself for the grand trial![5]

ليس منا من لم يحاسب نفسه كل يوم

An individual who does not judge himself every day is not of us![6]

Every night, we must turn back to our schedule for the day and judge ourselves for every minute and every action.

Third, detailing our sins gives us an outlet to alleviate our worries. If we allow our worries to take over and cloud our hearts, we will surely fall into despair. The best way to ease these worries and lift the boulder off our chests is to complain of our state to the dearest companion – the one who will always listen, but never air our secrets. How beautiful is it for a servant to take his Lord as his companion?

---

[4] *The Holy Quran*, 66:8.

[5] Al-'Amili, *Wasa'el al-Shi'a*, 16:99.

[6] Al-Majlisi, *Bihar al-Anwar*, 68:259.

We ask God Almighty to shower us with His love and affection, and continue to show forbearance in the face of all of our misdeeds.

Divine Beauty

الحَمْدُ للهِ مالِكِ المُلْكِ، مُجْرِي الفُلْكِ، مُسَخِّرِ الرِّياحِ، فالِقِ الإصْباحِ،
دَيّانِ الدِّينِ، رَبِّ العالَمِينَ.

Praise be to God, the possessor of all sovereignty, the controller of ships, the disposer of winds, the creator of daybreak, the judge of faith, and the Lord of the worlds.

Our beloved Imam started this supplication with praise. He turns again to praise the Almighty at the midpoint of the supplication. Why does the Imam return to praise time and again?

Praise is a compliment given for a voluntary good. The basis for praise is our acknowledgment of God's benevolence toward us. Whenever we return to that acknowledgement, we turn back to praising our benevolent Lord.

Whenever the Imam describes an aspect of divine beauty, he returns to praise the Almighty. Before we can delve deeper into understanding divine beauty, we must first provide a philosophical premise.

Qualitative and Quantitative Knowledge

Quantitative knowledge provides information in terms of measured numbers. It answers the question of "how much?"

Qualitative knowledge provides information in terms of descriptions of properties and attributes.

For example, I might know an individual by knowing their height, weight, shoe size, and so forth. This is all quantitative information about them.

A psychologist may be able to assess the individual's inclinations, goals, thought pattern, relationships, ambitions, and the like. The psychologist can provide qualitative information about the individual.

When we look around us and observe the universe, we can describe it in quantitative and qualitative terms. Contemporary scientists focus mostly on quantitative studies. An astronomer, for example, seeks to understand cosmic objects – their numbers, sizes, projectiles, paths, speeds, and so forth. This information can be gathered with telescopes and other instruments.

We can also ask qualitative questions about the universe. How and when did it begin? Is it a set of scattered germs, or a woven tapestry of existence? Did it come to be by chance or through some design? Does it have a purpose or not?

Quantitative understandings of the world around us help us immensely. They allow us to comprehend and control our environments in ways that benefit our species. However, quantitative data do not provide us with an understanding of our relationship with the world around us. What is our responsibility toward this planet? Is there a shared purpose between the existence of humankind and the rest of the universe?

We need qualitative information in order to assess the trajectory of our lives. We need to evaluate whether or not our goals and ambitions match up with the purpose of creation. For that, we must use external and internal processes to gather qualitative data.

We can use our sensory experiences to gather some qualitative data about ourselves and the world around us. However, our senses only gather images of external objects. When we see ourselves in the mirror, we do not actually see ourselves, but our reflection. When you look at your friend, you do not capture his essence through your senses. Instead, you capture an image. The image you capture is based on your relative positions, the existence of any barriers, lighting, and so forth. The brain gathers different sensory experiences before it can make a determination about reality.

This is why philosophers say that we cannot have true knowledge of anything but ourselves. Any knowledge that I acquire about anything outside of me is incomplete. It is based on sensory experience and mental processes, both of which are prone to error.

On the other hand, my knowledge of myself does not rely on sensory experiences or mental processes. My knowledge of myself comes from within me without any intermediary. My knowledge of myself is not prone to error.

Reasoning with Beauty

We try to understand the universe around us so that we can better understand its creator. In doing so, we use both rational and personal methods.

We use reason to ponder on the universe we observe. Deep reflection and understanding of this world allow us to see that this world was not created in vain. As we read in the Holy Quran:

الَّذِينَ يَذْكُرُونَ اللَّهَ قِيَامًا وَقُعُودًا وَعَلَىٰ جُنُوبِهِمْ وَيَتَفَكَّرُونَ فِي خَلْقِ السَّمَاوَاتِ وَالْأَرْضِ رَبَّنَا مَا خَلَقْتَ هَٰذَا بَاطِلًا سُبْحَانَكَ فَقِنَا عَذَابَ النَّارِ

Those who remember Allah standing, sitting, and lying on their sides, and reflect on the creation of the heavens and the Earth [and say], 'Our Lord, You have not created this in vain! Immaculate are You! Save us from the punishment of the Fire.[1]

We observe the world around us and ponder on our sensory experiences. Through that, we can reach some understanding of God's beauty and the beauty of His creation.

Yet, we mentioned that sensory experience is an incomplete method of acquiring knowledge. It provides deficient information that is prone to error. We can only acquire real knowledge of ourselves. Therefore, we must use our real knowledge of ourselves to ponder on God's creation. This allows us to reach an understanding of His beauty that is based on real knowledge.

---

[1] *The Holy Quran, 3:191.*

This knowledge that stems from the self – call it personal knowledge – is more important to us than what we can acquire through sensory experience. Imam Ali is reported to have said,

من عرف نفسه عرف ربه

Whoever knows himself knows his Lord.[2]

المعرفة بالنفس أنفع المعرفتين

Knowledge of the self is the best of knowledge.[3]

Having identified knowledge as qualitative and quantitative, and that qualitative knowledge can be acquired by rational and personal methods, we see that the Imam is addressing both methods of knowledge in the supplication.

The Imam begins by addressing the rational method of gaining qualitative knowledge. He says, "Praise be to God, the possessor of all sovereignty." We have addressed the idea of sovereignty in a previous chapter. The Imam continues to showcase several instances of divine sovereignty:

الحَمْدُ للهِ مالِكِ المُلْكِ، مُجْرِي الفُلْكِ، مُسَخِّرِ الرِّياحِ، فالِقِ الإصْباحِ، دَيّانِ الدِّينِ، رَبِّ العالَمِينَ.

Praise be to God, the possessor of all sovereignty, the controller of ships, the disposer of winds, the creator of daybreak, the judge of faith, and the Lord of the worlds.

Each of these instances is a form of beauty that we observe in the world.

Creation and Legislation

The Imam speaks of both creative and legislative sovereignty in this segment. He speaks of God's creation of material objects, as well as His legislative sovereignty over faith and judgment. God Almighty is "the

---

[2] *Al-Aamudi, Ghurar al-Hikam, 232.*
[3] *Ibid.*

judge of faith." He legislated religion for us and provided us with the beliefs and practices we must observe.

Why does the Imam address both creative and legislative sovereignty in this segment? Our understanding is that the Imam is trying to show a direct link between the two concepts.

To understand this link, let us first ask the following question: how do we prove that a person has a right to anything? How do we know that person A has the right of ownership over a piece of property? How do we prove that person B has a right to some payment from another person?

An individual's right – a legal matter – is directly linked to an existing reality. This can be understood in terms of efficient and final causes. We spoke about the four causes – material, formal, efficient, and final – in a previous chapter. We said that an outcome's efficient cause includes the actors that bring about that outcome. Its final cause is the reason why that outcome was brought about. For example, the carpenter is the efficient cause of the creation of a chair. The final cause for the chair is to be a seat and source of comfort for the user.

We can properly say that an individual has a right to a certain thing if we can point out an efficient and a final causal effect between the individual and the object. Let us take a few examples.

When a child is born, we find that its mother begins to lactate. A physiological effect in the mother's body begins to prepare food for the newborn infant. The infant – out of pure biology and instinct – can suckle and digest their mother's milk. There is no need for anyone to teach the mother how to lactate or teach the infant how to suckle. The two physiological effects arise for a common purpose – to ensure that the infant gets its proper nutrition. Therefore, nurture of the infant is the final cause for the breastfeeding process.

Moving on to the next step of the analysis, we look to see if there is a proper efficient cause for breastfeeding. Is the mother properly lactat-

ing? Is the infant able to digest its mother's milk? There may be a physiological obstacle for either the mother or the baby to participate in the
breastfeeding process. If there is such an obstacle, there is no efficient
cause for breastfeeding. However, if the mother is capable of breastfeeding and the baby is able to take in and use that milk, then the efficient cause does exist.

When both the final and efficient causes exist, we can say that the infant
has a right to its mother's milk. The milk exists for the purpose of feeding the child and there is no circumstance that makes breastfeeding
impossible or unnecessary. Therefore, the child must be afforded its
right to nutrition through its mother's milk.

The bottom line is that the existence of an efficient cause and a final
cause between an individual and an object meant that the individual
has a right to that object. Therefore, there is a link between causal links
and legal rights.

Let us take another example. If we look at human physiology, we find
that we are able to eat and digest different plants. Our molar teeth are
made to grind leaves and nuts. Our stomachs are made to digest food
and absorb its nutrients. There is a final cause between our digestive
system and plant life. This leads us to deduce that we have a right to
find sustenance in eating fruits and vegetables. If we wish to make use
of this right, then we have to put the efficient cause into action and use
our abilities to gather or grow food. This is why we find some traditions
that say,

من أحيا أرضا مواتا فهي له

Whoever brings life to a dead earth, it shall be his.[4]

In modern legal systems, this right is called 'homesteading.' When no
one is making proper and efficient use of land, an individual can come
in and claim it as their rightful property through sustained proper use
and possession.

---

[4] *Al-Makki, al-Fusool al-Muhimma*, 2:461.

The point is that there is a direct link between real objects and causes, and legal rights.

Going back to the supplication, we see that the Imam starts by pointing out the wellspring of divine beauty – His sovereignty. He then goes on to showcase instances of divine beauty in creation, then in legislation. In other words, God Almighty is worthy of praise for the beauty of His creation and legislation, two things which are inextricably linked.

Why Ships?

Here, a person might say, 'I understand that the Imam is speaking about divine beauty and creation. But why does he mention ships as an example of that? Ships are a human invention and not a natural occurrence. Why cite them as an instance of divine beauty?'

This emphasis on ships is not limited to this supplication. God Almighty says in the Holy Quran:

وَسَخَّرَ لَكُمُ الْفُلْكَ لِتَجْرِيَ فِي الْبَحْرِ بِأَمْرِهِ

And He disposed the ships for you[r benefit] so that they may sail at sea by His command.[5]

وَآيَةٌ لَّهُمْ أَنَّا حَمَلْنَا ذُرِّيَّتَهُمْ فِي الْفُلْكِ الْمَشْحُونِ ۞ وَخَلَقْنَا لَهُم مِّن مِّثْلِهِ مَا يَرْكَبُونَ

A sign for them is that We carried their progeny in the laden ship, and We have created for them what is similar to it, which they ride.[6]

God's emphasis on ships is like His emphasis on pens and writing. He says,

وَالْقَلَمِ وَمَا يَسْطُرُونَ

By the pen and what they write.[7]

---

[5] The Holy Quran, 14:32.

[6] The Holy Quran, 36:41-42.

[7] The Holy Quran, 68:1.

It is not because of a particular uniqueness to ships and pens. Rather, it is an allusion to the gift of creativity and invention that God granted to mankind. When God mentions ships as a divine blessing, He is in fact referring to what is behind the ship. He is reminding us that He gave us the ability to create such magnificent and useful inventions.

Islam and the Environment

God Almighty is the Lord of the worlds who created the seas, earth, winds, and celestial bodies. When the Imam reminds us of this fact in this segment of the supplication, we should stop and reflect on our relationship with nature and our environment.

Many people think that modern legal systems have made strides in incorporating environmental protections into their laws. They think that Islam concerns itself with ritual worships and spiritual obligations, without any concern for thorny contemporary issues such as climate change.

This is a false impression of our faith. Just reading and reflecting on this segment of the supplication shows us Islam's emphasis and concern with the environment:

الحَمْدُ للهِ مالِكِ المُلْكِ، مُجْرِي الفُلْكِ، مُسَخِّرِ الرِّياحِ، فالِقِ الاِصْباحِ، دَيّانِ الدِّينِ، رَبِّ العالَمِينَ.

Praise be to God, the possessor of all sovereignty, the controller of ships, the disposer of winds, the creator of daybreak, the judge of faith, and the Lord of the worlds.

The Imam is describing a state of environmental balance that allows mankind to reach its goals. God Almighty gave us the creative mind to build our ships, but He also taught us that nature is a loving mother, to be relied on but not abused. Her winds come and go – sometimes calmly and sometimes with force – to catch our sails and move our ships. The sun rises to show us our path, and sets so that we can map our journeys by the stars.

Notice Imam Ali's beautiful words on nature. He says,

فإنكم مسؤولون حتى عن البقاع والبهائم

You shall be questioned even about the lands and the beasts.[8]

On the Day of Judgment, we will not be questioned only about our prayers and fasts. Divine questioning does not stop at charity and social interactions. We will be questioned about how we treated the earth we walked on and the animals we came across.

When Imam Ali appointed his companion Malik al-Ashtar as governor of Egypt, he gave him a letter as an instrument of appointment. It read:

هذَا مَا أَمَرَ بِهِ عَبْدُ اللهِ عَلِيٌّ أَمِيرُ الْمُؤْمِنِينَ، مَالِكُ بْنُ الْحَارِثِ الأَشْتَرَ فِي عَهْدِهِ إِلَيْهِ، حِينَ وَلاَّهُ مِصْرَ: جِبْوَةَ خَرَاجِهَا، وَجِهَادَ عَدُوِّهَا، وَاسْتِصْلاَحَ أَهْلِهَا، وَعِمَارَةَ بِلاَدِهَا

This is what God's servant, Ali, the Commander of the Faithful, has ordered Malik ibn al-Harith al-Ashtar in his instrument [of appointment] when he made him Governor of Egypt – for the collection of its revenues, fighting against its enemies, seeking the good of its people, and developing its lands.[9]

Compare between the words of Imam Ali and his enemy Muawiya ibn Abu Sufyan. Muawiya would say:

By God, I did not fight you so that you may pray or fast, so that you may perform pilgrimage or pay alms, for you already do that. I fought you because I wish to rule over you. God has given me that, despite your wishes.[10]

Imam Ali would tell the citizens of Egypt that his appointed governor is not meant to subjugate them. Instead, he is meant to serve the land and its people.

---

[8] *Al-Radi, Nahj al-Balagha, 242, Sermon 167.*

[9] *Al-Radi, Nahj al-Balagha, 426, Letter 53.*

[10] *Al-Majlisi, Bihar al-Anwar, 44:48.*

This is the beauty of our faith and the shining examples that God appointed for us to follow!

An Immaculate
Supplicant

الحَمْدُ للهِ عَلَى حِلْمِهِ بَعْدَ عِلْمِهِ، وَالحَمْدُ للهِ عَلَى عَفْوِهِ بَعْدَ قُدْرَتِهِ، وَالحَمْدُ
للهِ عَلَى طُولِ أَنَاتِهِ فِي غَضَبِهِ، وَهُوَ قَادِرٌ عَلَى مَا يُرِيدُ.

Praise be to God for His forbearance in light of His all-awareness. Praise be to God for His amnesty, despite His omnipotence. Praise be to God for the long respite He allows in spite of provocation. Surely, He is able to do what He wills.

This segment of the supplication takes us to a topic often discussed by scholars – the intention behind our Immaculate Imams' supplications.

Many people ask, if our Immaculate Imams do not commit any mistake or slip into any sin, why do they supplicate so much – always asking for forgiveness and clemency?

They cry, weep, and faint during the supplications. If our Imams are immaculate, why do they weep and supplicate, asking for forgiveness?

Let us address three answers to this question.

Immaculate Teachers

Many scholars have mentioned that one reason for the Imams' supplications is education. The Imams teach us our religion in their gatherings, informing us of our religious duties of obligations, prohibitions, and the like. They do the same when they are on their prayer mats.

They teach us through their supplications. They teach us how to speak to God and supplicate to Him. They teach us how to beseech and glorify Him. They teach us the language that we should use with our Lord. Thus, they are not seeking forgiveness for any misdeed, but are teaching us how to seek forgiveness for ours.

This answer falls short when we look at the state of our Imams during supplication. Traditions tell us that Imam Ali would weep in his prayers to the point of fainting. Imam al-Hussain would supplicate on Mount Arafa and cry until those around him felt pity for his state.

If they were simply teaching us how to supplicate, would they reach such a high spiritual and emotional state? Would they weep so much that those around them felt pity for them?

It is difficult to believe that teaching is the sole reason behind our Immaculate Imams' supplications, especially when they reach such a high spiritual and emotional state.

Spiritual Sins

Sin can be categorized into four types: legal, rational, formal, and spiritual. Each of these types has a type of forgiveness and clemency that goes along with it.

Legal sins are transgressions against God's commands. A legal sin would be to forgo an obligation or to commit a prohibition. Such a sin would not be committed by an Immaculate Imam – an individual who God appointed as a role model for the rest of His servants.

Rational sins are breaches of rational principles that have been applied when a divine command is not known. What happens when we doubt whether a thing is permissible or forbidden? There are certain rational principles that jurists apply in such cases.

For example, what should we do if we doubt whether it is permissible or forbidden for a man to completely shave his beard? Let us assume that the individual did not search for the adequate evidence that would allow him to come to a reasonable conclusion about the issue. He shaved his beard, doubting whether this act was permitted or forbidden. He did not commit a legal sin because he did not know of any divine command against shaving. Still, he committed a rational sin because he acted on doubt. He approached a course of action fully aware that he might be sinning, but chose to act without first seeking to clear his doubts. This irrational behavior is what scholars call a rational sin.

Formal sins result from the failure to observe proper form and etiquette when dealing with God Almighty. This type of sin is most evident in the story of Adam and Eve. God said to them,

وَلَا تَقْرَبَا هَذِهِ الشَّجَرَةَ فَتَكُونَا مِنَ الظَّالِمِينَ

Do not approach this tree, lest you should be among the wrongdoers.[1]

This was not a divine command not to eat from the tree. It was an advisory statement. God told them that if they approach the tree, they could end up becoming of the wrongdoers. The proper etiquette and form would be to heed God's divine advice, even though to act against would not be a legal or rational sin. Still, Adam did not observe the proper form with God – a grave error when seen in light of his high status.

وَعَصَى آدَمُ رَبَّهُ فَغَوَى

Adam disobeyed his Lord, and went amiss.[2]

Finally, a **spiritual sin** is something completely different from the other three. A lover commits a spiritual sin when they are occupied with anything other than their beloved.

Our Immaculate Imams' relationship with God Almighty is that of a lover with his beloved. Their connection is so pure and sublime that everything in their lives is driven by the passion of divine love. If they spend any moment occupied with anything other than their beloved Lord, they feel that as the heaviest of sins. They weep and supplicate, asking God to forgive them that moment of shortcoming.

This second answer is also unsatisfactory. God Almighty had created them as lights – circling around His throne and glorifying Him – before the creation of any physical body. Would they ever lose sight of their

---

[1] *The Holy Quran, 2:35.*
[2] *The Holy Quran, 20:121.*

Lord, even for a moment? We cannot imagine that someone like the Holy Prophet or the Commander of the Faithful would ever forget the Almighty – even for a moment. Imam Ali would say,

ما رأيت شيئًا إلا ورأيت الله قبله وبعده وفوقه وتحته وفيه

I have not seen a thing except that I saw God before, after, above, under, and in it.[3]

How can an individual who always sees God before their eyes ever be occupied with anything other than their Lord? Let us ponder on that question as we read the deepest proclamations of faith that come with his supplications. He would say:

مَتَى غِبْتَ حَتَّى تَحْتَاجَ إِلَى دَلِيلٍ يَدُلُّ عَلَيْكَ ؟ وَمَتَى كَانَتِ الآثَارُ هِيَ الَّتِي تُوصِلُ إِلَيْكَ ؟

When have You ever been absent so that You may need a guide to point to You? When have [You ever been far-off so that] traces lead to You?[4]

Our Immaculate Imams spend every moment in their lives thinking of their Lord and glorifying Him. Even when they eat, drink, or commit any other act – whether obligatory, recommended, or permissible – God Almighty is always at the forefront of their minds. Everything that they do is with the intention of seeking closeness to Him. They are never distracted or occupied by anything but Him.

The Collective

So why do our Immaculate Imams supplicate and ask for forgiveness while weeping with such vigor?

The third and proper answer is that they are supplicating, not in light of their individual existence, but as a mirror for the rest of creation. To

---

[3] *Al-Mazandarani, Sharh Usool al-Kafi, 3:83.*

[4] *Ibn Tawus, al-Iqbal, 349.*

properly understand this point, let us first address three supporting concepts.

First, we have mentioned previously that the relationship between the Imams and the rest of existence is that of a condition with its subject. God Almighty emanates existence to the entire universe, yet He willed for them to be a condition precedent for the existence of all other creations. God Almighty created them as lights before any other creature. He linked the entire universe to the radiant existence of the Holy Household – what is sometimes referred to as "the Muhammadan Truth" or "the Throne."

الَّذِي خَلَقَ السَّمَاوَاتِ وَالْأَرْضَ وَمَا بَيْنَهُمَا فِي سِتَّةِ أَيَّامٍ ثُمَّ اسْتَوَىٰ عَلَى الْعَرْشِ

He, who created the heavens and the Earth and whatever is between them in six days, and then settled on the Throne.[5]

The radiant existence of the Holy Household was a condition for the creation of everything else. This was not due to any fault in God's omnipotence, but because He wished to give them such a high and noble status.

God Almighty made marriage a precondition for procreation. He could have created each one of us without need for parents. Yet He chose for us to be families and generations – each dependent on its predecessors. God made medicine a precondition for wellbeing, even though He could dispense health to whomever He wishes.

God's choice to make His creations interdependent does not compromise His omnipotence in the least. He created the light of the Holy Prophet and his blessed family, making them a condition to the rest of creation. As we read in al-Ziyara al-Jami'a al-Kabeera:

---

[5] *The Holy Quran, 25:59.*

بكم فتح الله وبكم يختم وبكم ينزل الغيث وبكم يمسك السماء أن تقع على الأرض إلا بإذنه

God created you in the first place and He shall seal creation with you. On account of you, He sent down the abundant rain [of His mercy], and by you He prevents the sky from falling down over the Earth, unless He permits.[6]

Second, as God made them a precondition for all creation, they are dominant amongst all creation. They grasp the soul of every living thing, especially the believers. They are a condition to every soul, including the believers.

ذِكْرُكُمْ فِي الذَّاكِرِينَ وَأَسْمَاؤُكُمْ فِي الْأَسْمَاءِ وَأَجْسَادُكُمْ فِي الْأَجْسَادِ وَأَرْوَاحُكُمْ فِي الْأَرْوَاحِ وَأَنْفُسُكُمْ فِي النُّفُوسِ وَآثَارُكُمْ فِي الْآثَارِ وَقُبُورُكُمْ فِي الْقُبُورِ فَمَا أَحْلَى أَسْمَاءَكُمْ وَأَكْرَمَ أَنْفُسَكُمْ وَأَعْظَمَ شَأْنَكُمْ وَأَجَلَّ خَطَرَكُمْ وَأَوْفَى عَهْدَكُمْ وَأَصْدَقَ وَعْدَكُمْ

Your mentioning is amongst mentions! Your names are amongst names! Your figures are amongst figures! Your souls are amongst souls! Your selves are amongst selves! Your traditions are amongst traditions! Your graves are amongst graves! O' how sweet are your names! How noble are your selves! How grand is your position! How magnificent is your station! How trustworthy is your covenant! How true is your promise![7]

These verses of the visitation refer to their conditionality to the rest of creation, and their dominance and grasp over it.

Third, they feel the pains and sins of the believers. Because of their position of conditionality and grasp over creation, they speak as a reflection of the believers.

Their souls are dominant over all other souls, grasping their pain and suffering. They feel our pains and ache for our aches. In fact, their love

---

[6] *Al-Qummi, Mafateeh al-Jinan, al-Ziyara al-Jami'a al-Kabeera.*
[7] *Ibid.*

and affection for the believers is so great that they are hurt by our sins more than we are.

Imagine a mother who sees her son taking the wrong path. How hurt is she by his addiction? How much does it pain her to see him arrested and imprisoned? How much does she weep for him when he lies dead, the gang violence finally catching up to him? How helpless does she feel when she could not get to him? How much does she blame herself for not being able to protect him?

Their love for us is like this and greater. Every one of our misdeeds is like an arrow we aim at our Imam's heart.

They are pained by our sins more than we are. They regret our actions more than we do. They feel pain for our pain. They experience sorrow for our sorrows. They seek repentance for our repentance. God Almighty describes this trait of the Holy Prophet, saying:

لَقَدْ جَاءَكُمْ رَسُولٌ مِّنْ أَنفُسِكُمْ عَزِيزٌ عَلَيْهِ مَا عَنِتُّمْ حَرِيصٌ عَلَيْكُم بِالْمُؤْمِنِينَ رَءُوفٌ رَّحِيمٌ

There has certainly come to you an apostle from among yourselves. Grievous to him is your distress; he has deep concern for you, and is most kind and merciful to the faithful.[8]

Our Immaculate Imams supplicate and weep, not in respect to their own existence, but with respective to the collective. They weep for us and seek forgiveness for us due to their deep connection with every single one of us.

The Commander of the Faithful's Example

Imam Ali al-Sajjad would always reflect on the example of his grandfather Ali ibn Abu Talib. When he read the manuscripts that described Imam Ali's worships, he would cry and say,

---

[8] *The Holy Quran*, 9:128.

من يقدر على عبادتك يا أمير المؤمنين

Who has the ability to worship like you, O' Commander of the Faithful?![9]

How could an individual like Ali ibn Abu Talib – whose staple meal was dry bread with a sprinkle of either salt or vinegar – have the strength to worship God for hours on end?

His piety and austerity were miraculous. No one can be or act like him. He would write to one of his governors:

أَلَا وَإِنَّ لِكُلِّ مَأْمُومٍ إِمَاماً، يَقْتَدِي بِهِ، وَيَسْتَضِيءُ بِنُورِ عِلْمِهِ. أَلَا وَإِنَّ إِمَامَكُمْ قَدِ اكْتَفَى مِنْ دُنْيَاهُ بِطِمْرَيْهِ، وَمِنْ طُعْمِهِ بِقُرْصَيْهِ. أَلَا وَإِنَّكُمْ لَا تَقْدِرُونَ عَلَى ذلِكَ، وَلكِنْ أَعِينُونِي بِوَرَعٍ وَاجْتِهَادٍ، وَعِفَّةٍ وَسَدَادٍ

Surely, every follower has an imam whom he follows and from the brightness of whose knowledge he takes light. Surely, your imam has contented himself with two shabby pieces of cloth out of his world and two loaves for his meal. Certainly, you cannot bear this – but at least support me in piety, exertion, chastity, and uprightness.[10]

His love is a safeguard for us from the fires of Hell. By following the Commander of the Faithful, we hope to gain the greatest rewards of the hereafter. As the Holy Prophet said,

يا علي أنت وشيعتك الفائزون يوم القيامة

O' Ali! You and your followers are the victors on the Day of Resurrection.[11]

We also read in Du'a al-Nudba:

---

[9] Al-Majlisi, *Bihar al-Anwar*, 46:75.

[10] Al-Radi, *Nahj al-Balagha*, Letter 45.

[11] Al-Majlisi, *Bihar al-Anwar*, 31:336.

وشيعتك على منابر من نور مبيضة وجوههم حولي في الجنة، وهم جيراني، ولولا
أنت يا علي لم يُعرف المؤمنون بعدي

Your adherents shall be on pedestals of light, bright-faced,
around me in Paradise, and they shall be my neighbors.
Were it not for you, O' Ali, true believers would not be
recognized after me![12]

We ask God Almighty to count us amongst the lovers and followers of
the Commander of the Faithful, Ali ibn Abu Talib.

---

[12] *Ibn Tawus, al-Iqbal, 296.*

So Far Yet So Near

الحَمْدُ لِلَّهِ خَالِقِ الخَلْقِ بَاسِطِ الرِّزْقِ، فَالِقِ الإِصْبَاحِ، ذِي الجَلالِ
وَالإِكْرَامِ، وَالفَضْلِ وَالإِنْعَامِ، الَّذِي بَعُدَ فَلا يُرَى، وَقَرُبَ فَشَهِدَ النَّجْوَى،
تَبَارَكَ وَتَعَالَى.

**Praise be to God, the creator of all creation, who expands
sustenance, who starts the day, the owner of majesty, magnanimity, favors, and bounties. He is far from being visible [to the eye], yet so near that He hears every whisper.
He is the most Blessed and High.**

The Imam speaks of God's creation and sustenance of everything in
existence. What is the link between those two concepts?

Mentioning creation and sustenance together is a reference to God's
promise to provide sustenance to all His creations. God mentions this
promise in the following verse:

وَمَا مِن دَابَّةٍ فِي الأَرْضِ إِلَّا عَلَى اللَّهِ رِزْقُهَا

*There is no animal on the Earth, but that its sustenance lies
with Allah.* [1]

God has made it incumbent upon Himself to grant every creature its
sustenance. In another verse He says,

وَفِي السَّمَاءِ رِزْقُكُمْ وَمَا تُوعَدُونَ ❁ فَوَرَبِّ السَّمَاءِ وَالأَرْضِ إِنَّهُ لَحَقٌّ مِثْلَ مَا أَنَّكُمْ
تَنطِقُونَ

*And in the sky is your provision and what you are
promised. By the Lord of the sky and the Earth, it is indeed
the truth, just as [it is a fact that] you speak.* [2]

Therefore, God has made it a right of every creature to receive its sustenance from Him. He made a promise that He will provide sustenance, and He does not break a promise.

---

[1] *The Holy Quran, 11:6.*

[2] *The Holy Quran, 51:22-23.*

Still, there seem to be some Quranic verses that contradict this fact. God says in His Holy Book:

وَلَوْ بَسَطَ اللَّهُ الرِّزْقَ لِعِبَادِهِ لَبَغَوْا فِي الْأَرْضِ وَلَكِن يُنَزِّلُ بِقَدَرٍ مَّا يَشَاءُ

Were Allah to expand the provision for [all] His servants,
they would surely create havoc on the Earth. But He sends
down in a [precise] measure whatever He wishes.[3]

How do we reconcile between this verse and the Imam's
supplication? Does God 'expand' His sustenance and make it
freely available? Or does He provide it in a limited and
precise measure?

The answer is that the holy verse and the supplications are speaking of two aspects of sustenance. The holy verse denies that sustenance is freely available to all creatures and in equal measure. Instead, it emphasizes God's creation of an interdependent world. Had God made all sustenance of equal measure for every individual – where people did not rely on one another – then mankind would wreak havoc on this world. Our economic interdependence necessitates that we make peace with one another, a fact that modern history has clearly proven. God says in the Holy Quran,

كَلَّا إِنَّ الْإِنسَانَ لَيَطْغَى ❁ أَن رَّآهُ اسْتَغْنَى

Indeed, man becomes rebellious when he considers himself
without need.[4]

Therefore, God Almighty made us dependent on one another. He apportioned sustenance between His creations, each with a precise measure. He says:

---

[3] The Holy Quran, 42:27.
[4] The Holy Quran, 96:6-7.

أَهُمْ يَقْسِمُونَ رَحْمَتَ رَبِّكَ ۚ نَحْنُ قَسَمْنَا بَيْنَهُم مَّعِيشَتَهُمْ فِي الْحَيَاةِ الدُّنْيَا ۚ وَرَفَعْنَا
بَعْضَهُمْ فَوْقَ بَعْضٍ دَرَجَاتٍ لِّيَتَّخِذَ بَعْضُهُم بَعْضًا سُخْرِيًّا ۗ وَرَحْمَتُ رَبِّكَ خَيْرٌ مِّمَّا
يَجْمَعُونَ

Is it they who dispense the mercy of your Lord? It is We who
have dispensed among them their livelihood in the present
life, and raised some of them above others in rank, so that
some may take others into service, and your Lord's mercy
is better than what they amass. [5]

The Quranic verses speak of God Almighty apportioning sustenance
for His creatures in due measure. When they say that God did not "expand the provision for [all] His servants," they mean that He did not
make each individual independent in sustenance.

What does the Imam mean when he uses similar words? There are two
possible meanings.

The Imam could be referring to the fact that God provides sustenance
without asking for any compensation. God does not need any payment
or favor from us. He sustains us simply out of His will and mercy. He
says,

وَتَرْزُقُ مَن تَشَاءُ بِغَيْرِ حِسَابٍ

You provide for whomever You wish without any
reckoning. [6]

Without reckoning does not mean without limits or measure. It means
that He is not looking for any kind of repayment. He says,

وَكُلُّ شَيْءٍ عِندَهُ بِمِقْدَارٍ

everything is by [precise] measure with Him. [7]

إِنَّا كُلَّ شَيْءٍ خَلَقْنَاهُ بِقَدَرٍ

Indeed, We have created everything in a measure. [8]

---

[5] The Holy Quran, 43:32.
[6] The Holy Quran, 3:27.
[7] The Holy Quran, 13:8.
[8] The Holy Quran, 54:49.

وَإِن مِّن شَيْءٍ إِلَّا عِندَنَا خَزَائِنُهُ وَمَا نُنَزِّلُهُ إِلَّا بِقَدَرٍ مَّعْلُومٍ

There is not a thing but that its sources are with Us, and
We do not send it down except in a known measure.[9]

God does not create anything without a limit or measure. However, He
does not seek any compensation for all the blessing He bestows:

مَا خَلَقْتُ الْجِنَّ وَالْإِنسَ إِلَّا لِيَعْبُدُونِ ✦ مَا أُرِيدُ مِنْهُم مِّن رِّزْقٍ وَمَا أُرِيدُ أَن
يُطْعِمُونِ ✦ إِنَّ اللَّهَ هُوَ الرَّزَّاقُ ذُو الْقُوَّةِ الْمَتِينُ

I did not create the jinn and the humans except that they
may worship Me. I desire no provision from them, nor do I
desire that they should feed Me. Indeed, it is Allah who is
the All-provider, Powerful and All-strong.[10]

God does not ask us for compensation. In fact, we cannot imagine anything that could compensate Him for all His favors.

Even our worship of God cannot be thought of as repayment for His
blessings. Worship itself is a blessing from Him. He allowed us the ability to remember Him and glorify His name. When everything we have
is from God, we cannot imagine that anything we do can ever compensate Him.

Therefore, God gives sustenance to all creation without any reckoning
– without asking for any repayment or compensation.

Another possible understanding for the Imam's words is that God
made natural wealth a gift to mankind. He provided metals, wildlife,
and so forth. He did not apportion natural wealth amongst people, but
made it freely available to all mankind. A narration attributed to the
Holy Prophet says,

الناس شركاء في ثلاث: الماء والنار والكلأ

People are partners in three things: water, fire, and grazing
[pastures].[11]

---

[9] The Holy Quran, 15:21.

[10] The Holy Quran, 51:56-58.

[11] Al-Nouri, Mustadrak al-Wasa'el, 17:114.

Our scholars say that this is meant as an example and not an exhaustive list.

The Holy Quran makes it clear that natural wealth belongs to Him and His prophet. God says,

يَسْأَلُونَكَ عَنِ الْأَنْفَالِ ۖ قُلِ الْأَنْفَالُ لِلَّهِ وَالرَّسُولِ

[When] they ask you concerning the anfaal, say: 'The anfaal belong to Allah and the Apostle.' [12]

The Holy Prophet and the Immaculate Imams in turn gave away their right to this wealth to the rest of mankind. They said, for example,

من أحيا أرضا مواتا فهي له

Whoever brings life to a dead earth, it shall be his. [13]

Everything on this Earth is for God. He gave it to us so that we make use of it on our journey towards Him. He says,

هُوَ الَّذِي خَلَقَ لَكُم مَّا فِي الْأَرْضِ جَمِيعًا ثُمَّ اسْتَوَىٰ إِلَى السَّمَاءِ فَسَوَّاهُنَّ سَبْعَ سَمَاوَاتٍ ۚ وَهُوَ بِكُلِّ شَيْءٍ عَلِيمٌ

It is He who created for you all that is in the Earth, then He turned to the heaven and fashioned it into seven heavens, and He has knowledge of all things. [14]

If we study the traditions of our Immaculate Imams, we can conclude that a proper apportionment of this wealth would eradicate poverty from this world. Imam Ali would say:

إِنَّ اللهَ سُبْحَانَهُ فَرَضَ فِي أَمْوَالِ الْأَغْنِيَاءِ أَقْوَاتَ الْفُقَرَاءِ، فَمَا جَاعَ فَقِيرٌ إِلَّا بِمَا مُتِّعَ بِهِ غَنِيٌّ، وَاللهُ تَعَالَى سَائِلُهُمْ عَنْ ذَلِكَ

Allah, the Glorified, has fixed the livelihood of the destitute in the wealth of the rich. Consequently, whenever a

---

[12] *The Holy Quran, 8:1.*
[13] *Al-Makki, al-Fusool al-Muhimma, 2:461.*
[14] *The Holy Quran, 2:29.*

destitute remains hungry, it is by what was enjoyed by the rich. Allah, the Sublime, will question them about it.[15]

As God says in the Holy Quran,

خُذْ مِنْ أَمْوَالِهِمْ صَدَقَةً تُطَهِّرُهُمْ وَتُزَكِّيهِم بِهَا

Take charity from their possessions to cleanse them and purify them thereby.[16]

It is natural for charity to purify the soul. It teaches us the principles of sacrifice and generosity, allowing us to rid ourselves from miserliness.

Charity also allows us to cleanse ourselves and our wealth. That is because, whether we know it or not, some part of our wealth does not belong to us. It belongs to the poor, who were not allowed to enjoy it due to the improper division of natural wealth. Had the Earth's natural bounties been properly apportioned, that money would not be in my bank account, but with some other poor individual.

When you take this money and give it to its proper owner, you are purifying yourself and your wealth. You are removing everything that does not belong to you. This is a reference to God's legislative provision of sustenance to His creatures.

Majesty and Beauty

God's divine attributes can be divided into attributes of majesty and attributes of beauty.

Attributes of majesty are those that exalt Him from any deficiency. He is of no need. He is not ignorant, incapable, or vulnerable in any way.

Attributes of beauty describe God's infinite perfections. He is all-living, omnipotent, omniscient, and omnibenevolent.

There are some who might look at their sustenance and think that they are independent of God. They lose sight of the source of their existence and think that God is either a fiction or a weakling. They look at their

---

[15] Al-Radi, *Nahj al-Balagha, Short Saying 328.*
[16] *The Holy Quran, 9:103.*

wealth and think that it will never fade. They see the bounties that have been given and think that God cannot take them away.

The Imam says,

الْحَمْدُ لِلَّهِ خَالِقِ الْخَلْقِ بَاسِطِ الرِّزْقِ، فَالِقِ الإِصْبَاحِ، ذِي الْجَلَالِ وَالإِكْرَامِ، وَالْفَضْلِ وَالإِنْعَامِ

Praise be to God, the creator of all creation, who expands sustenance, who starts the day, the owner of majesty, magnanimity, favors, and bounties.

The Imam mentions God's majesty and magnanimity to remind us of His attributes of majesty and beauty. He provides for us, not because He must or because we deserve it. His provision of favor and bounties is completely out of His will and generosity.

So Far Yet So Near

We have mentioned before that God Almighty is infinite, having no bounds or limits of any sort. Because He is so, He cannot be seen. For us to be able to see anything, that thing must have a recognizable boundary. If we are to sense anything, it must be limited in some way. When we cannot see or sense an object, we naturally think that it is far and beyond reach.

His limitless nature also means that He envelops the entirety of His creation. Everything in creation is within His grasp. This means that He is so close to everything that He witnesses every action, and hears every whisper.

His exalted existence can be thought of as both near and far. As the Imam describes:

الَّذِي بَعُدَ فَلَا يُرَى، وَقَرُبَ فَشَهِدَ النَّجْوَى، تَبَارَكَ وَتَعَالَى

He is far from being visible [to the eye], yet so near that He hears every whisper. He is the most Blessed and High.

He is far from being limited in anyway. Yet, He is so close to His limited creatures. His nearness to us is that of complete awareness, knowledge, and power. As He says in His Holy Book:

وَإِذَا سَأَلَكَ عِبَادِي عَنِّي فَإِنِّي قَرِيبٌ ۖ أُجِيبُ دَعْوَةَ الدَّاعِ إِذَا دَعَانِ ۖ
فَلْيَسْتَجِيبُوا لِي وَلْيُؤْمِنُوا بِي لَعَلَّهُمْ يَرْشُدُونَ

When My servants ask you about Me, [tell them that] I am indeed nearmost. I answer the supplicant's call when he calls Me. So, let them respond to Me, and let them have faith in Me, so that they may fare rightly.[17]

At the same time, He cannot be limited by our sight. He says,

لَّا تُدْرِكُهُ الْأَبْصَارُ وَهُوَ يُدْرِكُ الْأَبْصَارَ ۖ وَهُوَ اللَّطِيفُ الْخَبِيرُ

The sights do not apprehend Him, yet He apprehends the sights, and He is the All-attentive, the All-aware.[18]

Have you seen your Lord?

Imam Ali was once asked, "Have you seen your Lord?" He responded,

وكيف اعبد ربا لم أره؟ لم تره الأبصار بمشاهدة العيان ولكن رأته القلوب بحقائق
الإيمان

How would I worship a Lord who I have not seen? He was never witnessed with the vision of the eyes, but He was seen by the hearts through the truths of faith.

Our physical sight might not be able to apprehend Him. Still, our hearts can seek to know of His majesty. This sight of the heart is described in the Holy Quran,

مَا كَذَبَ الْفُؤَادُ مَا رَأَىٰ

The heart did not deny what it saw.[19]

Imam Ali saw his Lord with the sight of his heart. He would say,

---

[17] *The Holy Quran, 2:186.*

[18] *The Holy Quran, 6:103.*

[19] *The Holy Quran, 53:11.*

ما رأيت شيئا إلا ورأيت الله قبله وبعده وفوقه وتحته وفيه

I have not seen a thing except that I saw God before, after,
above, under, and in it. [20]

Awareness of God Almighty filled Imam Ali's every limb. It enlight-
ened his heart with love. This divine love manifested itself in his every
action.

When it came to his austerity, ibn Abbas says that he saw him once
fixing his shoes. The Imam asked ibn Abbas about the value of his torn
shoe. Ibn Abbas thought nothing of it and said, "It is worthless." The
Imam replied,

والله لَهِيَ أَحَبُّ إِليَّ من إمرتكم، إلاَّ أَن أُقيم حقًّا، أوْ أدفع باطلاً

By God, it should have been dearer to me than ruling over
you but for the fact that I may establish right and ward off
wrong. [21]

What benefit is authority if it is not used to for the benefit of others?
He would fix his shoe, patch his shirt, and say,

والله لَقَد رَقَّمتُ مِدْرَعَتي هذِهِ حَتَّى اسْتَحْيَيْتُ مِنْ رَاقِعِهَا

By Allah, I have been putting patches in my shirts so much
that now I feel shy of the patcher. [22]

In terms of his courage, the love of God had exceeded his attachment
to the world. When God informed His Messenger of a looming assas-
sination attempt, the Holy Prophet would go to his cousin Ali and say,

أوَ تبيتُ على فراشي يا علي؟ قال: أوَ تسلم يا رسول الله؟ قال: الحمد
لله الذي جعل نفسي فداء لنفس رسول الله (ص)

[The Messenger of God] said, 'Will you sleep in my place,
O' Ali?' [Ali] said, 'Will you be safe, O' Messenger of God?'
He replied, 'Yes.' [Ali] said, 'Praise be to God who made
my soul a sacrifice for the soul of the Messenger of God!'

---

[20] Al-Mazandarani, *Sharh Usool al-Kafi,* 3:83.

[21] Al-Radi, *Nahj al-Balagha,* Sermon 33.

[22] Al-Radi, *Nahj al-Balagha,* Sermon 160.

At that moment, God said to His angels Gabriel and Michael,

انظرا إلى حبيبي علي بن أبي طالب، قد آثر رسول الله على نفسه، وبات في فراشه، انزلا واحفظاه

Look unto My beloved Ali ibn Abi Talib! He preferred the Messenger of God over himself and slept on [the Messenger's] bed! Go down and protect him![23]

To memorialize that stance, God said in the Holy Quran,

وَمِنَ النَّاسِ مَن يَشْرِي نَفْسَهُ ابْتِغَاءَ مَرْضَاتِ اللَّهِ

And among the people is he who sells his soul seeking the pleasure of Allah.[24]

Imam Ali would march into battle without hesitation, for the sake of putting an end to sedition. Lady Fatima would describe him in her famous sermon,

فإِذا فَغَرَتْ فَاغِرَةٌ مِنَ الْمُشْرِكِينَ قَذَف أخاهُ في لَهَواتِها، فَلا يَنْكَفِعُ حَتَّى يَطَأَ صِماخَها بِأَخْمَصِهِ، ويُخْمِدَ لَهَبَهَا بِسَيْفِهِ

Whenever a gate [of sedition] was opened by the polytheists, [the Messenger of God] would strike its discords with his brother [Ali], who would not stop until he trod its head with the sole of his feet, and extinguished its flames with his sword.[25]

May God allow us to continue on the path of our master Ali and his blessed progeny.

---

[23] Al-Majlisi, *Bihar al-Anwar*, 19:95.

[24] *The Holy Quran*, 2:207.

[25] Al-Mu'tazili, *Sharh Nahj al-Balagha*, 16:249.

Might & Grandeur

الحَمْدُ للهِ الَّذِي لَيْسَ لَهُ مُنازِعٌ يُعادِلُهُ، وَلا شَبِيهٌ يُشاكِلُهُ، وَلا ظَهِيرٌ
يُعاضِدُهُ، قَهَرَ بِعِزَّتِهِ الأَعِزّاءَ، وَتَواضَعَ لِعَظَمَتِهِ العُظَماءُ، فَبَلَغَ بِقُدْرَتِهِ ما
يَشاءُ.

**Praise be to God, who has no equal to challenge Him, nor
is there an image comparable to Him, nor a helper to assist Him. He dominates the powerful by His might, and
disgraced are the great before His grandeur; so He,
through His omnipotence, fulfills that which He wills.**

What is the difference between this segment of the supplication and
previous ones? In a previous segment, the Imam said,

الحَمْدُ للهِ الَّذِي لا مُضادَّ لَهُ في مُلْكِهِ وَلا مُنازِعَ لَهُ في أَمْرِهِ، الحَمْدُ للهِ الَّذِي لا
شَرِيكَ لَهُ في خَلْقِهِ وَلا شَبِيهَ لَهُ في عَظَمَتِهِ

*All praise be to God, who has no opposition to His
sovereignty, nor any challenge to His commands, nor a
partner in His creation, nor is there anything similar to
Him in His greatness.*

What is the difference between God having no challenger and no opposition?

In the previous segment, we spoke of God's sovereignty and that no
one can ever oppose Him. Anyone who wished to do so remained fully
within the realm of His omnipotence. Therefore, there can never be
any real opposition to Him.

In the segment in question, we are denying any equal who could challenge God. There are numerous verses which address this issue. For
example, the Holy Quran says,

لَوْ كَانَ فِيهِمَا آلِهَةٌ إِلَّا اللَّهُ لَفَسَدَتَا

Had there been any gods in them other than Allah, they would surely have fallen apart.[1]

The verse states that if there were multiple gods – each with its own power, knowledge, and wisdom – then there would be distinct actions for each. Each deity would seek to build its own system, destroying the harmony of the world. Therefore, a multitude of deities would naturally lead to the corruption and destruction of the world.

What if there were a multitude of deities who have agreed to cooperate? Could they not create a harmonious world?

Let us assume that a pantheon of deities agrees that each of them will control a segment of the world. One will control the sun, another the seas, another fertility, and so forth – like the pantheons of ancient polytheistic religions. Here, we must ask the following question; is each of these deities able to influence the realm of the others? Or is each one restricted to its own realm?

If each deity can influence and control things that are presumably under the influence of the others, then we will reach the same conclusion that the Quranic verse above spoke to. Each of these deities will act and create in a way that suits its own purposes. This divergence will disrupt the harmony of the world and everything will fall apart. This concept can easily be seen in the myths of ancient polytheistic religions – especially in reference to trickster deities who seek to subvert the work of the others.

What if each of these deities was restricted to its own realm? What if each deity can independently influence a certain segment of the world – a segment that cannot be influenced by any other?

This would again result in disharmony in the world. If the deities of the sun, rain, wind, and fertility acted separately, how could they create a proper system for the universe where agriculture can prosper? In fact,

---

[1] *The Holy Quran*, 21:22.

we recognize that the world runs not on a multitude of systems, but on one.

We cannot imagine a world where a multitude of deities can properly exist.

None Like Him

In this segment the Imam says, "nor is there an image comparable to Him." In the previous segment, he said, "is there anything similar to Him in His greatness." What is the difference between the two phrases?

The latter quote denies the existence of anything that can match God's greatness. The former is much broader, denying the existence of anything that can match Him in any way. As He says in His Holy Book,

لَيْسَ كَمِثْلِهِ شَيْءٌ

Nothing is like Him. [2]

Nothing is like Him. There was never anything like Him, nor can there ever be anything like Him. He is the omnipotent, who has no fault in His power. He is the omniscient, that nothing is hidden from. He is the all-living, who will never cease. Nothing is like Him, because everything beside Him is in need of Him. Everything beside Him is deficient in some way, while He is the all-perfect.

Not only does this mean that there is nothing like Him. It also means that He does not need any aid or helper. We are the powerless while He is the omnipotent. We cannot claim to be of any help or use to Him in any sense.

Divine Dominance

قَهَرَ بِعِزَّتِهِ الْأَعِزَّاءَ، وَتَوَاضَعَ لِعَظَمَتِهِ الْعُظَمَاءُ، فَبَلَغَ بِقُدْرَتِهِ مَا يَشَاءُ.

He dominates the powerful by His might, and disgraced are the great before His grandeur; so He, through His omnipotence, fulfills that which He wills.

---

[2] *The Holy Quran*, 42:11.

Divine dominance is different from the dominance of one creature over another. In our physical world, domination means the forceful infliction of some effect on an object. For example, fire dominates objects by burning them.

God's dominance over His creatures is not tied to the worldly system of cause and effect. God Almighty created each creation with a finite and limited existence. His dominance over all creation existed since the first instance of His emanation of existence upon them. God's dominance is an attribute of His essence and is not limited to the world of cause and effect.

This segment of the supplication highlights two important aspects of God's dominance – its absoluteness and its universality.

God Almighty's dominance is absolute and has no conditions. Our power and ability are always limited in some sense. For example, our ability to eat is conditioned on having a properly working digestive system. If our jaws or our intestines were not working properly, we would not be able to eat properly. Our food may even become a threat to us if our diets are imbalanced.

God's dominance has no condition or limit. If it was conditioned on anything, it would dissipate if the condition is not met. This contradicts our understanding of God as the necessary existent, whose omnipotence is His essence.

God Almighty's dominance is also universal. Our scholars say that divine omnipotence does not attach to impossibilities. What does that mean?

A man once came to Imam Ali and asked, "Can your Lord put the entire world inside of an egg without making the world any smaller or the egg any bigger?" The Imam replied,

إن الله تبارك وتعالى لا ينسب إلى العجز، والذي سألتني لا يكون

God Almighty cannot be described as unable. As for what you asked, it cannot happen.[3]

The Imam's response is that God is omnipotent and there is no limit to His power. However, things that are impossible in themselves are not able to receive his power and emanation. A logical impossibility simply cannot occur, and that does not impair His omnipotence in the least. The questioner is asking whether there can be an egg that is both smaller and bigger than the universe. That is a logical contradiction and cannot occur.

Of course, God can create the most wondrous beings. The same question was asked of Imam al-Rida. He responded,

نعم وفي أصغر من البيضة، وقد جعلها في عينك وهي أقل من البيضة، لأنك إذا فتحتها عاينت السماء والأرض وما بينها، ولو شاء لأعماك عنها

Yes, and [He is able to do so] in what is even smaller than an egg. He has placed [the universe] in your eyes, which are smaller than an egg. When you open them, you see the heavens, the Earth, and what is in between them. Had He willed, He would have blinded your sight from doing so.[4]

Beseeching the Immaculate

Does our beseeching the Holy Prophet and his Immaculate Family contradict our belief in divine omnipotence?

Definitely not. We see examples of this in the life of our Holy Prophet, who would beseech the prophets before him. When the mother of Imam Ali, Fatima bint Asad, passed away, he prayed for her and said:

---

[3] Al-Majlisi, *Bihar al-Anwar*, 4:143.
[4] *Ibid.*

الله الذي يحيي ويميت وهو الحي الذي لا يموت، اغفر لأمي فاطمة بنت أسد
ووسع عليها مدخلها بحق نبيك والأنبياء من قبلي فإنك أرحم الراحمين

God is He who dispenses life and death, while He is the all-living who will never die! Forgive my mother, Fatima bint Asad, and expand for her this new dwelling by the right of Your prophet and the prophets before me. Surely, you are the most merciful![5]

Evidence of the permissibility of beseeching God's prophets and righteous servants exists in the Holy Quran. God says in His Holy Book,

يَا أَيُّهَا الَّذِينَ آمَنُوا اتَّقُوا اللَّهَ وَابْتَغُوا إِلَيْهِ الْوَسِيلَةَ

O you who have faith! Be wary of Allah, and seek the means of recourse to Him.[6]

The means of recourse to God are varied. Our prayer in the mosque is a means of recourse to Him, as it is more valuable than prayer at home. Our prayers and supplications on the Nights of Power are a means of recourse to Him, because they hold greater rewards than the same acts preformed on any other night.

Just as a place or a time might be a means to God, so too is the remembrance of God's appointed servants. When we call "O' Ali," we do not invoke him independently of God. We invoke him as a means to God – just as God asked us to seek the means to Him. Imam Ali does not aid us independently, but by the power and ability granted to him by God.

We ask God to allow us to seek the means of recourse to Him, by the right of the Holy Prophet and his Immaculate Progeny.

---

[5] *Al-Tabarani, al-Mu'jam al-Kabeer*, 24:352.

[6] *The Holy Quran*, 5:35.

Divine Compassion

الحَمْدُ للهِ الَّذِي يُجِيبُني حِينَ أُنادِيهِ، وَيَسْتُرُ عَلَيَّ كُلَّ عَوْرَةٍ وأَنا أَعْصِيهِ، وَيُعَظِّمُ النِّعْمَةَ عَلَيَّ فَلا أُجازِيهِ، فَكَمْ مِنْ مَوْهِبَةٍ هَنِيئَةٍ قَدْ أَعْطانِي، وَعَظِيمَةٍ مَخُوفَةٍ قَدْ كَفانِي، وَبَهْجَةٍ مُونِقَةٍ قَدْ أَرانِي، فَأُثْنِي عَلَيْهِ حامِداً وَأَذْكُرُهُ مُسَبِّحاً.

Praise be to God, who answers to me whenever I call Him, covers up my all my shortcomings while I disobey Him, and increases His blessings on me when I cannot repay Him. O' how many obvious favors has He granted me? From how many terrible dangers has He protected me? How many blossoming joys has He shown me? I sing His praises and recite His glorifications!

When the Immaculate Imam mentions our relationship with God time and again, he is attempting to show us how our Lord deals with us with mercy and love. What is the difference between merciful dealings and loving dealings?

Merciful Dealings

Mercy follows from lordship, while chastisement follows from creation. In other words, God Almighty showers His creations with mercy, without any action on the part of the creation. He simply grants mercy, out of His position as Lord of all things. His chastisement, on the other hand, is not doled out, except to those who incurred it. He says:

عَذابِي أُصِيبُ بِهِ مَنْ أَشاءُ ۖ وَرَحْمَتِي وَسِعَتْ كُلَّ شَيْءٍ ۚ فَسَأَكْتُبُها لِلَّذِينَ يَتَّقُونَ

I visit My punishment on whomever I wish, but My mercy embraces all things. Soon I shall appoint it for those who are Godwary.[1]

---

[1] *The Holy Quran, 7:156.*

That is why the Imam emphasizes that mercy does not need to be initiated by the individual. It encompasses each one of us, not for our deeds, but by God's grace. The Imam says:

فَكُمْ مِنْ مَوْهِبَةٍ هَنِيئَةٍ قَدْ أَعْطَانِي، وَعَظِيمَةٍ مَخُوفَةٍ قَدْ كَفَانِي، وَبَهْجَةٍ مونِقَةٍ قَدْ أَرَانِي

O' how many obvious favors has He granted me? From how many terrible dangers has He protected me? How many blossoming joys has He shown me?

The Imam enumerates God's bounties. He shows that some are obvious material favors, like health and wealth. Others are psychological favors, like safety and contentment.

God's mercy can also be divided into granted and earned. His granted mercy encompasses all creation, without an exception. His earned mercy is earned by the servant in some way. He referred to His earned mercy in the verse above – "My mercy embraces all things. Soon I shall appoint it for those who are Godwary."[2] He also says:

وَمَن يَتَّقِ اللَّهَ يَجْعَل لَّهُ مَخْرَجًا

Whoever is wary of Allah, He shall make for him a way out [of the adversities of the world and the Hereafter].[3]

وَالَّذِينَ جَاهَدُوا فِينَا لَنَهْدِيَنَّهُمْ سُبُلَنَا

As for those who strive in Us, We shall surely guide them in Our ways.[4]

كَتَبَ رَبُّكُمْ عَلَى نَفْسِهِ الرَّحْمَةَ ۖ أَنَّهُ مَنْ عَمِلَ مِنكُمْ سُوءًا بِجَهَالَةٍ ثُمَّ تَابَ مِن بَعْدِهِ وَأَصْلَحَ فَأَنَّهُ غَفُورٌ رَّحِيمٌ

Your Lord has made mercy incumbent upon Himself: whoever of you commits an evil [deed] out of ignorance and then repents after that and reforms, then He is indeed all-forgiving, all-merciful.[5]

---

[2] *The Holy Quran, 7:156.*
[3] *The Holy Quran, 65:2.*
[4] *The Holy Quran, 29:69.*
[5] *The Holy Quran, 6:54.*

If we study the Quranic verses that address God's mercy and chastisement, we will find that they address the two concepts in different manners. God's statements about His mercy are absolute. But when it comes to His chastisement, His words become somewhat ambiguous. For example, He says:

وَإِذْ تَأَذَّنَ رَبُّكُمْ لَئِن شَكَرْتُمْ لَأَزِيدَنَّكُمْ ۖ وَلَئِن كَفَرْتُمْ إِنَّ عَذَابِي لَشَدِيدٌ

And when your Lord proclaimed, 'If you are grateful, I will surely enhance you [in blessing], but if you are ungrateful, My punishment is indeed severe.'[6]

God does say, "If you are grateful I will [bless you]." Yet, He does not say, "If you are ungrateful, I will punish you." He promises His blessings. But when it comes to punishment, He describes it, but does not promise it.

There is an inherent link between gratefulness and mercy. There is no such inherent link between ungratefulness and chastisement. The Imam highlights this fact in the supplication. He states,

الْحَمْدُ لِلَّهِ الَّذِي يُجِيبُنِي حِينَ أُنَادِيهِ، وَيَسْتُرُ عَلَيَّ كُلَّ عَوْرَةٍ وَأَنَا أَعْصِيهِ، وَيُعَظِّمُ النِّعْمَةَ عَلَيَّ فَلَا أُجَازِيهِ

Praise be to God, who answers to me whenever I call Him, covers up my all my shortcomings while I disobey Him, and increases His blessings on me when I cannot repay Him.

No matter how ungrateful I am, He continues to cover up my shortcomings. He increases His sustenance and treats me with the greatest forbearance and mercy.

Loving Dealings

God Almighty loves His servants, even though they persist in disobedience. He is like a parent who loves His children unconditionally.

Love is an existential force of gravity that draws everything towards perfection. An individual loves everything that brings them closer to

---

[6] *The Holy Quran*, 14:7.

beauty and perfection. Why is it that we love food? Because it allows us to energize our bodies, and also for the aesthetic value of its taste. We love the opposite gender because they complete us physically and emotionally. We love wealth because it perfects our power to get what we want.

Therefore, we love for the purpose of perfecting ourselves. Our desires drive us towards enjoying food, intimacy, and wealth, because these things complete something within us.

Our love fluctuates with the degree of our needs. We need information to better our decision-making. That is why we humans love to learn.

So, what about our love for God? He is the source of all perfection and the fulfiller of every need. He is thus the greatest object of love we can imagine.

If our love for food, intimacy, and wealth are based on our desire for perfection, God Almighty is the all-perfect and the source of every perfection, so He is more deserving of our love than anything else.

If our love is based on our need, He is the creator and sustainer. There is no need that He cannot fulfill. If it were not for His blessings, we would not be able to fulfill any need.

Therefore, God is the most deserving of our love. He says,

وَالَّذِينَ آمَنُوا أَشَدُّ حُبًّا لِلَّهِ

The faithful have a more ardent love for Allah.[7]

What about God's divine love? Where does it stem from and what is its object?

As we said, love is an existential force of gravity that draws everything towards perfection. God Almighty loves Himself because He is the most perfect. He loves His creations because they are manifestations and signs of His perfection. As He says in the Holy Quran,

---

[7] *The Holy Quran*, 2:165.

سَنُرِيهِمْ آيَاتِنَا فِي الْآفَاقِ وَفِي أَنفُسِهِمْ حَتَّىٰ يَتَبَيَّنَ لَهُمْ أَنَّهُ الْحَقُّ ۗ أَوَلَمْ يَكْفِ بِرَبِّكَ أَنَّهُ عَلَىٰ كُلِّ شَيْءٍ شَهِيدٌ

Soon We shall show them Our signs in the horizons and in their own souls until it becomes clear to them that He is the Real. Is it not sufficient that your Lord is witness to all things?[8]

The more a creature becomes reflective of divine perfection, the more God loves that creature. He says,

قُلْ إِن كُنتُمْ تُحِبُّونَ اللَّهَ فَاتَّبِعُونِي يُحْبِبْكُمُ اللَّهُ

Say, 'If you love Allah, then follow me; Allah will love you.'[9]

His Most Beloved

This is why God's love for the Holy Prophet and his Immaculate Progeny is so great. They are the greatest signs of His perfection and beauty. And because they are God's most beloved creatures, we hold them as our most beloved signs to God. How can we not love them? Especially when the Holy Quran calls us and says,

قُل لَّا أَسْأَلُكُمْ عَلَيْهِ أَجْرًا إِلَّا الْمَوَدَّةَ فِي الْقُرْبَىٰ

Say, 'I do not ask you any reward for it except the love of [my] relatives.'[10]

We cannot stop ourselves from loving the Holy Prophet, who Imam Ali would describe by saying:

---

[8] *The Holy Quran*, 41:53.

[9] *The Holy Quran*, 3:31.

[10] *The Holy Quran*, 42:23.

كان أجود الناس كفا وأجرأ الناس صدرا وأصدق الناس لهجة وأوفاهم ذمة وألينهم
عريكة وأكرمهم عشرة ومن رآه بديهة هابه ومن خالطه فعرفه أحبه لم أر مثله قبله
ولا بعده

*Amongst the people, he held the most generous palm, the
most courageous heart, the most truthful expression, the
most trustworthy custody, the kindest disposition, and the
most honorable company. Whoever saw him was
intuitively awestricken. Whoever lived with and knew him
loved him. I have not seen anyone like him, neither before
nor after him.* [11]

Anas narrates that a nomad came to Medina one day and asked the
Holy Prophet about the Day of Judgment. It was the time of prayer, so
the Holy Prophet led prayer then turned and asked about the questioner. He asked the nomad about what he prepared for that day. The
nomad said, "By God, I have not prepared for it with much work –
neither prayers nor fasting. However, I do love God and His messenger!" The Holy Prophet said,

المرء مع من أحب

*Every individual shall be with whomever he loves [on the
Day of Judgment]!* [12]

God Almighty says,

وَمَن يُطِعِ اللَّهَ وَالرَّسُولَ فَأُولَٰئِكَ مَعَ الَّذِينَ أَنْعَمَ اللَّهُ عَلَيْهِم مِّنَ النَّبِيِّينَ وَالصِّدِّيقِينَ
وَالشُّهَدَاءِ وَالصَّالِحِينَ ۚ وَحَسُنَ أُولَٰئِكَ رَفِيقًا

*Whoever obeys Allah and the Apostle—they are with those
whom Allah has blessed, including the prophets and the
truthful, the martyrs and the righteous, and excellent
companions are they!* [13]

---

[11] Al-Majlisi, *Bihar al-Anwar*, 16:231.

[12] Al-Majlisi, *Bihar al-Anwar*, 17:13.

[13] *The Holy Quran*, 4:69.

That is why God has placed such great emphasis on the love of the His Messenger and the family of His Messenger. The Holy Prophet is narrated to have said:

من مات على حب آل محمد مات شهيدا، ألا ومن مات على حب آل محمد مات تائبا، ألا ومن مات على حب آل محمد مات مغفورا له، ألا ومن مات على حب آل محمد كان مع النبيين والصديقين والشهداء والصالحين، ألا ومن مات على حب آل محمد حفت به الملائكة، ألا ومن مات على بغض آل محمد جاء يوم القيامة مكتوب بين عينيه آيس من رحمة الله

He who dies with love of the family of Muhammad is a Martyr. Surely, he who dies with love of the family of Muhammad dies repentant. Surely, he who dies with love of the family of Muhammad is forgiven. Surely, he who dies with love of the family of Muhammad shall be amongst the prophets, the truthful, the martyrs, and the righteous. Surely, he who dies with love of the family of Muhammad shall be surrounded by angels. Surely, he who dies with hatred for the family of Muhammad shall arrive on the Day of Judgment with a stamp on his forehead that reads, 'Outcast from the Mercy of God.'[14]

We have prepared our love for the Holy Household as our provisions for our journey to the afterlife. There is no better provision than this. Still, we must work to maintain this until the moment we pass on. Yes, we have no better provision, but we can spoil our provisions with persistent sin and disobedience. We beseech God,

اللهم اجعل خير أعمالنا آخرها وخير أعمالنا خواتيمها وخير أيامنا يوم نلقاك

O' God, make the best of our deeds the last of them, the best [part] of our deeds their outcomes, and the best of our days the day in which we meet You.[15]

[14] Al-Majlisi, *Bihar al-Anwar*, 23:233.

[15] Al-Majlisi, *Bihar al-Anwar*, 94:277.

We must seek to protect and increase these provisions by reciting the blessed supplication of salawat – sending peace and blessings upon the Holy Prophet and his family. Imam al-Rida said,

من لم يقدر على ما يكفر به ذنوبه فليكثر من الصلاة على محمد وآل محمد، فإنها تهدم الذنوب هدما

Whoever cannot find anything to atone for his sins, let him persist in praying for blessings upon Muhammad and the family of Muhammad. Surely, it dismantles sin a [firm] dismantlement.[16]

A man once asked the Holy Prophet about the following verse:

إِنَّ اللَّهَ وَمَلَائِكَتَهُ يُصَلُّونَ عَلَى النَّبِيِّ

Indeed, Allah and His angels bless the Prophet.[17]

He asked the Holy Prophet, "How do we bless you?" The Holy Prophet replied:

قل: اللهم صل على محمد وآل محمد كما صليت على إبراهيم إنك حميد مجيد وبارك على محمد وآل محمد كما باركت على إبراهيم إنك حميد مجيد

Say, 'O' God, bless Muhammad and the family of Muhammad just as you blessed Abraham – surely, You are all-laudable, all-glorious. Elevate Muhammad and the family of Muhammad just as you elevated Abraham – surely, You are all-laudable, all-glorious.'[18]

We ask God to send His peace and blessings upon Muhammad and the family of Muhammad, surely, He is all-laudable, all-glorious.

---

[16] Al-'Amili, *Wasa'el al-Shi'a*, 7:194.

[17] *The Holy Quran*, 33:56.

[18] Al-Majlisi, *Bihar al-Anwar*, 27:258.

Divine Veil

الحَمْدُ للهِ الَّذِي لا يُهتَكُ حِجابُهُ، وَلا يُغْلَقُ بابُهُ، وَلا يُرَدُّ سائِلُهُ، وَلا يُخَيِّبُ آمِلَهُ.

Praise be to God. None can pierce His veil. None can shut His [ever-open] doors. None who beseech Him are ever turned down. None who have hope in Him are ever disappointed.

The Holy Quran says,

وَإِذَا قَرَأْتَ الْقُرْآنَ جَعَلْنَا بَيْنَكَ وَبَيْنَ الَّذِينَ لا يُؤْمِنُونَ بِالآخِرَةِ حِجَابًا مَسْتُورًا

When you recite the Quran, We draw a hidden veil between you and those who do not believe in the Hereafter.[1]

This blessed verse tells us that people are of two types. There are those who repented from any sin, for whom the doors of supplication opened. Then, ther are others, who persisted in sinning, so that God placed a veil between Himself and them. In other words, disobedience placed in their hearts a form of repulsion from worship, supplication, and repentance.

Our hearts belong to God Almighty. Nothing should enter them but Him and what He allows. He has the power and right to do with them as He pleases. When a servant persists in disobedience and transgression, God places a veil on his heart so that it does not long for repentance and mercy.

God may also look at His obedient servants and support them in maintaining their hearts with His love. He ensures that their hearts do not welcome anyone but Him and what He allows. He says,

وَاعْلَمُوا أَنَّ اللَّهَ يَحُولُ بَيْنَ الْمَرْءِ وَقَلْبِهِ

Know that Allah intervenes between a man and his heart.[2]

---

[1] *The Holy Quran*, 17:45.

[2] *The Holy Quran*, 8:24.

A person might desire a thing, yet God may intervene to ensure that the desire is not fulfilled. This is evident in some of our noble traditions. Imam Ali is reported as saying,

عَرَفْتُ اللهَ سُبْحَانَهُ بِفَسْخِ الْعَزَائِمِ

I have come to know God, the Glorified, to be the breaker of determinations.[3]

Many times, an individual might make a decision and resolve to undertake some endeavor. They get close to their goal, but do not end up following through at the end. That is a reflection of God's veil, which cannot be pierced.

At the same time, there are people who God blessed with the will to worship and supplicate, perhaps due to the effort they placed in trying to please Him. For such individuals, God's doors are always open.

In this segment of the supplication, God Almighty is highlighting His control over our supplications. He has the ability either to answer or reject our calls. Sometimes, we pray for things that are truly beneficial for us. God answers those supplications. But when what we ask for is in fact detrimental to us, God's mercy dictates that He reject our calls.

This is another understanding of God's impenetrable veil. If He does not want to answer a supplication, no one can force Him to. If He does want to answer a supplication, no one can stop Him. He says,

مَّا يَفْتَحِ اللَّهُ لِلنَّاسِ مِن رَّحْمَةٍ فَلَا مُمْسِكَ لَهَا ۖ وَمَا يُمْسِكْ فَلَا مُرْسِلَ لَهُ مِن بَعْدِهِ ۚ وَهُوَ الْعَزِيزُ الْحَكِيمُ

Whatever mercy Allah unfolds for the people, no one can withhold it; and whatever He withholds, no one can release it except Him, and He is the All-mighty, the All-wise.[4]

God Almighty's lordship is different from what we may see in other beings. A person may have legal lordship and mastery over another, such as parents' guardianship over their children. On the other hand,

---

[3] Al-Radi, *Nahj al-Balagha, Short Saying* 250.

[4] *The Holy Quran*, 35:2.

God Almighty's lordship stems from His creatorship. It is real lordship as opposed to legal lordship. God says,

ذَٰلِكُمُ اللَّهُ رَبُّكُمْ خَالِقُ كُلِّ شَيْءٍ

That is Allah, your Lord, the creator of all things.[5]

We addressed this topic in a previous chapter. What is important to remember here is that God's divine lordship, which stems from His creatorship, cannot be breached or contravened in any way. No matter how much we rebel and we try to be our own masters, we cannot escape His power and authority. No matter what we do, we can never pierce the veils of His lordship.

We ask God Almighty to keep the doors of supplication open for us, so that we may continue to call on Him in times of hardship and ease.

---

[5] *The Holy Quran,* 40:62.

Divine Justice

الحَمْدُ للهِ الَّذِي يُؤْمِنُ الخَائِفِينَ، وَيُنَجِّي الصَّالِحِينَ، وَيَرْفَعُ المُسْتَضْعَفِينَ، وَيَضَعُ المُسْتَكْبِرِينَ، وَيُهْلِكُ مُلُوكًا وَيَسْتَخْلِفُ آخَرِينَ.

Praise be to God, who protects the frightened, helps the righteous, promotes the meek, demeans the arrogant, and destroys kings to replace them with others.

As the reader has seen so far, this supplication contains a multitude of sublime descriptions of God's divine attributes. In this segment of the supplication, we turn to the idea of divine justice – an integral aspect of our creed.

Can God Almighty be described as just or oppressive?

Among humans, we can describe an individual as just or oppressive. We are limited creatures, with each having rights and obligations due to others. If an individual usurps the right of another, we can describe that action as oppressive. This is dictated by both rational principles and social norms.

Thus, if we act within the scope of our own rights, we are acting justly. If we act in transgression of another's rights, we are acting unjustly and oppressively.

Ownership and Sovereignty

Some might say that God cannot be described as unjust, no matter what He decides to do. After all, everything in the universe is under His ownership and sovereignty. It is His right to do as He pleases with everything that He owns. Even if He chooses to place the most devout servants in Hellfire and the most disobedient rebels in Paradise, that would not be injustice. We are all His creations, and He may do with us as He pleases.

This is a false belief that has been debated since the early years of Islam. We will address the flaws in the argument in detail. However, we must first clarify the meaning of ownership and sovereignty.

God Almighty describes Himself as both owner and sovereign of this world. He says:

مَلِكِ يَوْمِ الدِّينِ

Sovereign of the Day of Retribution.[1]

تَبَارَكَ الَّذِي بِيَدِهِ الْمُلْكُ وَهُوَ عَلَىٰ كُلِّ شَيْءٍ قَدِيرٌ

Blessed is He in whose hands is all sovereignty, and He has power over all things.[2]

قُلِ اللَّهُمَّ مَالِكَ الْمُلْكِ

Say, 'O Allah, Master of all sovereignty!'[3]

Legal scholars define ownership as the right to possess, control, exclude, enjoy, and dispose of an object. Owning a piece of land means I can live on it, farm it, exclude others from entering it, sell its crops, or even sell the whole piece of land.

God possesses everything within the grasp of His omnipotence. He controls the life and sustenance of every being. He places rules on what each creature can and cannot do. He demands that His creatures worship Him. He can end any creature's existence at any time.

All of God's creations rely on Him for existence and sustenance. He is the real owner of everything in existence. He is the sovereign that controls and commands as He pleases.

Justice and Oppression

Let us turn back to the question. God Almighty is the true owner and sovereign over all things. He has the right to control and dispose of His creations as He wills. How can we ever describe any of His actions as unjust?

Answering this question requires addressing three premises.

---

[1] *The Holy Quran*, 1:4.

[2] *The Holy Quran*, 67:1.

[3] *The Holy Quran*, 3:26.

First, mankind requires a system for us to balance our personal interests and communal interests. Otherwise, each of us will always pursue self-interest without regard to communal interests, disturbing the existence of society.

This system must be effective. It must provide a deterrence against actions that would disrupt the system. It must provide incentives for everyone to follow its rules. Otherwise, the system would not be of any value.

Second, the system must be set by God Almighty. Why would He not set such a system? It cannot be out of ignorance, as He is the omniscient and all-wise. It cannot be out of inability, as He is omnipotent and all-capable. It cannot be out of miserliness, as He is the most generous.

It also cannot be that God is relying on the human mind to create a system. He knows that our intellects are limited and cannot set a perfect system – one that justly addresses all citizens, of all times and all cultures. Human experience has shown this to be a fact.

There is no reason for God to withhold giving us such a system. Therefore, this system, which is necessary for the wellbeing of mankind, must be set by our Almighty Lord.

Third, God legislates with the incentive of Paradise and deterrent of Hellfire. He says,

$$فَمَن يَعْمَلْ مِثْقَالَ ذَرَّةٍ خَيْرًا يَرَهُ ۞ وَمَن يَعْمَلْ مِثْقَالَ ذَرَّةٍ شَرًّا يَرَهُ$$

So, whoever does an atom's weight of good will see it, and whoever does an atom's weight of evil will see it.[4]

God Almighty established a legal system for mankind, with deterrents and incentives, rewards and punishments. Those rewards and punishments are most evidently seen in the hereafter.

The question is, would God abolish this system and decide to forgo any judgement?

---

[4] *The Holy Quran, 99:8.*

God Almighty promised and foretold of His judgment. He warned of His severe punishment in Hellfire, and His endless rewards in Paradise. To breach His promise would be a contradiction and a form of dishonesty. God Almighty is sublime over such faults. He is the all-powerful, all-knowing, all-wise, all-merciful, and all-benevolent. He would never break a promise.

This is the meaning of God's justice. He will never break His promise. He might forgive a disobedient servant if he were a proper recipient of such forgiveness. However, He would never rob anyone of their promised rewards.

Therefore, His justice lies in that He will abide by the system of rewards and punishments that He set. Injustice would be for Him not to abide by His own system.

Justice is to place everything in its correct place. All of God's actions – whether reward, punishment, or promise – advance the interests of the universe He created. Not creating reward and punishment would have been an act of injustice, as there would be no system of guidance for mankind – something which we direly need and which God can provide. Similarly, not applying the system of reward and punishment would also be an act of injustice, as it would not be placing things in their correct place. If God Almighty were to allow Satan to enter Paradise, while the prophets were sent to Hellfire – that would be an obvious injustice. It would be a breach of God's divine promise. It is impossible for God, the all-perfect, to break any promise or commit any injustice.

Justice is to give everything its due right. Injustice is the opposite. The divine legislative system determines the right of every creature based on the interest of the greater system of creation. It is true that God is the owner and sovereign over all things. However, He can still put in place a system of rights for His creatures and act accordingly. This does not take away any of His power, but is a manifestation of His mercy and justice.

Necessity of Justice

Theologians say that justice is a must for God Almighty and that injustice is an impossibility for Him. Is this true?

It could be said that human reason cannot be so audacious as to judge God's actions. He does as He wills with His creatures. It would be even more ludicrous to claim that any man can set rules as to what God can and cannot do! We cannot claim that we have any sovereignty over Him. We therefore cannot claim to set rules for Him or judge Him in any way.

In answering this misconception, we must first clarify that no one is claiming to set any rules on what God can and cannot do. He may do as He wishes – everyone agrees on that. However, we seek to understand His actions and attributes. When we say that justice is a must and injustice is an impossibility, we are not setting rules, but making observations about reality.

In addition, to say that justice is a must for Him and that injustice is an evil that cannot come from Him is to say that He made all this incumbent upon Himself. We do not claim to judge Him. We are merely observing His actions and promises.

Reason recognizes that God Almighty always acts in according to universal interests and never against them. Reason also recognizes that actions that advance universal interests are just, and that others are unjust. Reason understands that justice is a beauty and an attribute of the all-perfect. Reason therefore concludes that all of His actions are just and none of His actions are unjust.

We are not seeking to oblige God to any rational principles. Instead, we are using reason to understand divine actions and attributes.

We ask God Almighty to bless us with His rewards and protect us from His punishment.

The Philosophy of
Punishment

الحَمْدُ للهِ قاصِمِ الجَبّارِينَ، مُبِيرِ الظّالِمِينَ، مُدْرِكِ الهارِبِينَ، نَكالِ الظّالِمِينَ، صَرِيخِ المُسْتَصْرِخِينَ، مَوْضِعِ حاجاتِ الطّالِبِينَ، مُعْتَمَدِ المُؤْمِنِينَ.

Praise be to God, breaker of tyrants, ender of oppressors, capturer of runaways, punisher of oppressors, aid to those who cry out for help, target of beseechers' requests, and patron of the faithful.

No one can escape God's power. No matter where we attempt to run away, we cannot escape His kingdom. He is the capturer of runaways, bringing them to the court of His justice. He is the punisher of the oppressors and those who disobey His commands.

There are numerous questions about God's punishment.

Mankind's disobedience is limited. No matter how much we might sin, we can only do so for the limited period of our lives. If we disobey and sin for 50 or 70 years, why should we suffer eternal punishment? God Almighty says,

وَمَا هُم بِخَارِجِينَ مِنَ النَّارِ

And they shall not leave the Fire. [1]

How can we understand that a limited being can cause eternal punishment for itself?

We also know that God is the all-merciful and most forbearing. If His mercy is boundless, would that not mean that He will forgive all sin and never punish a soul? How is eternal punishment compatible with His grace and mercy? If His mercy embraces all things, why would it not embrace the oppressors? God Almighty says,

---

[1] *The Holy Quran*, 2:167.

عَذَابِي أُصِيبُ بِهِ مَنْ أَشَاءُ ۚ وَرَحْمَتِي وَسِعَتْ كُلَّ شَيْءٍ

I visit My punishment on whomever I wish, but My mercy embraces all things.[2]

Manifestation of Sin

Philosophers and mystics say that our very misdeeds are manifested as punishment. Philosophers say that what we experience as punishment in the hereafter is in fact no more than a manifestation of our misdeeds in this world. We build our fires and prepare our brimstone by our own hands. As God says,

إِنَّمَا تُجْزَوْنَ مَا كُنتُمْ تَعْمَلُونَ

You are only being requited for what you used to do.[3]

An individual may drink alcohol in this world. That alcohol will manifest itself as boiling oil in the hereafter. A person's choice to drink in this world is their choice to drink in the hereafter. The same idea applies to all other misdeeds.

The same idea also applies to divine rewards. Our prayers and fasts in this world manifest themselves as the palaces and fruits of the hereafter.

Mystics interpret this idea somewhat differently. They say that each of us takes a different path in this world that results in the molding of our souls in a particular fashion. This is what they call 'essential movement.' They say that if an individual spends their life in worship, that worship becomes part of their very essence. God says,

فَمَن شَرَحَ اللَّهُ صَدْرَهُ لِلْإِسْلَامِ فَهُوَ عَلَىٰ نُورٍ مِّن رَّبِّهِ

Is someone whose breast Allah has opened to Islam so that he follows a light from His Lord...?[4]

---

[2] *The Holy Quran,* 7:156.

[3] *The Holy Quran,* 52:16.

[4] *The Holy Quran,* 39:22.

A person who spends their life in worship gains a new light from their Lord every day. That light mixes with their essence and may even become their essence. After a lifetime of worship, they become a beacon of light.

That is why when a number of companions asked Imam al-Hadi who they should take the teachings of their faith from, the Imam said:

اصمدا في دينكما على كل مسنٍّ في حبنا وكل كثير القدم في أمرنا، فإنهم كافوكما إن شاء الله

Rely in your faith on every individual who grew old in our love and has a long history in our matter [of Imamah]. They shall suffice you, God willing.[5]

When an individual spends their life drinking from the pools of their love, it will mix with their blood and become part of their. The light of their love becomes part and parcel of their being.

Conversely, if a person spends their life in disobedience, those sins also become part of their very essence. This is what God refers to when He says:

قُلْ هَلْ أُنَبِّئُكُم بِشَرٍّ مِّن ذَٰلِكَ مَثُوبَةً عِندَ اللَّهِ ۚ مَن لَّعَنَهُ اللَّهُ وَغَضِبَ عَلَيْهِ وَجَعَلَ مِنْهُمُ الْقِرَدَةَ وَالْخَنَازِيرَ وَعَبَدَ الطَّاغُوتَ

Say, 'Shall I inform you concerning something worse than that as a requital from Allah? Those whom Allah has cursed and with whom He is wrathful, and turned some of whom into apes and swine, and worshippers of fake deities!'[6]

These individuals did not turn into physical apes and swine, because of the impossibility of change of one species to another, but took on the characteristics and essence of these beasts. When we disregard God's commands and act like animals – with no worries but our carnal desires – that beastliness becomes part of our character and essence.

---

[5] Al-'Amili, Wasa'el al-Shi'a, 27:151.
[6] The Holy Quran, 5:60.

Let us turn back to the question: how does the disobedience of a limited number of years justify eternal punishment?

The answer is that disobedience is not the direct cause of punishment. Rather, it is the deformed essence of the individual that becomes deserving of eternal punishment. Disobedience disfigures the sinner's soul, such that it becomes unfit for anything but Hellfire. Thus, we can say that disobedience is an indirect cause of punishment.

That is why Imam al-Sadiq is reported to have said:

إنما خلد أهل النار في النار لان نياتهم كانت في الدنيا لو خلدوا فيها أن يعصوا الله أبدا، وإنما خلد أهل الجنة في الجنة لان نياتهم كانت في الدنيا لو بقوا أن يطيعوا الله أبدا ما بقوا، فالنيات تخلد هؤلاء وهؤلاء، ثم تلا قوله تعالى:

﴿وقل كل يعمل على شاكلته﴾

قال: على نيته.

The people of Hellfire were made to dwell therein for eternity because it was their intention – had they been allowed to live in this world for eternity – to disobey God eternally. The people of Paradise were made to dwell therein for eternity because it was their intention – had they been allowed to live in this world for eternity – to obey God eternally. It was intention that eternalized both the former and latter. 'Say,
"Everyone acts according to his character."
He said: His intention.' [7]

The noble tradition does not mean that people are punished for their intentions. Rather, a person's intention to disobey for all eternity is evidence that their essence has devolved into a beastly form. The converse is true with the obedient believers.

---

[7] Al-Majlisi, *Bihar al-Anwar*, 8:347.

Mercy and Punishment

Mercy is an emanation upon a proper recipient. He showers His mercy on all creation. At the same time, He favors His servants with the beneficence of His guidance and rewards.

The question remains, how is God's infinite mercy compatible with the punishment? How is it compatible with the idea of eternal punishment specifically?

First, as we have mentioned, mercy can be thought about as both general and special. General mercy is dispensed to all creation. Special mercy, which includes guidance and reward, is dispensed only to those who are able to receive it. When it comes to the disobedient, they do not receive God's special mercy – not because God does not dispense it, but because the disobedient have cast themselves outside of its purview. Persistence in disobedience deforms the soul to the point that it can no longer receive God's favors.

Second, general mercy includes emanating existence to anything that is able to receive it. The disobedient are able to receive existence. God created them and allowed them to disobey, a mercy in and of itself.

Punishment is either temporary or eternal. Temporary punishment is a form of purification for the soul. It is a mercy for the soul, because it allows it to take on a more beautiful form.

Eternal punishment can also be seen as a mercy upon others. God's wisdom dictated that He create this world, and allow mankind to walk on it with the freedom to choose righteousness or deviance. Each individual has the ability to either choose righteousness and rise to the greatest levels of creation, or choose deviance and fall to a worse level than the beasts. God says:

وَلَقَدْ ذَرَأْنَا لِجَهَنَّمَ كَثِيرًا مِّنَ الْجِنِّ وَالْإِنسِ ۖ لَهُمْ قُلُوبٌ لَّا يَفْقَهُونَ بِهَا وَلَهُمْ أَعْيُنٌ لَّا يُبْصِرُونَ بِهَا وَلَهُمْ آذَانٌ لَّا يَسْمَعُونَ بِهَا ۚ أُولَٰئِكَ كَالْأَنْعَامِ بَلْ هُمْ أَضَلُّ ۚ أُولَٰئِكَ هُمُ الْغَافِلُونَ

Certainly, We have winnowed out for Hell many of the jinn and humans: they have hearts with which they do not understand, they have eyes with which they do not see, they have ears with which they do not hear. They are like cattle; indeed, they are more astray. It is they who are the heedless.[8]

The creation of such a system is a blessing to everyone within it. The system would not be complete without some form of final judgement. Punishment of the disobedient is a mercy, because it is part of a grand merciful system.

Third, eternal punishment for the denizens of Hellfire is a mercy for the dwellers of Paradise.

God Almighty promised us rivers of wine and honey, grand castles, eternal partners, and so much more. Yet, all this is not the crux of divine reward. Those are only physical manifestations of the true treasure – closeness and knowledge of God Almighty. As the believers continue to dwell in Paradise, they increase in proximity and knowledge of their Lord. Thus, the true mercy is knowledge of God and His attributes.

As we live in Paradise – God willing – we will continue to live in the bliss of His rewards. We will experience His mercy, generosity, and magnanimity. This allows us to grow closer to Him by better understanding His attributes.

But God also has other attributes that He manifests. Greater knowledge of those attributes is also a mercy and reward for the believers. So how can the dwellers of Paradise better understand the divine attributes of God, the Dominant, the Debaser, the Reckoner, and the Avenger?

---

[8] *The Holy Quran*, 7:179.

God manifests those attributes by inflicting His wrath on the most wretched transgressors against His commands. The dwellers of Paradise see this manifestation of God's attributes and grow closer to Him. Therefore, God's infliction of punishment on the disobedient is a mercy for the obedient.

We ask God Almighty to count us amongst His obedient servants and safeguard us against the debasement of His punishment.

Divine Attributes

الحَمْدُ للهِ الَّذِي مِنْ خَشْيَتِهِ تَرْعَدُ السَّماءُ وَسُكَّانُها، وَتَرْجُفُ الأَرْضُ وَعُمَّارُها، وَتَمُوجُ البِحارُ وَمَنْ يَسْبَحُ فِي غَمَراتِها. الحَمْدُ للهِ الَّذِي هَدانا لِهذا، وَما كُنّا لِنَهْتَدِيَ لَوْلا أَنْ هَدانا اللهُ. الحَمْدُ للهِ الَّذِي يَخْلُقُ وَلَمْ يُخْلَقْ، وَيَرْزُقُ وَلا يُرْزَقُ، وَيُطْعِمُ وَلا يُطْعَمُ، وَيُمِيتُ الأَحْياءَ وَيُحْيِي المَوْتى وَهُوَ حَيٌّ لا يَمُوتُ، بِيَدِهِ الخَيْرُ وَهُوَ عَلى كُلِّ شَيْءٍ قَدِيرٌ.

Praise be to God. Out of fear of Him, the heavens and their denizens quiver, the Earth and its inhabitants tremble, the oceans and all that swims in their depths shudder. Praise be to God, who has guided us to this. Certainly, we could not have been guided if God had not guided us. Praise be to God, who creates but is not created, gives sustenance but needs no provisions, gives food but takes no nourishment, and makes the living die and brings the dead to life while He is the ever-living – there is no death for Him. In His hands is all beneficence and He is able to do all things.

In previous chapters, we have spoken of God's oneness, mercy, sovereignty, and justice. Let us take this opportunity to address some other divine attributes.

Oneness in Worship

Our scholars say that divine oneness can be understood in four distinct ways. He is one in essence. He is one in attributes, with nothing like Him. He is one in His actions. He is also one in worship – meaning that there is no one deserving of worship but Him.

The Imam addressed each of these understandings in some part of the supplication.

Regarding oneness of essence he said, "Praise be to God, who has no... image comparable to Him."

Regarding oneness of attributes he said, "nor is there anything similar to Him in His greatness."

He referred to oneness in action when he said, "All praise be to God, who has no opposition to His sovereignty, nor any challenge to His commands."

In this segment, the Imam is addressing oneness in worship. He said,

الْحَمْدُ للهِ الَّذِي مِنْ خَشْيَتِهِ تَرْعَدُ السَّمَاءُ وَسُكَّانُهَا، وَتَرْجُفُ الأَرْضُ وَعُمَّارُهَا،
وَتَمُوجُ الْبِحَارُ وَمَنْ يَسْبَحُ فِي غَمَرَاتِهَا.

Praise be to God. Out of fear of Him, the heavens and their
denizens quiver, the Earth and its inhabitants tremble, the
oceans and all that swims in their depths shudder.

Worship is of two kinds – involuntary and voluntary. Human beings are given the choice to worship Him voluntarily through prayers, fasts, and the like. However, everything in the universe worships Him in some way. Because these things do not have the quality of free will, we call their worship involuntary. God says,

وَإِن مِّن شَيْءٍ إِلَّا يُسَبِّحُ بِحَمْدِهِ وَلَٰكِن لَّا تَفْقَهُونَ تَسْبِيحَهُمْ

There is not a thing but celebrates His praise, but you do
not understand their glorification.[1]

Philosophers say that there is a correlation between existence and goodness. Where there is existence, there is goodness. Where there is goodness, there is existence. From this, philosophers conclude that wherever there is existence, there is some form of awareness. Thus, there is nothing in creation that is not aware at some level.

With this awareness, all creatures praise God and thank Him. Each creation is able to recognize divine beauty by recognizing its own existence. That is a form of glorification of the Almighty. God says:

---

[1] *The Holy Quran*, 17:44.

لَوْ أَنزَلْنَا هَٰذَا الْقُرْآنَ عَلَىٰ جَبَلٍ لَّرَأَيْتَهُ خَاشِعًا مُّتَصَدِّعًا مِّنْ خَشْيَةِ اللَّهِ ۚ وَتِلْكَ
الْأَمْثَالُ نَضْرِبُهَا لِلنَّاسِ لَعَلَّهُمْ يَتَفَكَّرُونَ

*Had We sent down this Quran upon a mountain, you
would have seen it humbled [and] go to pieces with the fear
of Allah. We draw such comparisons for mankind, so that
they may reflect.*[2]

These verses refer to creation's involuntary worship of its Creator. The
segment of the supplication is referring to that concept. The fear and
awe of all creation – causing the heavens to tremble and the oceans to
shudder – is their involuntary worship.

God Almighty is also the only being deserving of being worshipped
voluntarily. He says,

مَا خَلَقْتُ الْجِنَّ وَالْإِنسَ إِلَّا لِيَعْبُدُونِ

*I did not create the jinn and the humans except that they
may worship Me.*[3]

Guidance and Self-Sufficiency

The Imam continues and says:

الْحَمْدُ لِلَّهِ الَّذِي هَدَانَا لِهَٰذَا، وَمَا كُنَّا لِنَهْتَدِيَ لَوْلَا أَنْ هَدَانَا اللَّهُ

*Praise be to God, who has guided us to this. Certainly, we
could not have been guided if God had not guided us.*

God Almighty says,

قَالَ رَبُّنَا الَّذِي أَعْطَىٰ كُلَّ شَيْءٍ خَلْقَهُ ثُمَّ هَدَىٰ

*He said, 'Our Lord is He who gave everything its creation
and then guided it.'*[4]

God created everything then blessed it with His guidance. He created
everything then guided it to its purpose – that of attaining perfection.

---

[2] *The Holy Quran*, 59:21.

[3] *The Holy Quran*, 51:56.

[4] *The Holy Quran*, 20:50.

The perfection of a thing comes with its knowledge of its Lord. Every creature was made to know its Lord, and was guided to that knowledge.

God Almighty guided us to know that everything in this world is striving toward that perfection. Everything in this world is striving to know its Lord.

How can mankind not take the path of guidance that everything in existence strives on? How can we reject knowing our Lord?

As our Imam taught us to supplicate,

اللهم عرفني نفسك فإنك إن لم تعرفني نفسك لم أعرف نبيك

O' God, allow me to know You, for if You do not allow me to know You, I shall not know Your prophet. [5]

The Imam then goes on to describe God's self-sufficiency. He said:

الحَمْدُ لله الَّذِي يَخْلُقُ وَلَمْ يُخْلَقْ، وَيَرْزُقُ وَلا يُرْزَقُ، وَيُطْعِمُ وَلا يُطْعَمُ، وَيُمِيتُ الأَحْياءَ وَيُحْيِي المَوْتَى وَهُوَ حَيٌّ لا يَمُوتُ، بِيَدِهِ الخَيْرُ وَهُوَ عَلَى كُلِّ شَيْءٍ قَدِيرٌ.

Praise be to God, who creates but is not created, gives sustenance but needs no provisions, gives food but takes no nourishment, and makes the living die and brings the dead to life while He is the ever-living – there is no death for Him. In His hands is all beneficence and He is able to do all things.

We have mentioned God's self-sufficiency in previous chapters. We said that a limitless being – omnipotent, omniscient, and all-living – has no dependency on any other being. Therefore, He creates but was not created. He sustains but needs no sustenance. He feeds but needs no nourishment. Surely, He is capable of all things!

---

[5] *Al-Kulayni, al-Kafi, 1:337.*

Appointed
Guardians

اللَّهُمَّ صَلِّ عَلَى مُحَمَّدٍ عَبْدِكَ وَرَسُولِكَ، وَأَمِينِكَ وَصَفِيِّكَ، وَحَبِيبِكَ وَخِيرَتِكَ مِنْ خَلْقِكَ، وَحَافِظِ سِرِّكَ وَمُبَلِّغِ رِسَالاتِكَ، أَفْضَلَ وَأَحْسَنَ وَأَجْمَلَ وَأَكْمَلَ وَأَزْكَى وَأَنْمَى وَأَطْيَبَ وَأَطْهَرَ وَأَسْنَى وَأَكْثَرَ مَا صَلَّيْتَ وَبَارَكْتَ وَتَرَحَّمْتَ وَتَحَنَّنْتَ وَسَلَّمْتَ عَلَى أَحَدٍ مِنْ عِبَادِكَ وَأَنْبِيَائِكَ وَرُسُلِكَ وَصَفْوَتِكَ وَأَهْلِ الْكَرَامَةِ عَلَيْكَ مِنْ خَلْقِكَ.

O' God, send blessings on Muhammad – Your servant, messenger, trustee, friend, beloved, chosen amongst Your creatures, keeper of Your secrets, and deliverer of Your messages – the most superior, exquisite, beautiful, perfect, upright, prospering, pleasant, pure, sublime, and numerous amongst what You have blessed, sanctified, treated mercifully, dealt with affectionately, and saluted any of Your servants, prophets, messengers, friends, and those honored by You from among Your creatures.

The Imam starts with *salawat* – praying for blessings upon his grandfather, the Holy Prophet. He later continues to make that prayer for the rest of the Immaculate Imams.

Salawat

What is the meaning and importance of salawat?

God Almighty says in the Holy Quran:

إِنَّ اللَّهَ وَمَلَائِكَتَهُ يُصَلُّونَ عَلَى النَّبِيِّ ۚ يَا أَيُّهَا الَّذِينَ آمَنُوا صَلُّوا عَلَيْهِ وَسَلِّمُوا تَسْلِيمًا

Indeed, Allah and His angels bless the Prophet; O you who have faith! Invoke blessings on him and invoke Peace upon him in a worthy manner.[1]

---

[1] The Holy Quran, 33:56.

Imam al-Sadiq is reported to have said in clarifying this verse:

الصلاة من الله عز وجل رحمة، ومن الملائكة تزكية، ومن الناس دعاء

Blessings from God, the glorious and majestic, are a mercy.
From the angels, they are praise. From the people, they are
prayers.[2]

Therefore, when we recite the salawat, we are praying for the Holy
Prophet and his Immaculate Progeny. We are asking God to honor
them and raise their status.

Why do we repeat this prayer so often?

First, it is a means of thanking the Holy Household for everything they
gave us. They are the conditions of emanation, both existentially and
legislatively. Without them, we would not have been created. Without
their knowledge, divine commands would not have reached us. Without their efforts and sacrifices, God's religion would not have survived
to this day. The Holy Prophet said:

إني مخلف فيكم الثقلين كتاب الله وعترتي أهل بيتي، ما إن تمسكتم بها لن تضلوا
بعدي أبدا، وقد أنبأني اللطيف الخبير أنها لن يفترقا حتى يردا عليّ الحوض،
فانظروا كيف تخلفوني فيها

Verily, I am leaving among you the Two Weighty Things,
the Book of God and my kindred (`itrah), my household.
Indeed, if you hold firmly to the two, you will never stray
after me. The most kind and all-aware God has told me
that the two will never separate until they come back to me
by the Pool [of al-Kawthar on the Day of Judgment]. So be
mindful of how you deal with them after me.[3]

It is also reported that the Holy Prophet said:

---

[2] Al-Kashani, al-Tafseer al-Kafi, 4:201.
[3] Al-Kulayni, al-Kafi, 2:415.

في كل خلف من أمتي عدل من أهل بيتي ينفي عن هذا الدين تحريف الغالين
وانتحال المبطلين وتأويل الجهال، وإن أئمتكم وفدكم إلى الله فانظروا من توفدون في
دينكم وصلاتكم

In every succeeding generation of my nation, there is a counterpart from my household who shall protect this religion against the distortions of fanatics, the deceit of corrupters, and the interpretations of the ignorant. Your leaders are your delegation to God, so be mindful who you select as the delegation of your faith and prayers.[4]

How do we thank them for everything that they sacrificed for the sake of this religion and its adherents? Our prayers for them are a method of thanks and a sign of appreciation for everything they offered.

Second, our prayers for them are a way to observe God's command to hold them with affection. God says,

قُل لَّا أَسْأَلُكُمْ عَلَيْهِ أَجْرًا إِلَّا الْمَوَدَّةَ فِي الْقُرْبَىٰ

Say, 'I do not ask you any reward for it except the love of [my] relatives.'[5]

Our prayers for them are a display of our affection. We must pray for them as a means of observing God's command in that regard. That is why some traditions say:

من لم يقدر على ما يكفر به ذنوبه فليكثر من الصلاة على محمد وآل محمد، فإنها
تهدم الذنوب هدما

Whoever cannot find anything to atone for his sins, let him persist in praying for blessings upon Muhammad and the family of Muhammad. Surely, it dismantles sin a [firm] dismantlement.[6]

Third, our prayers are a means of establishing a spiritual connection with them. Whenever a servant has a connection to a great individual,

---

[4] Al-Majlisi, *Bihar al-Anwar*, 23:31.

[5] *The Holy Quran*, 42:23.

[6] Al-'Amili, *Wasa'el al-Shi'a*, 7:194.

that great individual will look after and care for the servant. Our prayers for them establish a spiritual connection with them, and they will surely look after whoever looks up to them.

The Commander of the Faithful

The Imam then continued to mention some of the traits and attributes of the Commander of the Faithful, Imam Ali. He said,

اللّٰهُمَّ وَصَلِّ عَلى عَلِيٍّ أَمِيرَ الْمُؤْمِنِينَ، وَوَصِيِّ رَسُولِ رَبِّ الْعالَمِينَ، عَبْدِكَ وَوَلِيّكَ وَأَخِي رَسُولِكَ وَحُجَّتِكَ عَلَى خَلْقِكَ وَآيَتِكَ الْكُبْرَى وَالنَّبَأِ الْعَظِيمِ

O' God send blessings on Ali, the Commander of the Faithful, the successor to the Messenger of the Lord of the worlds, Your servant and representative, the brother of Your Messenger, Your proof upon your creatures, Your greatest sign, and the great tiding from You.

The supplication mentions Imam Ali as the Commander of the Faithful and successor to the Holy Prophet before mentioning his role as servant of God. However, we know that servitude to God is a prerequisite to these other lofty statuses. As our traditions say about Prophet Abraham:

إن الله اتخذ ابراهيم عبدا قبل أن يتخذه نبيا، وإن الله اتخذه نبيا قبل أن يتخذه رسولا، وإن الله اتخذه رسولا قبل أن يتخذه خليلا، وإن الله اتخذه خليلا قبل أن يتخذه إماما

Surely, God took Abraham as a servant before He took him as a prophet. God took him as prophet before He took him as a messenger. God took him as a messenger before He took him as a friend. God took him as a friend before He took him as an imam.[7]

---

7 Al-Kulayni, al-Kafi, 1:175.

227

Imam Ali's servitude to God is precedent to his position of commander and successor. Still, those traits were mentioned before servitude. Why? There are a few possible explanations.

Servitude can be understood in two ways. The first instance of servitude comes from the moment of creation. Everything is at God's service once He emanates existence onto it. However, voluntary servitude to God that comes through following His divine commands comes after those commands are clarified. Thus, prophethood and guidance are prerequisites to servitude, as those positions elucidate what servitude means. As the Holy Quran says,

إِنَّمَا أَنتَ مُنذِرٌ ةٌ وَلِكُلِّ قَوْمٍ هَادٍ

You are only a warner, and there is a guide for every people.[8]

Therefore, it can be understood that Imam Ali's position of guidance and successorship are precedent to his servitude.

Mentioning the positions of imamah and commandership at the forefront could be a reference to their distinction amongst all other traits. A person might believe that Imam Ali is a servant of God and the brother of His Messenger, yet not believe in his imamah. However, Imam Ali's imamah and successorship are integral to truly knowing his stature and position. The Holy Prophet said,

من مات ولم يعرف إمام زمانه مات ميته جاهلية

Whoever passes not knowing the imam of his time has passed as if he were still in the Age of Ignorance.[9]

It is also narrated that Imam al-Sadiq said,

---

[8] The Holy Quran, 13:7.

[9] Al-'Amili, Wasa'el al-Shi'a, 16:246.

أما لو أن رجلا صام نهاره وقام ليله وتصدق بجميع ماله وحج جميع دهره ولم يعرف
ولاية ولي الله فيواله وتكون جميع أعماله بدلالته إليه ما كان له على الله ثواب ولا
كان من أهل الإيمان

Alas, a man may fast his days, wake his nights [in worship], give away his entire wealth as charity, and perform the pilgrimage his entire life, yet if he does not know the authority of God's vicegerent and abide by it and act in accordance to his guidance – such a man would have no rewards with God and would not be amongst the people of faith.[10]

Whether deeds are accepted or not is contingent on acceptance of Imam Ali's imamah and guidance.

Finally, we know that God Almighty chose the Holy Prophet and his Immaculate Household for their sublime roles before He created the rest of the universe. Imam Ali was chosen as an Imam before the creation of mankind. As we read in the Grand Comprehensive Visitation,

خَلَقَكُمُ الله أَنْوَاراً فَجَعَلَكُمْ بِعَرْشِهِ مُحَدِّقِينَ حَتَّى مَنَّ عَلَيْنَا بِكُمْ فَجَعَلَكُمْ فِي بُيُوتٍ أَذِنَ
الله أَنْ تُرْفَعَ وَيُذْكَرَ فِيهَا اسْمُهُ

Allah created you as lights and kept you closely attached with His Throne until He, out of His favor, bestowed you upon us – placing you in houses that He allowed to be elevated and for His name to be mentioned therein.[11]

Therefore, their selection as Imams preceded their servitude. Therefore, it would be proper to speak of imamah before speaking of servitude.

A Glimpse of Ali's Character

We see in this segment of the supplication that the Imam is recounting a number of traits of the Commander of the Faithful, many of which

---

[10] Al-'Amili, Wasa'el al-Shi'a, 27:42.

[11] Al-Qummi, Mafateeh al-Jinan, al-Ziyara al-Jami'a.

have the same or similar meanings. What is the difference between the traits of commandership, successorship, proof, and guardianship? An appointed successor of the Holy Prophet is doubtlessly a commander, proof, and guardian. Thus, these titles all refer to Imam Ali's position as the chosen successor of the Holy Prophet. So why all these labels?

Our scholars say that there are words that generally convey the same meaning, but each provides a distinct meaning when they are used in the same sentence. This is especially true in the Arabic language. For example, the words poor and destitute generally convey the same meaning. However, a person may be asked to 'feed the poor and the destitute.' If the two words were meant to convey the same meaning, then using both would be unnecessary and ineloquent. However, they can be used together to convey slightly different meanings. In this case, poor could mean 'someone who cannot afford a reasonably comfortable life.' Destitute could mean 'someone who cannot afford the basic necessities of life.' Those two definitions are very similar, but there are precise distinctions between the two.

All this is to say that the Imam lists these labels for Imam Ali in order to convey a number of precise qualities. All these qualities stem from the fact that Imam Ali is the chosen successor of the Holy Prophet by God's will. However, each label carries a precise meaning that we must understand.

General Authority. The appointed successor of the Holy Prophet is doubtlessly possessed with authority over the Muslims. He has authority over the lives and wealth of the believers. As the Holy Quran states,

النَّبِيُّ أَوْلَىٰ بِالْمُؤْمِنِينَ مِنْ أَنْفُسِهِمْ

The Prophet possesses more authority over the faithful than their own souls.[12]

The same holds for the Holy Prophet's successors. They hold greater authority over each Muslim than we do over ourselves. If they exercise their authority over us – if they give even the simplest commands – we

---

[12] *The Holy Quran, 33:6.*

have no option but to follow. Such is the authority of the Holy Prophet, as well as of all of his appointed successors.

The title of 'Commander of the Faithful' rings especially true because of this. He has the ability to command as he sees fit, and we have no power to reject any of his orders.

Lifted Veils. Imam Ali is also an individual who has been shown the dominion of the heavens and the Earth. The Holy Quran says,

وَكَذَٰلِكَ نُرِي إِبْرَاهِيمَ مَلَكُوتَ السَّمَاوَاتِ وَالْأَرْضِ وَلِيَكُونَ مِنَ الْمُوقِنِينَ

Thus, did We show Abraham the dominions of the heavens and the Earth, that he might be of those who possess certitude.[13]

The Imam has the power to see all worlds. He sees the worlds of the angels, jinn, spirits, and so forth. He also sees the realities of Paradise and Hellfire; he sees the reality of everything. Moreover, he is able to influence these worlds as he sees fit. He possesses creational authority over all things.

His ability to see and influence the realms of existence, along with the authority he holds over the souls of the believers, means that he has the ability to impart guidance. He can emanate the light of guidance to the believers, pulling them closer to their Almighty Lord.

This is true for Imam Ali as well as all of the other Imams. It is true for our living twelfth Imam, who says:

وأما وجه الإنتفاع بي في غيبتي فكالانتفاع بالشمس إذا غيّبتها عن الأبصار السحاب، وإني لأمان لأهل الأرض كما أن النجوم أمان لأهل السماء

As for benefitting from me in my occultation, it is like benefitting from the Sun when it is shielded from vision by the clouds. Surely, I am a safeguard for the denizens of the Earth as the stars are a safeguard for the denizens of the heavens.[14]

---

[13] *The Holy Quran*, 6:75.
[14] *Al-Majlisi, Bihar al-Anwar*, 52:92.

Even in his occultation, our twelfth Imam exercises his power of guidance, and his authority over the believers.

This should not be surprising to us. The Imam is a force of guidance, just as Satan is a force of misguidance. Just as Satan whispers to us to indulge in our desires, the Imam imparts the light of guidance that reminds us of our Lord's commands.

Therefore, in addition to Imam Ali's position as Commander of the Faithful, he is also God's representative, who imparts guidance.

Successorship. The Holy Prophet came to deliver a divine message and groom a corps of followers who will ensure the message's survival. However, after many years of toiling for that goal, the Holy Prophet passed on to join the company of his merciful Lord. Who is it that was to take on the role of continuing to teach the nation and groom its leaders?

Before the Holy Prophet passed, he had to deliver to the people a successor who would take care of them after him. He did deliver that message on a day known as the Day of Ghadeer. When the Holy Prophet delivered that command, the following verse was revealed:

الْيَوْمَ يَئِسَ الَّذِينَ كَفَرُوا مِن دِينِكُمْ فَلَا تَخْشَوْهُمْ وَاخْشَوْنِ ۚ الْيَوْمَ أَكْمَلْتُ لَكُمْ دِينَكُمْ وَأَتْمَمْتُ عَلَيْكُمْ نِعْمَتِي وَرَضِيتُ لَكُمُ الْإِسْلَامَ دِينًا

Today the faithless have despaired of your religion. So do not fear them, but fear Me. Today I have perfected your religion for you, and I have completed My blessing upon you, and I have approved Islam as your religion.[15]

Thus, Imam Ali's successorship is the completion of faith and a sign of divine approval. Without an explicit appointment, how were we to know who the successor should be?

Imam Ali's successorship is a pointer to our eternal need for God's blessings, and His eternal emanations upon us – the greatest of which is the blessing of faith and its guardians.

---

[15] *The Holy Quran*, 5:3.

Truthfulness. The Holy Prophet and the Imams are immaculate in their knowledge, actions, and teachings. They are immaculate in knowledge in that they are never heedless. They never forget and are never confused. Otherwise, they would not be the most perfect teachers that God appointed for His servants. This is the meaning of the verse,

وَمَا يَنطِقُ عَنِ الْهَوَىٰ ۞ إِنْ هُوَ إِلَّا وَحْيٌ يُوحَىٰ

Nor does he speak out of [his own] desire: it is just a revelation that is revealed [to him].[16]

In other words, they never err in delivering and teaching the message of their Lord.

In addition, their actions are also immaculate. Whatever they do is a proof upon mankind. Their actions are based on a true and unerring knowledge of reality. Thus, seeing their actions reveals to us reality with clarity. If they take a certain action, we know that their action is at the least permissible, or maybe even obligatory. If they forbid someone from something, we know that thing is forbidden by God.

Thus, their words and actions are proof upon mankind.

Imam Ali's Attributes

Many of the attributes mentioned in the supplication are also mentioned in the noble traditions. Let us address them one by one.

The Commander of the Faithful. It is narrated that Imam al-Rida said,

قال رسول الله (ص): يا علي إنك سيد المسلمين وإمام المتقين وقائد الغر المحجلين ويعسوب الدين

O' Ali, you are the master of the Muslims, the imam of the pious, the leader of noble believers, and the commander of faith.[17]

It is also narrated that the Holy Prophet would say,

---

[16] *The Holy Quran, 53:4.*

[17] *Al-Majlisi, Bihar al-Anwar, 40:24.*

ما أنزل الله آية وفيها ﴿ يَا أَيُّهَا الَّذِينَ آمَنُوا ﴾ إلا وعلي رأسها وأميرها

Whenever God revealed a verse that says, 'O' you who have faith,' Ali is its pinnacle and master. [18]

The Successor. When the Holy Prophet was first commanded to deliver the message, he was asked to start with his near of kin. The verse was revealed,

وَأَنذِرْ عَشِيرَتَكَ الْأَقْرَبِينَ

Warn the nearest of your kinsfolk. [19]

The Holy Prophet gathered his clan and delivered the message to them. Imam Ali narrates the events of that day. He recounted that the Holy Prophet said:

يا بني عبد المطلب إني والله ما أعلم شابا في العرب جاء قومه بأفضل مما جئتكم به، إني قد جئتكم بخير الدنيا والآخرة وقد أمرني الله أن أدعوكم إليه، فأيكم يؤازرني على هذا الأمر على أن يكون أخي ووصيي وخليفتي فيكم

O' clan of Abdulmuttalib! By God, I do not know of a young Arab man who came to his people with anything better that what I have brought to you. I came with the best of this world and the hereafter, and God has commanded me to call you to it. Who will support me in this matter, so that he may be my brother, vicegerent, and successor amongst you?

Imam Ali recalled that everyone went quiet. He was the youngest amongst them, but the firmest in faith. At that moment he said,

أنا يا نبي الله أكون وزيرك عليه

O' prophet of God! I will be your supporter.

The Holy Prophet placed his hand on Ali's neck and said,

---

[18] Al-Majlisi, *Bihar al-Anwar*, 35:350.
[19] *The Holy Quran*, 26:214.

إن هذا أخي ووصيي وخليفتي فيكم فاسمعوا له وأطيعوا

This is my brother, vicegerent, and successor amongst you.
Listen to him and obey.[20]

This tradition, known as Hadith al-Dar, is recounted by Muslims of all sects in their books. It is one of many instances where Imam Ali is named as successor.

The Messenger's Brother. When the Holy Prophet migrated from Mecca to Medina, he gathered the Muslims of the time. He ordered them in pairs and established brotherhood amongst them – pairing between the *muhajirun* and *ansar*,[21] black and white, noblemen and commoners. In one narration, Imam Ali recalls:

آخى رسول الله (ص) بين أصحابه وتركني، فقلت: يا رسول الله (ص) آخيت
بين أصحابك وتركتني فردا لا أخ لي، فقال: إنما اخترتك لنفسي، أنت أخي وأنا
أخوك، فإن حاجّك أحد فقل: إني عبد الله وأخو رسول الله (ص)

The Messenger of God established brotherhood between his
companions and overlooked me. I said, 'O' Messenger of
God, you established brotherhood amongst your
companions, but left me alone without a brother.' He said,
'Rather, I chose you for myself. You are my brother and I
am your brother. If anyone were to challenge you, say: "I
am the servant of God and the brother of the Messenger of
God!"'[22]

The Holy Prophet did this to show all the Muslims the great status that Imam Ali had. He had sacrificed so much in support of the Holy

---

[20] Al-Majlisi, Bihar al-Anwar, 18:192.

[21] The terms muhajirun and ansar are used to refer to two groups of Muslims at the time of the migration of the Holy Prophet from Mecca to Medina. The ansar were the inhabitants of the city of Medina at the time of the Prophet's migration to the city. They aided the Prophet and allowed him to establish his capital in their city, and so they came to be known as the ansar – literally, supporters – of the Prophet. The term is usually used to distinguish them from the muhajirun – literally, migrants – who came from Mecca along with the Prophet and lived along-side their ansar brethren in Medina. The two groups are not inclusive of all Muslims – many converted to Islam and continued to live outside the boundaries of these two cities. –Eds.

[22] Al-Hilli, Nahj al-Haq, 217.

Prophet and would continue to do so for the sake of Islam. He held such a high status that he shared all the attributes of the Holy Prophet – with the exception of prophethood.

This is why the Holy Quran referred to Imam Ali as the Prophet's self. It says:

فَمَنْ حَاجَّكَ فِيهِ مِن بَعْدِ مَا جَاءَكَ مِنَ الْعِلْمِ فَقُلْ تَعَالَوْا نَدْعُ أَبْنَاءَنَا وَأَبْنَاءَكُمْ وَنِسَاءَنَا وَنِسَاءَكُمْ وَأَنفُسَنَا وَأَنفُسَكُمْ ثُمَّ نَبْتَهِلْ فَنَجْعَل لَّعْنَتَ اللَّهِ عَلَى الْكَاذِبِينَ

Should anyone argue with you concerning him, after the knowledge that has come to you, say, 'Come! Let us call our sons and your sons, our women and your women, our souls and your souls, then let us pray earnestly, and call down Allah's curse upon the liars.' [23]

At this event, the Holy Prophet would bring his sons (al-Hassan and al-Hussain), his women (Lady Fatima), and his self (Imam Ali).

This means that Imam Ali shares all the merits of the Holy Prophet. The only exception to that rule is prophethood – the Holy Quran and the noble traditions specifically say that the Holy Prophet Muhammad is the last of prophets. Thus, our beloved Prophet is greater than Imam Ali, because he holds that high honor. However, they remain equal in all other merits.

The Holy Prophet is greater than all other creations, including the other prophets and messengers. Imam Ali – being equal in merit to the Holy Prophet in almost every way – is also greater than all the other prophets and messengers, with the exception of the Holy Prophet of Islam.

God's Representative. It is narrated that a poor man once entered the mosque of the Holy Prophet in Medina during the Prophet's lifetime. The man asked if anyone could help him buy any food. The Holy Prophet did not have anything to give the man. Everyone in the mosque was either as poor as he was, or unwilling to help the man.

---

[23] *The Holy Quran*, 3:61.

The poor man finally came to Imam Ali, who was busy with his prayer. Still, in the midst of prayer and in the state of prostration, the Imam stretched his right hand and pointed for the man to take his signet ring.

The Holy Prophet saw what happened. He was overjoyed by the actions of his brother, Ali. He turned to the heavens and said:

إن أخي موسى سألك ﴿رَبِّ اشْرَحْ لِي صَدْرِي ✤ وَيَسِّرْ لِي أَمْرِي ✤ وَاحْلُلْ عُقْدَةً مِّن لِّسَانِي ✤ يَفْقَهُوا قَوْلِي ✤ وَاجْعَل لِّي وَزِيرًا مِّنْ أَهْلِي ✤ هَارُونَ أَخِي ✤ اشْدُدْ بِهِ أَزْرِي ✤ وَأَشْرِكْهُ فِي أَمْرِي﴾ فأنزلت عليه ﴿سَنَشُدُّ عَضُدَكَ بِأَخِيكَ وَنَجْعَلُ لَكُمَا سُلْطَانًا﴾ وأنا أدعوك رب اشرح لي صدري ويسر لي أمري واجعل لي وزيرا من أهلي عليا أخي اشدد به أزري وأشركه في أمري

My brother, Moses, asked you, 'My Lord! Open my breast for me. Make my task easy for me. Remove the hitch from my tongue, [so that] they may understand my speech. Appoint for me a minister from my family, Aaron, my brother. Strengthen my back through him, and make him my associate in my task.' You revealed to him, 'We will strengthen your arm by means of your brother, and invest both of you with such authority.' I ask you, My Lord! Open my breast for me. Make my task easy for me. Appoint for me a minister from my family, Ali, my brother. Strengthen my back through him, and make him my associate in my task.[24]

Before the Holy Prophet finished speaking those words, the archangel Gabriel came to him with the following revelation,

---

[24] Al-Hasakani, *Shawahid al-Tanzil*, 1:230.

إِنَّمَا وَلِيُّكُمُ اللَّهُ وَرَسُولُهُ وَالَّذِينَ آمَنُوا الَّذِينَ يُقِيمُونَ الصَّلَاةَ وَيُؤْتُونَ الزَّكَاةَ وَهُمْ رَاكِعُونَ

Your guardian is only Allah, His Apostle, and the faithful
who maintain the prayer and give the zakat while bowing
down. [25]

Some people ask, 'How could Imam Ali do that when he is in his prayer? Should he not have been concentrating on his prayers rather than on what is going on around him?'

Imam Ali was not preoccupied by a worldly matter away from his worship. Rather, he combined two types of worship at once. His servility in his prayer did not stop him from praising and worshipping God through giving charity. This is evidence of his connection to God, and not a distraction.

The Great Tiding. We read in the Holy Quran,

عَمَّ يَتَسَاءَلُونَ ❖ عَنِ النَّبَإِ الْعَظِيمِ ❖ الَّذِي هُمْ فِيهِ مُخْتَلِفُونَ

What is it that they are questioning each other about?! [Is
it] about the Great Tiding, the one about which they
differ? [26]

What is the great tiding that people were arguing about? Our narrations tell us that this great tiding was none other than Imam Ali and his authority over the Muslims. God Almighty called it a great tiding, because even at the time of revelation there were those who held deep hatred towards Ali ibn Abu Talib. As we read in Du'a al-Nudba:

فَأَوْدَعَ قُلُوبَهُمْ أَحْقَاداً بَدْرِيَّةً وَخَيْبَرِيَّةً وَحُنَيْنِيَّةً وَغَيْرَهُنَّ فَأَضَبَّتْ عَلَى عَدَاوَتِهِ وَأَكَبَّتْ عَلَى مُنَابَذَتِهِ

He therefore filled in their hearts with malice from the
battles of Badr, Khaybar, and Hunayn, as well as others.

---

[25] The Holy Quran, 5:55.
[26] The Holy Quran, 78:3.

Therefore, they continued to oppose him and dedicated to resist him.[27]

As Lady Fatima said in her famous sermon after the passing of the Holy Prophet:

[كلما] فغرت فاغرة من المشركين، قذف أخاه في لهواتها، فلا ينكفئ حتى يطأ
صماخها بأخمصه، ويخمد لهبها بسيفه، مكدودا في ذات الله، ومجتهدا في أمر الله،
قريبا من رسول الله، سيد أولياء الله، مشمرا ناصحا، مجدا كادحا، وأنتم في
رفاهية من العيش، وادعون فاكهون آمنون، تتربصون بنا الدوائر، وتتوكفون
الاخبار، وتنكصون عند النزال، وتفرون عند القتال

Whenever a gate [of sedition] was opened by the polytheists, [the Messenger of God] would strike its discords with his brother [Ali], who would not stop until he treads its head with the sole of his feet, and extinguishes its flames with his sword. He was toiling for the sake of God, diligent in God's affair, close to the Messenger of God, master over God's vicegerents, earnest and sincere, persistent and tireless. Meanwhile, you lived luxuriously in calmness, joy, and peace. Still, you watched for a reversal of our fortunes and yearned for news [of our tragedies]. You fled at every challenger and retreated at every battle.[28]

The great tiding is the authority and imamah of the Commander of the Faithful. Every person will be asked about it on the Day of Judgment. It is narrated that the Holy Prophet said:

يا علي إن أول ما يُسأل عنه العبد بعد موته شهادة أن لا إله إلا الله وأن محمدا
رسول الله وأنك ولي المؤمنين بما جعله الله وجعلته، فمن أقرّ بذلك وكان معتقده
صار الى النعيم الذي لا زوال له

O' Ali, the first thing that a servant is asked about [after death] is the testaments that there is no god but God, that

---

[27] Al-Qummi, *Mafateeh al-Jinan, Du'a al-Nudba.*
[28] Al-Majlisi, *Bihar al-Anwar,* 29:223.

Muhammad is the Messenger of God, and that you are the master of the believers by the decree of God and my decree. Whoever testifies to this and holds it as his creed, he will be led to bliss which shall never fade. [29]

O' God, allow us to remain steadfast on the path of Ali ibn Abu Talib, and grant us his intercession on a day when neither wealth nor children will avail!

---

[29] Al-Mazandarani, al-Manaqib, 3:34.

Supplication...[1]

---

[1] *This part of the supplication was not addressed by the author. We leave it here for your reference.*

اللَّهُمَّ وَصَلِّ عَلَى عَلِيٍّ أَمِيرِ المُؤْمِنِينَ، وَوَصِيِّ رَسُولِ رَبِّ العَالَمِينَ، عَبْدِكَ وَوَلِيِّكَ وَأَخِي رَسُولِكَ وَحُجَّتِكَ عَلَى خَلْقِكَ وَآيَتِكَ الكُبْرَى وَالنَّبَأِ العَظِيمِ،

O' God send blessings on Ali, the Commander of the Faithful, the successor to the Messenger of the Lord of the worlds, Your servant and representative, the brother of Your Messenger, Your proof upon your creatures, Your greatest sign, and the great news from You.

وَصَلِّ عَلَى الصِّدِّيقَةِ الطَّاهِرَةِ فَاطِمَةَ سَيِّدَةِ نِسَاءِ العَالَمِينَ، وَصَلِّ عَلَى سِبْطَيِ الرَّحْمَةِ وَإِمَامَيِ الهُدَى الحَسَنِ وَالحُسَيْنِ سَيِّدَيْ شَبَابِ أَهْلِ الجَنَّةِ، وَصَلِّ عَلَى أَئِمَّةِ المُسْلِمِينَ عَلِيِّ بْنِ الحُسَيْنِ وَمُحَمَّدِ بْنِ عَلِيٍّ وَجَعْفَرِ بْنِ مُحَمَّدٍ وَمُوسَى بْنِ جَعْفَرٍ وَعَلِيِّ بْنِ مُوسَى وَمُحَمَّدِ بْنِ عَلِيٍّ وَعَلِيِّ بْنِ مُحَمَّدٍ وَالحَسَنِ بْنِ عَلِيٍّ وَالخَلَفِ الهَادِي المَهْدِيِّ، حُجَجِكَ عَلَى عِبَادِكَ وَأُمَنَائِكَ فِي بِلَادِكَ، صَلَاةً كَثِيرَةً دَائِمَةً.

O' God, send blessings on the truthful and pure Fatima, the leader of the women of the worlds. O' God, send blessings on the sons of 'the mercy unto the worlds,' the imams of guidance, al-Hassan and al-Hussain, the leaders of the youth of Paradise. O' God, send blessings on the imams of the Muslims, Ali ibn al-Hussain, Muhammad ibn Ali, Jafar ibn Muhammad, Musa ibn Jafar, Ali ibn Musa, Muhammad ibn Ali, Ali ibn Muhammad, al-Hassan ibn Ali, and the rightly guided successor, al-Mahdi – Your proofs over Your servants and Your trustees on Your Earth – blessings which are numerous and everlasting.

اللَّهُمَّ وَصَلِّ عَلَى وَلِيِّ أَمْرِكَ القَائِمِ المُؤَمَّلِ، وَالعَدْلِ المُنْتَظَرِ، وَحُفَّهُ بِمَلَائِكَتِكَ المُقَرَّبِينَ، وَأَيِّدْهُ بِرُوحِ القُدُسِ يَا رَبَّ العَالَمِينَ. اللَّهُمَّ اجْعَلْهُ الدَّاعِيَ إِلَى كِتَابِكَ، وَالقَائِمَ بِدِينِكَ، اسْتَخْلِفْهُ فِي الأَرْضِ كَمَا اسْتَخْلَفْتَ

الَّذِينَ مِنْ قَبْلِهِ، مَكِّنْ لَهُ دِينَهُ الَّذِي ارْتَضَيْتَهُ لَهُ، أَبْدِلْهُ مِنْ بَعْدِ خَوْفِهِ أَمْناً،
يَعْبُدُكَ لا يُشْرِكُ بِكَ شَيْئاً. اللّهُمَّ أَعِزَّهُ وَأَعْزِزْ بِهِ، وَانْصُرْهُ وَانْتَصِرْ بِهِ،
وَانْصُرْهُ نَصْراً عَزِيزاً، وَافْتَحْ لَهُ فَتْحاً يَسِيراً، وَاجْعَلْ لَهُ مِنْ لَدُنْكَ سُلْطاناً
نَصِيراً.

O' God, send blessings on the custodian of Your matter, the longed-for guardian and the awaited justice. Surround him by Your closest angels and assist him by the Holy Spirit, O' Lord of the worlds. O' God, make him the caller unto Your Book and the patron of Your religion. Make him the successor of the Earth, as You made successors before him. Establish for him his faith which You approved for him. Translate his fear into security, so that he may worship You and ascribes no partner to You. O' God, grant him might and grant might [to the believers] through him. Grant him victory and grant victory [to the believers] through him. Grant him a great victory and an effortless triumph. Grant him through this manifest authority.

Remember Your Beloved

اللَّهُمَّ وَصَلِّ عَلَى وَلِيِّ أَمْرِكَ القَائِمِ المُؤَمَّلِ، وَالعَدْلِ المُنْتَظَرِ، وَحُفَّهُ بِمَلَائِكَتِكَ المُقَرَّبِينَ، وَأَيِّدْهُ بِرُوحِ القُدُسِ يَا رَبَّ العَالَمِينَ. اللَّهُمَّ اجْعَلْهُ الدَّاعِيَ إِلَى كِتَابِكَ، وَالقَائِمَ بِدِينِكَ، اسْتَخْلِفْهُ فِي الأَرْضِ كَمَا اسْتَخْلَفْتَ الَّذِينَ مِنْ قَبْلِهِ، مَكِّنْ لَهُ دِينَهُ الَّذِي ارْتَضَيْتَهُ لَهُ، أَبْدِلْهُ مِنْ بَعْدِ خَوْفِهِ أَمْنَا، يَعْبُدُكَ لَا يُشْرِكُ بِكَ شَيْئًا. اللَّهُمَّ أَعِزَّهُ وَأَعْزِزْ بِهِ، وَانْصُرْهُ وَانْتَصِرْ بِهِ، وَانْصُرْهُ نَصْرًا عَزِيزًا، وَافْتَحْ لَهُ فَتْحًا يَسِيرًا، وَاجْعَلْ لَهُ مِنْ لَدُنْكَ سُلْطَانًا نَصِيرًا.

O' God, send blessings on the custodian of Your matter, the longed-for guardian and the awaited justice. Surround him by Your closest angels and assist him by the Holy Spirit, O' Lord of the worlds. O' God, make him the caller unto Your Book and the patron of Your religion. Make him the successor of the Earth, as You made successors before him. Establish for him his faith which You approved for him. Translate his fear into security, so that he may worship You and ascribes no partner to You. O' God, grant him might and grant might [to the believers] through him. Grant him victory and grant victory [to the believers] through him. Grant him a great victory and an effortless triumph. Grant him through this manifest authority.

This sublime supplication was written by our beloved twelfth Imam – the Awaited al-Mahdi. But why does the Imam praise himself and pray for himself in this segment? Does humility not require that he not mention all of this in a supplication that he teaches to his followers?

There are three perspectives in answering this question.

First, the Imam could be recounting these merits as a way of thanking God Almighty for His blessings.

When Imam al-Kadhim passed away, a number of Waqifites came to visit his son, Imam al-Rida. The Waqifites believed that Imam Musa ibn Ja'far al-Kadhim was a divinely appointed Imam, but they refused to accept the Imamah of Imam al-Rida. Instead, they said that Imam al-Kadhim went into occultation.

These Waqifites – Ali ibn Abu Hamza, ibn al-Sarraj, and ibn al-Makaari – came to Imam al-Rida and asked him about his father. When he told them that Imam al-Kadhim had passed away, they asked, "Are you an Imam whose authority was vested by God?" He told them that he was. They whispered amongst themselves, "He has empowered us against himself!" They thought that the Imam had acted with hubris when he told them that he was an imam. One of them said, "You have flaunted something which none of your forefathers had done before or talked about!"

The Imam replied:

بلى والله لقد تكلم به خير آبائي رسول الله صلى الله عليه وآله لما أمره الله أن ينذر عشيرته الأقرين جمع من أهل بيته أربعين رجلا وقال لهم: إني رسول الله إليكم فكان أشدهم تكذيبا وتأليبا عليه عمه أبو لهب، فقال لهم النبي صلى الله عليه وآله إن خدشني خدش فلست بنبي، فهذا أول ما أبدع لكم من آية النبوة، وأنا أقول: إن خدشني هارون خدشا فلست لإمام، فهذا أول ما أبدع لكم من آية الإمامة.

Rather, by God, the best of my forefathers, the Messenger of God, had spoken of it! When God commanded him to warn his near of kin, he gathered forty of his clansmen and said, 'I am the Messenger of God to you.' The greatest denier and instigator amongst them was his uncle, Abu Lahab. The Prophet said to them, 'If he [i.e. Abu Lahab] lays a finger on me, I am not a prophet!' That was the first sign of prophethood which he awed you with. Now I say

> *that if Harun lays a finger on me, I am not an Imam! This*
> *is the first sign of imamah which I shall awe you with!* [1]

Acknowledging God's blessings is not hubris. In fact, God Almighty asks us to speak of His blessings on all of us. He says,

وَأَمَّا بِنِعْمَةِ رَبِّكَ فَحَدِّثْ

As for your Lord's blessing, proclaim it! [2]

Secondly, we spoke in a previous chapter about the Imam's supplications as a reflection of collective existence and experience. Here, the Imam is supplicating in the tongue of the believers who are awaiting the end of his occultation. He is reflecting our hopes in his safe and blessed return. He is giving voice to the dreams of those whose hearts ache at not having the opportunity to see him.

Third, the Imam is drawing a link between our connection to him and our connection to God. He uses this segment of the supplication to show us that we cannot divide our love for God and our love for our Imam. It is impossible for a person to love God but not love His chosen servants!

When a person loves a thing, they also love everything that comes with it. No one can say, 'I love person A, but hate how he looks!' No one can say, 'I love person B, but hate her personality!' True love encompasses the object, and everything associated with it.

Can a person love God for His beauty and majesty, yet loath the signs of His beauty and majesty?! The greatest of His signs are the Holy Prophet and his Immaculate family. How can we claim to love God but not love them?

God's beauty and majesty are evident to us through the beauty and majesty of the Imam. He is God's greatest sign – there is no separating between God and His signs.

---

[1] Al-Majlisi, *Bihar al-Anwar*, 48:270.
[2] *The Holy Quran*, 93:11.

We ask God Almighty to remember His beloved servant – the Awaited Mahdi – and shower him with the greatest blessings and most perfect of bounties.

Supplication...[1]

---

[1] *This part of the supplication was not addressed by the author. We leave it here for your reference.*

251

اللَّهُمَّ أَظْهِرْ بِهِ دِينَكَ وَسُنَّةَ نَبِيِّكَ، حَتَّى لَا يَسْتَخْفِيَ بِشَيْءٍ مِنَ الْحَقِّ مَخَافَةَ أَحَدٍ مِنَ الْخَلْقِ.

O' God, empower Your religion and the tradition of Your prophet through him, such that he shall not hide any truth out of fear of any creature.

اللَّهُمَّ إِنَّا نَرْغَبُ إِلَيْكَ فِي دَوْلَةٍ كَرِيمَةٍ، تُعِزُّ بِهَا الْإِسْلَامَ وَأَهْلَهُ، وَتُذِلُّ بِهَا النِّفَاقَ وَأَهْلَهُ، وَتَجْعَلُنَا فِيهَا مِنَ الدُّعَاةِ إِلَى طَاعَتِكَ، وَالْقَادَةِ إِلَى سَبِيلِكَ، وَتَرْزُقُنَا بِهَا كَرَامَةَ الدُّنْيَا وَالْآخِرَةِ.

O' God, we ask of you for an honorable era where you distinguish Islam and its adherents and humiliate hypocrisy and its adherents. Allow us to be in it [i.e., that honorable era] amongst those who call toward Your obedience and the leaders in Your path. Bless us through it with the honor of this world and the next.

اللَّهُمَّ مَا عَرَّفْتَنَا مِنَ الْحَقِّ فَحَمِّلْنَاهُ، وَمَا قَصُرْنَا عَنْهُ فَبَلِّغْنَاهُ، اللَّهُمَّ الْمُمْ بِهِ شَعَثَنَا، وَاشْعَبْ بِهِ صَدْعَنَا، وَارْتُقْ بِهِ فَتْقَنَا، وَكَثِّرْ بِهِ قِلَّتَنَا، وَأَعْزِزْ بِهِ ذِلَّتَنَا، وَأَغْنِ بِهِ عَائِلَنَا، وَاقْضِ بِهِ عَنْ مُغْرَمِنَا، وَاجْبُرْ بِهِ فَقْرَنَا، وَسُدَّ بِهِ خَلَّتَنَا، وَيَسِّرْ بِهِ عُسْرَنَا، وَبَيِّضْ بِهِ وُجُوهَنَا، وَفُكَّ بِهِ أَسْرَنَا، وَأَنْجِحْ بِهِ طَلِبَتَنَا، وَأَنْجِزْ بِهِ مَوَاعِيدَنَا، وَاسْتَجِبْ بِهِ دَعْوَتَنَا، وَأَعْطِنَا بِهِ سُؤْلَنَا، وَبَلِّغْنَا بِهِ مِنَ الدُّنْيَا وَالْآخِرَةِ آمَالَنَا، وَأَعْطِنَا بِهِ فَوْقَ رَغْبَتِنَا،

O' God, allow us to bear what You have taught us of the truth, and teach us that which we have come short of. O' God, through him [i.e., al-Mahdi], unite our disunity, bond our rifts, remove our divsions, multiply our slightness, rectify our humility, support our destitute, shield our fugitives, mend our poverty, redress our shortcomings, ease our difficulties, brighten our faces, break our

252

bondage, respond to our pleas, fulfill our promises, answer our calls, give us our requests, fulfill our hopes in this
world and the hereafter, and give us more than what we
seek.

يا خَيْرَ المَسْؤُولِينَ وَأَوْسَعَ المُعْطِينَ، اشْفِ بِهِ صُدُورَنا، وَأَذْهِبْ بِهِ غَيْظَ
قُلُوبِنا، وَاهْدِنا بِهِ لِما اخْتُلِفَ فِيهِ مِنَ الحَقِّ بِإِذْنِكَ، إِنَّكَ تَهْدِي مَنْ تَشاءُ
إِلى صِراطٍ مُسْتَقِيمٍ، وَانْصُرْنا بِهِ عَلى عَدُوِّكَ وَعَدُوِّنا، إِلهَ الحَقِّ آمِينَ.

O' best of those who are beseeched and the most abundantly giving. Through him, cure our chests [of psychological ills], remove the rancor in our hearts, guide us to what
was disagreed upon of truth by Your leave – surely, You
guide whomever You wish to the straight path. Support us
with him over our enemies. God of truth, amen.

اللّهُمَّ إِنّا نَشْكُو إِلَيْكَ فَقْدَ نَبِيِّنا صَلَواتُكَ عَلَيْهِ وَآلِهِ، وَغَيْبَةَ وَلِيِّنا، وَكَثْرَةَ
عَدُوِّنا، وَقِلَّةَ عَدَدِنا، وَشِدَّةَ الفِتَنِ بِنا، وَتَظاهُرَ الزَّمانِ عَلَيْنا، فَصَلِّ عَلى
مُحَمَّدٍ وَآلِهِ، وَأَعِنّا عَلى ذلِكَ بِفَتْحٍ مِنْكَ تُعَجِّلُهُ، وَبِضُرٍّ تَكْشِفُهُ، وَنَصْرٍ
تُعِزُّهُ، وَسُلْطانِ حَقٍّ تُظْهِرُهُ، وَرَحْمَةٍ مِنْكَ تُجَلِّلُناها، وَعافِيَةٍ مِنْكَ
تُلْبِسُناها، بِرَحْمَتِكَ يا أَرْحَمَ الرّاحِمِينَ

O' God, we complain to you the departure of our Prophet
– may your blessings be upon him and his family – the absence of our guardian [our Imam], the multitude of our
enemies, the slightness of our numbers, the hardship of sedition for us, and the vicissitudes of time against us. So
send blessings on Muhammad and on his family. Help us
to overcome this state of affairs through Your quickening
of triumph, repelling of misfortunes, inaugurating victories, and empowering the authority of truth. Immerse us
with the bestowal of Your mercy. Dress us with the grant
of Your health. By Your mercy, O' most Merciful

Full Circle

The reader can see by now the great breadth of topics that this sublime supplication addresses. Most importantly, it provides guiding points of light for the supplicant's theological, spiritual, and social growth.

From a theological perspective, it tackles the major tenets of our faith:

- It speaks of God's oneness – "Praise be to God, who has not taken unto Himself a wife, nor a son…."
- It highlights God's justice – "Praise be to God, breaker of tyrants, ender of oppressors, capturer of runaways, punisher of oppressors…."
- It addresses the concept of prophethood – "O' God, send blessings on Muhammad – Your servant, messenger…."
- It speaks of the tenet of imamah – "O' God send blessings on Ali, the Commander of the Faithful…."
- It delves into the realm of the hereafter – "[Praise be to God who] makes the living die and brings the dead to life while He is the ever-living – there is no death for Him…."

From a spiritual perspective, the supplication addressed a number of key points:

- It teaches us to always be grateful for God's countless blessings – "Praise be to God, the creator of all creation, who makes sustenance freely available…."
- It teaches us to rely on God Almighty in all of our affairs – "Yet, when [Your answer] is delayed for me, I blame You out of my ignorance – although perhaps the delay is a blessing for me…."
- It teaches us to be repentant and seek forgiveness – "Praise be to God for His forbearance in light of His all-awareness. Praise be to God for His amnesty despite His omnipotence. Praise be to God for the long respite He allows in spite of provocation. Surely, He is able to do what He wills."

- It teaches us the importance of supplication – "Praise be to God, who answers to me whenever I call Him, covers up my all my shortcomings while I disobey Him...."

From a social perspective, the supplication addressed three important points:

First, the supplication teaches us to be empathetic towards others. The Imam says, "Praise be to God, who protects the frightened, helps the righteous, promotes the meek, demeans the arrogant, and destroys kings to replace them with others. Praise be to God, breaker of tyrants, ender of oppressors, capturer of runaways, punisher of oppressors, aid to those who cry out for help, target of beseechers' requests, and patron of the faithful."

Second, it teaches us that each of us should see ourselves as a tools for the creation of a better society. Our hopes for a world filled with peace and justice should drive us to be tools for that cause. The supplication says, "O' God, we ask of you for an honorable era where you distinguish Islam and its adherents, and humiliate hypocrisy and its adherents. Allow us to be in it amongst those who call toward Your obedience and the leaders in Your path. Bless us through it with the honor of this world and the next."

Third, the supplication highlights the points of weakness in society. We cannot reform our communities without first acknowledging their weaknesses. We must first identify the causes of social illness and seek to address them at the root. The supplication does that for us when it says, "O' God, we complain to you the departure of our Prophet – may your blessings be upon him and his family – the absence of our guardian [our Imam], the multitude of our enemies, the slightness of our numbers, the hardship of sedition for us, and the vicissitudes of time against us."

We have lost our divinely guided leadership! We lack dedicated individuals who will help in building our communities! The existence of disparate trends and internal conflicts have weakened whatever we may have.

Therefore, if we seek to build a righteous community, we must:

1. Be dedicated and devoted in following the path of our divinely guided leaders,

2. Strive to unify our communities and reject social conflicts, and

3. Focus on capacity-building to ensure the growth of a dedicated corps of individuals who will take on the mantle of building our communities.

This will allow us to avert some of the consequences of living in a time so far past the passing of our Holy Prophet, and in a state of being unable to directly communicate with our beloved Imam.

اللّهُمَّ إِنَّا نَشْكُو إِلَيْكَ فَقْدَ نَبِيِّنا صَلَواتُكَ عَلَيْهِ وَآلِهِ، وَغَيْبَةَ وَلِيِّنا، وَكَثْرَةَ عَدُوِّنا، وَقِلَّةَ عَدَدِنا، وَشِدَّةَ الفِتَنِ بِنا، وَتَظاهُرَ الزَّمانِ عَلَيْنا

O' God, we complain to you the departure of our Prophet – may your blessings be upon him and his family – the absence of our guardian [our Imam], the multitude of our enemies, the slightness of our numbers, the hardship of sedition for us, and the vicissitudes of time against us.

فَصَلِّ عَلى مُحَمَّدٍ وَآلِهِ، وَأَعِنّا عَلى ذلِكَ بِفَتْحٍ مِنْكَ تُعَجِّلُهُ، وَبِضُرٍّ تَكْشِفُهُ، وَنَصْرٍ تُعِزُّهُ، وَسُلْطانِ حَقٍّ تُظْهِرُهُ، وَرَحْمَةٍ مِنْكَ تُجَلِّلُناها، وَعافِيَةٍ مِنْكَ تُلْبِسُناها، بِرَحْمَتِكَ يا أَرْحَمَ الرّاحِمِينَ

So, send blessings on Muhammad and on his family. Help us to overcome this state of affairs through Your quickening of triumph, repelling of misfortunes, inaugurating victories, and empowering the authority of truth. Immerse us with the bestowal of Your mercy. Dress us with the grant of Your health. By Your mercy, O' most Merciful.

And all praise be to God, Lord of the worlds.

Translator's Note

Firstly, there are great structural differences between the original Arabic language of the book and the modern English language. Such structural differences make the task of literal translation burdensome, and create a final result that does not accurately capture the spirit and readability of the Arabic text. Because Sayyid al-Khabbaz's work could not be encapsulated in a direct or literal translation, adaptations were used freely to capture the meaning of the text without being bogged down in linguistic and structural variations.

The process of translation always begs us to find precise meanings for the passages that we translate. When we encounter the majesty of the Holy Quran, we find ourselves incapable of understanding its intricacies, let alone translating its true and deep meanings. We turned to the works of translators who have attempted to do this before. Although no translation can do justice to the Holy Quran, we found the translation of Ali Quli Qarai to be the most proper in understanding when compared to the interpretation of the text as derived by our grand scholars. As such, we decided to rely on Qarai's translations throughout this book, with minor adaptations that allowed us to weave the verses more properly with the rest of the work.

A second great limitation came with translating the narrations of the Holy Prophet Muhammad[1] and his Holy Household.[2] Their words are ever so deep and ever so powerful. We attempted to convey these passages to the reader in a tone that is understandable, without deviating from the essence of the words of these immaculate personalities. We pray that we were successful in this endeavor.

Finally, we want to take this opportunity to thank you for your support. As students of Islam and as translators of this text, our greatest purpose is to please God by passing along these teachings to others. By picking up this book, you have lent your crucial support to this endeavor. We hope that you will continue your support throughout the rest of this book, and we ask that you keep us in your prayers whenever you pick it up.

The Editorial and Translation Team,

The Mainstay Foundation

---

[1] *The reader should note that the supplication of Salawat (May God send his peace and blessings upon Muhammad and the Household of Muhammad) is usually recited at the mention of the Holy Prophet. This is normally marked in elaborate calligraphy in Arabic text, or with (s) in English text. While such marks do not appear in this book, we encourage the reader to recite this supplication whenever they come across the blessed name of our Holy Prophet.*

[2] *The reader should note that salutations (Peace be upon them) is usually recited at the mention of the Holy Household or any of its members. This is normally marked in elaborate calligraphy in Arabic text, or with (a) in English text. While such marks do not appear in this book, we encourage the reader to recite salutations whenever they come across any of those blessed names.*

Bibliography

Religious Scripture

The Holy Quran

Other Sources

Abtahi, Muhammad Baqir Al-Muwahhid. *Al-Sahifa Al-Sajjadia*. Qum: Namuna, 1411 AH.

Al-'Amili, Muhammad ibn al-Hassan al-Hurr. *Wasa'el al-Shi'a*.

Al-Aamudi, Abdulwahid ibn Muhammad. *Ghurar al-Hikam*.

Al-Hasakani, Ubaydullah ibn Adbullah. *Shawahid al-Tanzil*.

Al-Hilli, al-Hassan ibn Yousif. *Nahj al-Haq*.

Al-Kaf'ami, Ibrahim ibn Ali. *Al-Balad al-Ameen*.

Al-Kashani, Muhammad Muhsin. *Al-Tafseer al-Kafi*.

Al-Kulayni, Muhammad ibn Yaqoub. *Al-Kafi*. Tehran: Daar Al-Kutub Al-Islamiya, 1968.

Al-Majlisi, Muhammad Baqir. *Bihar Al-Anwar*. Beirut: Al-Wafaa, 1983.

Al-Makki, Ali ibn Muhammad ibn Ahmad al-Maliki. *Al-Fusool al-Muhimma*.

Al-Mazandarani, Muhammad ibn Ali. *Manaqib Aal Abu Talib*.

Al-Mazandarani, Muhammad Salih. *Sharh Usool al-Kafi*.

Al-Mu'tazili, ibn Abu al-Hadeed. *Sharh Nahj al-Balagha.*

Al-Nouri, Mirza Hussain. *Mustadrak al-Wasa'el.*

Al-Qummi, Abbas. *Mafateeh al-Jinan.*

Al-Radi, Muhammad ibn Al-Hussain. *Nahj Al-Balagha.* Qum: Daar Al-Thakhaer, 1412 AH.

Al-Sadouq, Muhammad ibn Ali. *Man La Yahdaruh Al-Faqih.* 2nd ed. Qum: Muasasat Al-Nashr Al-Islami.

Al-Sadouq, Muhammad ibn Ali. *Oyoon Akhbar Al-Rida.* Beirut: Al-A'lami, 1984.

Al-Tabarani, Suleiman ibn Ahmad. *Al-Mu'jam Al-Kabeer.* Daar Ihyaa Al-Torath Al-Arabi.

Ibn Tawus, Ali ibn Moussa. *'Ayn al-'Aabra.*

Ibn Tawus, Ali ibn Moussa. *Iqbal al-A'mal.*

www.ingramcontent.com/pod-product-compliance
Lightning Source LLC
Chambersburg PA
CBHW021220090426
42740CB00006B/303